DATE DUE

DEMCO 38-296

*Humor and
Revelation
in American
Literature*

Humor and Revelation in American Literature
The Puritan Connection

Pascal Covici, Jr.

UNIVERSITY OF MISSOURI PRESS
COLUMBIA AND LONDON

Library of Congress Cataloging-in-Publication Data

Covici, Pascal, 1930–
    Humor and revelation in American literature : the Puritan
  connection / Pascal Covici, Jr.
      p.   cm.
    Includes bibliographical references and index.
    ISBN 0-8262-1095-3 (alk. paper)
    1. American wit and humor—History and criticism.   2. Christian
  literature, American—Puritan authors—History and criticism.
  3. Wit and humor—Religious aspects—Christianity.   4. American
  literature—History and criticism.   5. Puritan movements in
  literature.   6. Puritans—New England—Humor.   7. Revelation in
  literature.   I. Title
  PS430.C68   1997
  817.009'382–dc20   96-43457
                                                           CIP

♾TM This paper meets the requirements of the
American National Standard for Permanence of Paper
for Printed Library Materials, Z39.48, 1984.

Jacket Design: Susan Ferber
Text Design: Mindy Shouse
Typesetter: BOOKCOMP
Printer and binder: Thomson-Shore, Inc.
Typefaces: Palatino and Dorchester script

The University of Missouri Press gratefully acknowledges
the generosity of the Fund for Faculty Excellence
of Dedman College at Southern Methodist University, Dallas.

For Joan
"Our Learned . . . Fortescue"

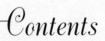

Contents

ACKNOWLEDGMENTS ix

INTRODUCTION 1
Loomings 1
Casting Off and Getting Under Way 4

I. **RELUCTANTLY INDEPENDENT**
THE RATTLING OF CHAINS 10

1. A Problem of Respect 10
2. Genteel and Vernacular
   Josiah Holland and Mark Twain 13
3. Responses, and Intimations of Crossing Over 23
4. American Self-Reliance? The Case of Hawthorne's Robin 28
5. Melville, the American Difference, and Richard Chase 36

II. **GOD'S CHOSEN PEOPLE**
THE ANGLICAN PERSPECTIVE 47

1. Megalomaniacal Fantasies . . . 47
2. Megalomania . . . With a British Accent 53
3. Ossa upon Pelion Concluded
   And Then? 57
4. Britain Versus the Bay Colony? Yes . . . and No 68

III. **CERTAINTY: DIVINE OR HUMAN?**
BISHOP BURNET AND THE MATTER OF CHOICE 73

1. Religiously Political, Politically Religious 73
2. Of Tolerance, Intolerance, and Bishop Fleetwood's
   Country Curate 75
3. Toleration, Belief, and the Power(lessness) of the Will 87

IV.   **VOICE, COUNTRY, AND CLASS**
      REAPPROACHING THE VERNACULAR   101

      1. Mather Proposes, Wise Disposes   101
      2. The Triumph of the Country
         Earthy and Conservative Vulgarity   113
      3. "The Simple Cobler" and the Masks of Wise,
         Versus Polly Baker
         Or, Humor Slips in When Theology Blinks   119
      4. From Wise and Franklin, Mark Twain's Triumphant
         Vernacular   127

V.   **THE BASIS OF LAUGHTER**
      WHAT'S SO FUNNY?   137

      1. How Do We Read Polly and Tom?   137
      2. Affectation, Again—and Certainty   143
      3. Disgust and Gentility   150
      4. Gentility, Ideality, and Responses to Mystery
         Nick Carraway and Jim Doggett   154
      5. Mystery Within   162
      6. Dr. Holland Once More, and the Plight of the Humorless 167

VI.   **THE PURITAN ROOTS OF AMERICAN HUMOR**   174

      1. Recognitions of the Self   174
      2. The Loneliness of the Solipsist
         No Laughing Matter   179
      3. Emerson's Saving Rejection of the "Noble Doubt"   190
      4. Thoreau's Recalcitrant Individual Fires His Pistols   197
      5. At the Heart of All, The Unknowable Remains   202
      6. Puritan Rejection of Puritan Reality—And What About Us? 211

      BIBLIOGRAPHY   217

      INDEX   223

Acknowledgments

Janet Barnes at Dr. Williams's Library, Gordon Square, London, and her staff, gave my wife and me valuable assistance and equally valuable friendship during and beyond a London winter. The staff of the North Reading Room of the British Library made possible the tracking down of the hundreds of occasional sermons we read, and an even greater number whose existence we simply noticed. London House, in Mecklenberg Square, provided a gracious, convenient, and affordable base from which to sally forth in search of texts, theaters, and pubs. Lyris and "Sweet William" Hopes, along with Val and Perce Russo, our Aussie pals in London, helped us retain sanity in the midst of assorted chaos. To Deans Gray and Bhat of Dedman College, SMU, I am grateful for generous support and for an unexpected leave that allowed me to complete the first draft of this book. Vic Doyno's careful reading of a late draft forced me to rethink many of my arguments as well as to pare down my long sentences and unscramble at least some of my involuted ones. I shall never attain his level of clarity, but he certainly pushed me toward it. Margaret Hamlin leaves me greatly in her debt for giving up precious vacation time to help root out at least some of the evidences of my muddiness, ignorance, and sloth. Those that remain reflect my own stubbornness. To my beloved research assistant, who put her own career on hold to help me explore her Anglican past, I am grateful not only for solid hours of uncomplaining labor but also for the initial impetus to this whole endeavor.

Humor and Revelation in American Literature

Introduction

LOOMINGS

American humor has its roots not just in British Anglican but also, and perhaps surprisingly, in American Puritan habits of mind. This is one of the conclusions I shall be drawing in what follows. To differentiate and to characterize what I am calling the Anglican and Puritan mental states, I suggest that a stronger insistence on the complexity of social and political issues forms part of the Anglican tradition, while the Puritan puts more weight in the scales of cosmic mystery and of the soul's dilemma. Also, a sharper focus on the self seems to distinguish the preoccupations of Puritan from Anglican sermons, always with the proviso that in all cases exceptions abound.

The Anglican absence of mystery, the absence of introspective trouble-making, will show itself not only in numerous sermons but—more usefully—in what happens to American humor, perhaps most clearly (but not at all exclusively) in the writings of Mark Twain. That is, the humor that most influenced Twain's immediate predecessors of the Old Southwest came directly out of the British eighteenth century, directly out of Henry Fielding's clearly stated concern with "affectation as the only source of the true ridiculous." Based on assumptions of clarity, of an amazing (to us) absence of mystery, surrounding the human psyche, this primary British influence on American humor held sway well into the nineteenth century. But then it turned out that long-dormant Puritan roots had been nourishing a very different sort of growth. The humor

1

of affectation, borrowed from England, gave way to humor, and to perceptions, of a very different sort. As we will see.

These central intuitions on which this study is based began in a random thought that seemed as if it might become a short essay. Mark Twain's humor, as I (and certainly many others) thought about it, had its genesis in what has come to be called the humor of the Old Southwest. The differences, however, proved to be more interesting than the similarities, and *Mark Twain's Humor: The Image of a World* essentially developed my initial sense of those differences. Then, a few years ago, in a seminar concerned with George Santayana's "The Genteel Tradition in American Philosophy" as a possible perspective on American literature, my students pushed me to think about connections between the Genteel Tradition and Calvinistic Puritanism that were by no means explicit in Santayana's essay. Both the Genteel Tradition and the Puritans showed a sense of certainty, of possessing inside information, about the workings of the universe and the intentions of the Almighty. In both, this sense manifested itself in an arrogant intolerance that, at least as much as any other quality, has led to consistently bad twentieth-century press for both Genteel Tradition and Puritans. Not surprisingly, much of the humor from which young Sam Clemens derived his early models had the same sort of arrogance, not so much about cosmic issues as about social and political truths. Written as it was primarily by representatives of genteel culture, and taking its lead from eighteenth-century British humor, how could it have been otherwise?

Now the random thought that led to this study: Like Twain's predecessors, the Puritans seemed very sure of their assumptions; but like Twain, they seemed also to reflect a sense of essential mystery. That is, the richness of American Puritan thought might have a great deal to do with the formative stages of American humor. A further step: Puritan insistence on the primacy of divine grace, as opposed to human works, emphasized the individual human soul and its isolated and problematic status in the mind of God. Communal considerations, as has been often shown and as we will see, counted for a great deal, too; but the Calvinist doctrines of predestination, election, free grace, justification, sanctification, et al., made for an emphasis different from that prevailing in the increasingly Arminian Anglican establishment. There, individual salvation came more and more to be seen as a matter of reward for proper behavior. Reverence for and obedience to authority seem to have formed an important part of the Anglican message. So: the rugged American soul, on its own before its Maker, stands in contrast to the conforming cringe of Anglicanism. Surely nothing is ever quite so simple as that! Still, what a delightfully unlikely notion: American humor, in its iconoclastic bumptiousness and focus on the foibles of the individual, has its origins in Puritan thought. There might be something to it, but . . . no. But then again, maybe. And so began a pleasant, at first only half-serious, effort to see what, if anything, might follow.

Meanwhile, two things happened. First, it became clearer and clearer to me that a surprisingly large sampling of American literature "works" very much the same way that humor does. Although most significant American authors do not generally receive the title of humorist—more and more of them, however, write humor—a great many of their works force readers into the same sudden shifts of perspective that humor brings about. This is probably a subject for another book; but, for now, I propose to assume, with only a very small suggestion of demonstration, that the revelations brought about by much American literature occur in large part because that literature functions in many of the ways that humor does, even when it is essentially very unfunny indeed.

Second, starting in the winter and spring of 1983, my wife and I discovered treasure in Dr. Williams's Library, Gordon Square, London, that developed into a gold-mine in the North Reading Room of the British Library. Initially, we were simply looking at British Anglican sermons of the early seventeenth century out of an interest in seeing what, if anything, the Anglicans were saying about the Independents, the Puritans. I had a "fishing license" in the form of a generous leave from my university, and my wife, with equal generosity, agreed to put her own teaching career on hold and act as my research assistant; we were having a wonderful time, cuddling up to the radiator in Dr. Williams's during chill January and February days and then thawing out in pubs and theaters in the evening. And then, as I say, we stumbled onto something. Not to spin this out any thinner, what we discovered was that seventeenth- and eighteenth-century Anglican bishops and priests, of all backgrounds and leanings, had been addressing their auditors in precisely those terms of communal divine favoritism and protection that, we had been taught, were attributable exclusively to New England Puritan ministers. God's new chosen people, His new Israel, it turned out, might well be the Puritan inhabitants of the Massachusetts Bay Colony if one were sitting in the Old South Church of Boston; but in St. Paul's of London, and in all the other—well, hundreds of other— Anglican houses of worship, those whom God held in the forefront of his consciousness for both protection and punishment, for both penalty and reward, explicitly his chosen people in the same Old Testament sense that infused the jeremiads of New England, were the Anglican people of Old England their very selves.

This we found both surprising and interesting. Between the two of us, we read and took notes on well over six hundred sermons, some of them considerably expanded for publication, some of the details of which the waiting world will find in my Chapter II. But why should anyone care, apart from the sheer historical jolt of the thing? Asking this question led to my own private jolt that, in turn, led to this book. Mark Twain, so quintessentially American, found the beginnings of his humor in the work of nineteenth-century Americans who were echoing the British eighteenth century. Seventeenth-century American Puritans echoed, in their most characteristically arrogant claims to divine guidance and nurture, the vocabulary and even the tone of the Anglican British seventeenth century. As most of us Americanists never get tired of telling our students, Ralph Waldo Emerson's "American Scholar Address," in calling for an artistic and intellectual independence from things European and especially from things British, was repeating—with, to be sure, far greater force and with a new, because very personal, spin— the same message that Phi Beta Kappa orators and magazine writers had been reiterating at least since the end of the War of 1812. Somehow, independence of cultural, religious, and maybe even psychological sorts seemed to be coming considerably more slowly than the political. Apart from essayists, who else in earlier America was seeing this?

The answer forms, in part, the substance of this book. Just as Americans have praised and blamed elitist order and praised and condemned democratic chaos, so have we valued independence—theological, political, cultural, psychological—while at the same time rejecting it. I believe that I am developing a usefully illuminating way of thinking about the effects of works by a number of American writers. If my central preoccupation has any value, readers will find themselves thinking of works, of writers, and of situations not herein mentioned that will add to a sense of this ambivalence and to an understanding of it as intimately, even indissolubly, linked with what I hope to show are the Puritan roots of American humor. Cultural outsiders, whether women or members of minority groups, as a matter of survival have dealt, and are dealing, with the gap between America's stated values and American behavior as they experience it. Accordingly, I focus upon some of the writers long regarded as among the usual suspects in any consideration of cultural hegemony. I want to explore not so much the hypocrisy as the ambivalence presented by our literature. Along the way, the centrality of Mark Twain to my sense of this ambivalence will become apparent. He does seem to be an archetypal American voice; many of his particular tunes continue to raise echoes.

CASTING OFF AND GETTING UNDER WAY

We Anglo-Americans can look to our literature to explain us to ourselves. Often, we do; often, we don't. One might wonder how, with "Covici" as a patronymic (Romanian and Roman) and "Pascal" in front of it, I can speak of "we" Anglo-Americans. Easily. So overpowering is the British experience behind being American that even as a second-generation arriviste, born and raised in the ethnic soup of New York City, I can claim as heritage the hesitancies and ambivalences of New England, the self-assurance and courtesy, and the violence, of Virginia. I'm suggesting a way of reading mainstream American literature that encourages readers to pay deliberate attention to questions about independence and dependence, questions central to the agenda of many a writer, whether consciously so or not. In considering these matters, I have found that humor, so often a matter of the mere use of vernacular dialect, entangles itself with thoughts and feelings about democracy and the competence of "ordinary" people. At whom and at what do readers and characters laugh? Why? With what effect? How strongly independent, how cringingly dependent, do our writers see us as being? Independent of, dependent on, what?

These have come to strike me as questions worth asking. Chapter I sets up ways in which several American writers make us aware of just how ambivalent we have been about independence from Britain and from British ways. It does so mostly by looking at three texts:

1. Mark Twain's Whittier Birthday Speech (delivered at the *Atlantic* dinner of 1877), in the contexts of Twain's humorous predecessors and of George Santayana's 1911 articulation of the Genteel Tradition. I use Josiah Holland (here and later) to represent both the Tradition and ways in which "gentility" leaked dissatisfaction with itself. The humor of the Old Southwest seemed at one time to lack respectability and ideality; but I find that, nowadays, it seems to echo a surprisingly solid dose of both. Curiously, though not unexpectedly, the spokespersons for ideality hankered after the raw experience that their traditions seemed to be denying them. The immediate reaction to Twain's speech suggests that proponents of gentility themselves express in their own way a certain ambivalence toward two specific embodiments of that vague genteel desideratum, ideality: (1) a longing for foreign models of thought and speech, and (2) a reverence for the past.

2. Nathaniel Hawthorne's "My Kinsman, Major Molineux" (1832) indicates that the desire for independence does not rule out a deeper desire for its opposite, and that Hawthorne, perhaps along with a number of his early readers, lamented the unruliness of mobs far more than he admired the idea of political independence. The psychological independence or dependence of the main character turns out to have political as well as personal significance. Both Twain and Hawthorne, in their apparently so different ways, suggest both a rejection of reverence for the past in a context of striving for independence and also the attractiveness of what is being rejected.

3. Herman Melville's story, "The Paradise of Bachelors and the Tartarus of Maids" (1855), exhibits, by embodying, ways in which British and American literary sensibilities differ significantly, as Richard Chase in 1957 suggested that they do. I'm concerned with a contrast between the realistic surface of Melville's "British" style and the favoring of meaning over mimesis when he writes "American." He presents both British and American enslavements as equally "real," but he works hard at distinguishing between the two. The contrast might well be stated as one between British materiality and American transcendentalism. Briefer glances in other directions—especially at Nathaniel Ward's *Simple Cobler of Aggawam* (1647)—indicate both a contrast between American and British Puritans and a curious bond between American Puritans and British Anglicans.

The next two chapters jump across the Atlantic. Chapter II, the fruit of the London experience I have already described, shows that British Anglicans were every bit as certain as the American Puritans that they were God's new chosen people, His Israelites. Sharing this peculiar view of their dependence upon the divine, and their certainty of knowing the divine will, made for a binding tie between Americans and Britons. Although the general principle that such a tie exists has long been a commonplace for students of history, literature, and general culture, I believe that this particular facet of that tie has not been noticed before. No one text is central, but the sermons delivered on specific occasions—November 5 (Guy Fawkes Day-Gunpowder Treason), January 30 (Beheading of Charles I), and May 29 (Restoration of the Stuart Monarchy)—demonstrate the point and set up early-eighteenth-century reactions that become accessible through an understanding of the well-named John Wise. But the significance of these Anglican sermons lies also in their differences from the Puritan. Despite those similarities—and they will be important to my argument—the differences count for a great deal on at least four fronts: (1) Anglican Arminianism removes the Calvinist mystery engulfing the human soul; (2) in doing so, it puts a premium on obedience and reverence; (3) further, the facts of British Anglican experience—1605 vs. 1688 vs. 1648—put a certain complexity in front of the auditors of the relevant "occasional" sermons; and (4) finally (for my purposes), Bishop Burnet's commentary (discussed in Chapter III) articulates mystery and complexity on a divine, on a cosmic, scale.

Chapter III focuses on British anticipations of independence that are implicit in the idea of toleration. Dealing with specific problems of voice and humor via Bishop Fleetwood's persona as "Curate of Salop" and Luke Milbourne's "railing sermons," in contrast to the "reasonable" voices of a few others, the chapter explores at length the paradoxical achievement of Bishop Burnet: his analysis leads to the startling conclusion that the Calvinist core of Church of England belief (Article 17, concerning the Calvinist doctrines of predestination and election) reveals itself as a primary basis for freedom of belief. Although theology tends to send most people into a fitful slumber, I hope that, by keeping the technicalities brief and the points concerning freedom and mystery paramount, I have allowed the paradox to throw its ray of light.

Chapter IV returns to this side of the Atlantic, dealing mostly with texts by John Wise, Nathaniel Ward, Benjamin Franklin, and Mark Twain. Various, often contradictory, attitudes toward vernacular speech, both as mark of social status and as indication of perceptiveness, will emerge as the mingled property of writers, readers, and narrators. By looking at what I see as five distinct personae through which Wise delivered his 1713 *Satyre* on the *Proposals* of 1705, and then at different but related masks of Ward, Franklin, and Twain, the chapter advances related arguments: (1) struggles to conform to and to oppose various conventions shape American humorous polemic, especially in its early showing up of wrong-headed rejection by various elites of the capacities of ordinary persons to think and act intelligently; (2) the basis for eighteenth-century British ridicule of affectation, as spelled out by Henry Fielding, shapes the nineteenth-century American humor of the Old Southwest (a matter that gets further treatment in Chapters V and VI); and (3) certainty about the human ability to "know" reality, implicit in such humor, establishes an unsuspected fellowship between humor and the Genteel Tradition, despite genteel rejection of humor, and its often vernacular trappings, as vulgar.

Chapter V initiates my taking issue with Santayana's sense that American humorists had nothing "solid" to put in place of the Genteel Tradition, and that, therefore, they posed no real threat to that tradition. The chapter starts with an extended look at genteel implications and manifestations in the humor of the Old Southwest, with special attention to George Washington Harris's Sut Lovingood. Harris keeps at the forefront of a reader's consciousness the emotion of genteel disgust in response to Sut's raucous and raunchy escapades. In many respects a pivotal writer, Harris constructs Sut's "adventures" so that they reaffirm the world of genteel propriety while apparently celebrating its antithesis. Less richly, and therefore more clearly, many of Harris's predecessors and contemporaries organized their humor around the showing up of affectation. Themselves certain of possessing both proper standards and adequate knowledge of reality, they revealed for their reader's delight the often painful and usually deserved misfortunes of their socially inferior protagonists or victims.

In contrast to the certainty implicit in the idea of affectation that underpins much of that humor, an aura of mystery and of the unknowable emerges through a number of East-West contrasts. The chapter also looks at works by F. Scott Fitzgerald, Thomas Bangs Thorpe, Herman Melville, Stephen Crane, and Mark Twain, and returns with new understanding to Josiah Holland and the ideal. Twain's Tom Sawyer, as both sympathetic victim and despised target in *Tom Sawyer Abroad*, seems especially useful. Genteel insistence on human ability to know the unknowable emerges as central to genteel ideality. Genteel ideality, in turn, begins to emerge as a villain in my presentation of American literature and American sensibility.

Chapter VI concludes the various quarrels and arguments started earlier. Melville, Hawthorne, Santayana, Poe, Emerson, Thoreau, Twain, the British Nathan Marshall (eighteenth century) and William Prynne (seventeenth century) all come into it, as do independence and humor. A subtle choice of symbolic indeterminacy over transcendental certainty in *Walden* gives special bite to Thoreau's quarrel with Emerson and to Emerson's disappointment with Thoreau. To what extent do we really want our children to go their own way? To what extent do we really want to escape from our parents? At times, independence seems to have a great deal to do with a willingness to accept our vernacular selves, to stop longing for elitist guardians who will somehow save us from the perceived realities of our material existence. At the same time, even Henry David Thoreau cautions against throwing out all guidance from the past. "We will not forget," he says in the first chapter of *Walden*, "that some Egyptian wheat was handed down to us by a mummy."

To be sure, it is not only ancient wheat but a considerable amount of outmoded chaff that our writers find growing in the dark places of the collective national psyche. The point is that they find both, and they show us both as they go about presenting what it may mean to feel and think "Americanly." The first sentence of the first chapter of this book finds what I trust is its earned answer near the end of Chapter VI: "Americans, finally, may be simply human beings, individuals who keep on denying part of what they have been, and becoming, in part, what they have denied." From an early but not unique cultural sense of divine chosenness to a subsequent, and related, sense of a noble struggle to embody various ideal constructions, we have kept looking to our writers to spell out our self-reliance as well as our sense of dependence. If self-awareness has value, then American literature generally has been of great value in showing us how confused and self-contradictory we have been and still are. In forcing upon readers a closer look at self, more of our principal national literary treasures than one might at first assume take a stance that is indistinguishable from humor. In order to reveal ourselves to ourselves, our literature seems often to surprise its readers into a fresh perspective in much the same way that humor does. No matter how actively readers engage in deconstructing and reconstructing texts, those texts are in large part constructed by their authors. This book offers a meditation upon some of our literature's revelation, and on some of the ways that our writers have engineered it.

I

Reluctantly Independent

The Rattling of Chains

1. A Problem of Respect

What is an American? What have our writers had to say on this extremely broad subject? By now, the question is familiar, the answers increasingly complex. Who knows what we are? Who cares? We exist, and that might seem enough, particularly given the tentative condition of human existence these days. But it was not always thus. One gets a fresh sense of what we have come from—and, therefore, of what we are—when one goes back to the nineteenth century, that time of exuberant expectancy, and then further back, to our colonial beginnings.

When we look at the literature of our land, we look at American thought, at avatars of the American soul. Because I believe that what I have to say will strike chords in my reader's mind, leading you to remember, to extrapolate from, to think carefully about, texts and authors to which and to whom I do not refer, I shall look closely at a few extremely traditional, canonical bits and pieces of American literary effort. Also, I shall deal, in part and in brief, with a large number of almost interchangeable seventeenth- and eighteenth-century Anglican sermons. If the drift of my observations has merit, its application to minority and feminist texts will be self-evident and strikingly axiomatic. Dependence and independence strike me as polarities helpful toward an understanding of American thought and feeling. If at times I equate respect for vernacular with independence, I intend also to make clear why I do so. With this sparse, loose, and deliberately undefined vocabulary for dealing with theological, political, cultural, and psychological issues, I propose to move into the intellectual morass of thought related to belonging to America. As Robert Frost said, "The land was ours before we were the land's."

If we are American in any significant way, as we have long claimed, then we must differ from our British cousins, our founders; and one way of studying American literature should entail a hard look at various refusals to break from Britain, a hard look at our awareness, and at our denial, of connections between Britain and America. I suppose that I am writing a declaration of dependence. We are familiar with the other kind of declaration, but I think that we would do well to examine our great ambivalence toward the ties that bind. Of this complex set of attitudes and values, the easiest to pin down comes under the general heading of provincialism, or colonialism. We were for a long time victims of the notion that life could be endured in the states (earlier, in the colonies) but really lived only in the mother country.

The case of William Byrd II, of Westover, Virginia, still strikes a responsive chord. He kept for years his own chambers in London, always planning to return, yet always buried beneath debt and administrative duties on his Virginia plantation. He wrote for and to a London readership; parts of his personal journal sound as if written to persuade himself—or, perhaps, to persuade that eventual London readership—that rural eighteenth-century Virginia had the cosmopolitan attractions of the finest city anywhere. Kenneth S. Lynn long ago showed that Byrd's *History of the Dividing Line* set the form that much subsequent American humor would take: an educated gentleman—self-controlled, aristocratic—shares with his readers his sophisticated laughter at the behavior of the uneducated boors of the frontier.[1] To say in serious conversation that something was first rate and also American was to utter a perceived contradiction, an oxymoron. The humor of exaggeration was something else: the boasts of the tall tale, in their hysterical insistence upon the great size, and therefore the automatic excellence, of all things American only confirmed our enslavement to Europe by rattling the chains so hard.

Even by the latter part of the nineteenth century, respect for American intellectual and moral culture—a kind of national self-respect—remained a battle to be fought by the few, for most of the eastern literary establishment still took for granted that American excellence lay in imitating the revered models of the Old World. In a book about

1. Kenneth S. Lynn, *Mark Twain and Southwestern Humor*, chap. 1, "The Style of a Gentleman."

the iconoclastic Theodore Dreiser, F. O. Matthiessen, speaking of what George Santayana had in 1911 labeled "the genteel tradition," saw the sterility latent in such reverence:

> Observing our dominant New England culture, Santayana believed that its deep-rooted error was that it separated thought from experience. Among the legacies of a colonial culture is the habit of thinking of creative sources as somehow remote from itself, of escaping from the hardness and rawness of everyday surroundings into an idealized picture of civilized refinement, of believing that the essence of beauty must lie in what James Russell Lowell read about in Keats rather than in what Walt Whitman saw in the streets of Brooklyn. The inescapable result of this is to make art an adornment rather than an organic expression of life, to confuse it with politeness and delicacy.[2]

And this, in turn, led not simply to an undervaluing of American expression but to its absolute denigration.

Now that American vernacular, even American slang, has permeated and begun to dominate the English-speaking world (and bids fair to establish dominion even beyond those constantly expanding borders), tuning in to the conflicted voices of a century and more ago takes a fair amount of doing ("fair amount of doing" vs. "denigration": vernacular vs. standard genteel). It's hard, now, to realize that even William Dean Howells, that crusader for literary realism, that fearless fighter for the "commonplace," the ordinary, in American life as the proper material for fiction, expressed pride that we now "call a spade an agricultural instrument."[3] He lamented the loss of vigor but praised the rise of decency, associating vernacular usage with the vulgar and uncouth. Today, we take for granted the literary value of vernacular. During 1989, all manner of national and regional conferences celebrated the centennial of *A Connecticut Yankee in King Arthur's Court*. Four years earlier, *Adventures of Huckleberry Finn* enjoyed a similar occasion. Both of these justly revered works represent Mark Twain's triumph of the vernacular over refinement. In December 1977, however, I do not recall any ceremonial marking of another centenary perhaps even more significant in plotting the collision course between the voice of American vernacular humor and the genteel tradition. Before coming to the December 17, 1877, celebration of Whittier's seventieth birthday and the *Atlantic*'s twentieth anniversary, however, let us try to assess the extent to which Twain himself was a prisoner of that tradition, which held captive the literary establishment of the time.

2. F. O. Matthiessen, *Theodore Dreiser*, 62.
3. William Dean Howells, *Criticism and Fiction*, 154.

2. GENTEEL AND VERNACULAR
JOSIAH HOLLAND AND MARK TWAIN

As the verbal warrior on the side of the vernacular as opposed to the genteel, did Mark Twain see himself as a "mere" journalist, or a "mere" humorist, instead of as a Writer of Books? Was he a comedian or a moralist, or both? Was his proper vein "merely" the raucous Western tall tale? We need to recall his fear of poverty, his worry about offending and alienating friends and family, his anxieties over being misunderstood by his audience. We know that he became justly famous for his blistering temper and his deliciously outspoken diatribes aimed at genteel targets. We also know that he tried, however unsuccessfully, to conform to the external demands of his wife's sense of propriety, and that he valued her oversight of his occasional verbal slips. He was surprised, we have learned, when she said nothing in objection to Huck Finn's being combed "all to hell" at the end of the manuscript adventures of Tom Sawyer.

The part of genteel tradition represented by propriety alone, by shallow good manners and mere politeness, Twain could conform to easily enough. He could snarl restlessly at it, too, thereby warming the hearts of his equally restless readers without at all disturbing their foundations. A more important facet of the tradition, however, was what Santayana considered its decadent descent from Platonic idealism and New England transcendentalism. No matter how great the deviation of actual experience from the ideal, the archetype, the mental image of what "ought" to be, genteel literature tended to present the "ideal" rather than what William Dean Howells, by the 1880s, was calling "the real." Although we now think of Howells as a representative of gentility (he was, to Sinclair Lewis, a "church-mouse"), he was also the champion of literary realism, of what in one lively essay he called the presentation of the "real grasshopper," rather than of "the good old romantic cardboard grasshopper."[4] Howells's short story, "Editha," in 1905, would use the Spanish-American war (as Stephen Crane's *The Red Badge of Courage* [1895] had used the long-ended Civil War) to contrast the ideal realm—constructions in people's heads—with what war actually entailed, emphasizing the futility, indeed the danger, of trying to live in that ideal. Howells reminded his turn-of-the-century readers that romantic, idealizing preconceptions can kill.

These two facets of the genteel tradition, propriety and a prizing of the ideal, come together in the "official" view of the role of the humorist. In approved public opinion, humor was not to be taken as "serious literature." People like to laugh, but no one respects the clown.

4. Ibid., 12.

This was a matter of cultivated taste: people found satisfaction for their pretensions toward culture in genteel romance, in melodramatic stories, and in plays about European nobility and plantation aristocracy. At the same time, they enjoyed humor, but this enjoyment was a kind of slumming. Henry Nash Smith reports that "a biographer of Johnson J. Hooper (creator of Simon Suggs, [a southwestern scalawag,]) wrote in 1872: 'His ambition had been . . . to enjoy the respect of men; but he had unfortunately obtained a reputation [that is, of being a humorist] which cut off such hopes.' "[5] The humor represented by the works of Hooper and his fellows of what has come to be called "the Old Southwest" (a fluid region, shifting with time, and originally including places as far east as Pineville, Georgia, and Knoxville, Tennessee) leads by both influence and chronology to the humor of Mark Twain and provides through contrast (as West met East) an understanding of several causes of Twain's conflict with the genteel tradition. Let us think about Twain's humor in two different contexts: that of the humor of the Old Southwest; and also that of a specific socio-literary event, the Whittier seventieth birthday dinner, sponsored by the publisher of the prestigious *Atlantic Monthly* to celebrate jointly the venerable poet and the twentieth anniversary of Boston's most cultivated magazine, already a cultural institution.

In 1852, with "S.L.C." 's publication of "The Dandy Frightening the Squatter" in *The Boston Carpet-Bag*, young Sam Clemens, not yet 17, and not yet forming himself into Mark Twain, imitates the way of telling a story that he had encountered in all the journals, including those that circulated among the printshops up and down the river. He uses the voice of an educated observer—one of "us," in fact—who knows perfectly well what a steamboat is, and who also knows that vernacular words, like "woodyard" and "squatter," need the disinfecting isolation that only quotation marks can provide. This narrative voice presents the story in the proper English that characterizes the usual cultivated and trustworthy observer of uncouth backwoods behavior. On the other hand, this voice presents a pattern of action that upsets the usual sophisticated values implicit in such stories. The ignorant, uncouth squatter speaks—always inside quotation marks, of course— the ignorant, uncouth language fitting to his station. This man, who doesn't even know that "the approaching object" is indeed a steamboat, still gets the moral and physical best of the affected, but standard-speaking, "Dandy." The dandy plans to humiliate the squatter simply to impress the assembled ladies. But the dandy ends up in the river, a fool as well as a poltroon. Western-vernacular honesty and brawn have

5. Henry Nash Smith, *Mark Twain: The Development of a Writer*, 106.

triumphed over Eastern language and affectation. Rural sharpness—and violence—defeat urban wealth and pretension.

Unlike most of the writers of the humor of the Old Southwest, young Sam was a native of the region. He had not been educated in an Eastern college; he was no lawyer or doctor or circuit judge or banker or newspaper editor more or less new to the region, looking around and down on the barbarous habits of the frontier in order to report back to the delightedly horrified East. Accordingly, young Sam's story presents what was to become one of Mark Twain's commonplaces: the undoing of a greenhorn's pretensions by a laconic but savvy veteran of the place. In a sense, the events of the story undercut the traditional significance of the verbal strategies that frame the story's telling. If that introductory narrative voice favors either of the antagonists, the standard-speaking Easterner, rather than the vernacular-speaking squatter, ought to have that voice's vote. The arch tone of the quotation marks leads one to expect that the narrator will tell a story supportive of Eastern genteel values, but the dandy loses. Remember, in contrast, that thirteen years later, with the writing and rewriting of "The Celebrated Jumping Frog of Calaveras County," the professional writer Mark Twain would quite consciously use the stuffed-shirt tones of an all-business, no-pleasure, standard-speaking narrator to enhance his readers' delight in listening to a laid-back vernacular teller of events who enjoys a story simply for its own sake, and who also enjoys stringing along an unsuspecting, elevated narrator. Part of the later story's humor lies in the reader's realization that the standard-speaking narrator does not understand that he is being mocked. But young Sam was still a long way from the creation of garrulous old Simon Wheeler, whose way of telling serves to undercut Eastern pomposity. Sam's squatter of 1852 triumphs through the writer's reflexes, not through any deliberate narrative strategy.

In the traditional story of writers like Hooper, Hall, or Longstreet—the list could go on and on—the authority of the speaker of standard English usually establishes a moral and social distance between the reader and the vernacular character. In the wonderful episode in which Hooper has Simon Suggs attend a camp meeting, for example, the boorish country boobies get taken in by the equally boorish Simon, while the narrative voice emphasizes just how "low," how hopelessly far below the ideal of what true religion ought to be, he finds the whole sordid affair. No reader could doubt that such bumpkins as these deserved only contempt. Their language and their behavior all of a piece, the ideal was not in them: even slightly educated readers could feel relatively elevated, relatively genteel, in measuring themselves against such louts.

In contrast, consider the most popular American lecturer of the 1860s —"the most successful man of letters in the United States, measured either by the number of his readers or by the solid pecuniary rewards that had come to him."[6] The revered and respected Dr. Josiah G. Holland in 1861 published a collection of his lyceum lectures under the title of *Lessons in Life: A Series of Familiar Essays, By Timothy Titcomb.* (Timothy Titcomb was the pen name that Holland, at that time an editor of the *Springfield Republican,* used.) Holland's main point comes down to the propriety, indeed the necessity, of working to retain a vision of the ideal, no matter how inescapable the unfortunately "real" may appear to become. "Let us suppose," Dr. Holland suggests,

> that in a country journey we arrive at the summit of a hill, at whose foot lies a charming village imbosomed in trees from the midst of which rises the white spire of the village church. If we are in a poetical mood, we say: "How beautiful is this retirement! This quiet retreat, away from the world's distractions and great temptations, must be the abode of domestic and social virtue—the home of contentment, of peace, and of unquestioning Christian faith. Fortunate are those whose lot it is to be born and to pass their days here, and to be buried at last in the little graveyard behind the Church." As we see the children playing upon the grass, and the tidy matrons sitting in their doorways, and the farmers at work in the fields, and the quiet inn, with its brooding piazzas like wings waiting for the shelter of its guests, the scene fills us with a rare poetic delight.
>
> In the midst of our little rapture, however, a communicative villager comes along, and we question him. We are shocked to learn that the inn is a very bad place, with a drunken landlord, that there is a quarrel in the church which is about to drive the old pastor away, that there is not a man in the village who would not leave if he could sell his property, that the women give free rein to their propensity for scandal, and that half of the children of the place are down with the measles.[7]

But these "facts" do not affect Holland's way of seeing, his sense of what is "real," except to strengthen his determination to preserve his illusional vision: "The true poet," he goes on in the next paragraph,

> sees things not always as they are, but as they ought to be. He insists upon congruity and consistency. Such a life in such a spot, under such circumstances; and no unwarped and unpolluted mind can fail to see that the poet's ideal is the embodiment of God's will.[8]

Intent on his vision of "rare poetic delight," committed to the ideal, Holland refuses to notice the undercutting anticlimax of those measles that, for any vernacular humorist of the time, would by themselves have invalidated all sense of the scene's ideality. The "poet's ideal," the purely

6. Harriette M. Plunkett, *Josiah Gilbert Holland,* 72.

7. Cited by Smith, in *Mark Twain,* 6–7.

8. Josiah Gilbert Holland, *Lessons in Life: A Series of Familiar Essays,* 285–86 (from "The Poetic Test," 284–97, unchanged from the edition of 1861).

imaginary structure in the poet's head, has a religiously based validity: the particulars of a viewer's experience—the facets of reality that, to use Howells's words, "can be perceived by the senses"—do not count. Dr. Josiah Holland's preference for, and definition of, unpolluted minds will be turning up soon again.

Holland's way of seeing and of saying did not agree with Twain's, as a little sketch from the *Territorial Enterprise* of January 28, 1866, will confirm. Twain entitled it "Sabbath Reflections,"[9] making his point by a clever use of parentheses, so that the first part of the article can be read as two quite separate "reflections," one consisting of the ideal mental expectation, the cultural and literary stereotype, while the parenthetical parts offer the irritating reality that disturbs the senses and distracts the attention of the struggling writer. A very small portion of it will suffice:

> This is the Sabbath to-day. This is the day set apart by a benignant Creator for rest—for repose from the wearying toils of the week, and for calm and serious (Brown's dog has commenced to howl again—I wonder why Brown persists in keeping that dog chained up?) meditation upon those tremendous subjects pertaining to our future existence. How thankful we ought to be (There goes that rooster, now.) for this sweet respite; . . . .

And so on, through hens cackling, tom-cats fighting, and street-hawkers crying their wares. Then, "Sunday reflections! A man might as well try to reflect in Bedlam as in San Francisco when her millions of livestock are in tune." The ideal of the Sabbath can have no power over any sane person's perception of this reality. Twain concludes: "I have got to go now and report a sermon. I trust it will be pleasanter work than writing a letter on Sunday, while the dogs and cats and chickens are glorifying their Maker and raising the mischief." The power and the glorious humor of Twain's piece depend upon one's enjoying the juxtaposition. Refusing to deny the dramatic conflict between perceptions and style, as Holland had done, Twain celebrates the difference.

Then Twain came East, traveled to Europe and the Holy Land, published widely, married, and, in the early 1870s, settled into an elaborately built house in the Nook Farm literary community of West Hartford. Meanwhile, William Dean Howells, another arriviste, had signed on to the staff of the *Atlantic* (in 1865). The literary East welcomed him, in part because he seemed so "up" on the latest literary developments, in part because, as a young man grown up in Ohio before the Civil War had begun, he so reverently stood in awe of Eastern, which is to say Bostonian, literary culture as represented by the established vessels on

9. Reprinted in *Mark Twain's San Francisco*, 199–200, 201; the last paragraph of the "Reflections" appears at the end of "Neodamode," also in the *Enterprise* for January 28, 1866.

the *Atlantic*'s billows. After becoming editor, he had published Mark Twain's reminiscences of "Old Times on the Mississippi" in seven installments in 1874–1875, along with "A True Story" and several other pieces, and had admired *The Adventures of Tom Sawyer*. Twain especially appreciated appearing in print before the *Atlantic*'s readership "for the simple reason that it don't require a 'humorist' to paint himself stripèd & stand on his head every fifteen minutes."[10] That is, Twain hoped that he would be taken as a writer and thereby escape the pejorative label of humorist.

The *Atlantic* dinner of December 17, 1877, and Twain's speech there, bears reconsidering, however often the story has been told.[11] Fifty-eight men, all contributors or members of the staff, dined in Victorian opulence and ease. Then, after dinner, ladies and additional guests were admitted for the speeches. Henry O. Houghton, as publisher, welcomed them and introduced John Greenleaf Whittier, the guest of honor, who excused himself from speaking and asked Henry Wadsworth Longfellow to read a sonnet that Whittier had written for the occasion. Houghton next introduced William Dean Howells, his editor, as toastmaster, who introduced Ralph Waldo Emerson to recite Whittier's "Ichabod." There followed a short speech by Howells; Dr. Oliver Wendell Holmes read a new poem of his own; Charles Eliot Norton, a distinguished professor at Harvard, responded with a toast to James Russell Lowell, absent as Minister to Spain. Howells read several letters from guests unable to attend. The evening could not have pampered more thoroughly the pretensions of the "establishment" to gentility and dignity: everyone attending probably felt a pleasant thrill of self-satisfaction simply to have been included.

Then came Howells's introduction of Twain, the only non-"old boy," the only new kid on the block:

> And now, gentlemen, I will not ask the good friend of us all, to whom I am about to turn, to help us to forget these absent fellow-contributors, but I think I may properly appeal for oblivion from our vain regrets at their absence to the humorist, whose name is known wherever our tongue is spoken, and who has, perhaps, done more kindness to our race, lifted from it more crushing care, rescued it from more gloom, and banished from it more wretchedness than all the professional philanthropists that have live[d]; a humorist who never makes you blush to have enjoyed his joke; whose generous wit has no meanness in it, whose fun is never at the cost of anything honestly high or good, but comes from the soundest of

---

10. Mark Twain, December 8, 1874, *Mark Twain–Howells Letters*, 1: 49.
11. I summarize and quote from Henry Nash Smith's account in *Mark Twain*, chap. 5, "The California Bull and the Gracious Singers."

hearts and the clearest of heads. Mr. Clemens, gentlemen, whom we all know as Mark Twain, will address you.

This is an extremely curious introduction. "The good friend of us all, . . . whom we all know as Mark Twain," had barely met most of the assembled guests. Howells, who did know him very well—their friendship by 1877 was firmly secured, and would last until Twain's death, after which Howells would refer in print to his friend as "the Lincoln of our literature"—appears to be concealing and expressing an eleventh-hour fear that Twain might indeed shock the company, before whom Howells was sponsoring him, by making fun of some cherished ideals. Henry Nash Smith refers to the introduction as "Howells' admonition" and as "an obvious reference to the role of the man of letters in New England and therefore in American culture." "Since the occasion was intended to honor Whittier, and through him, the vocation of literature as represented by the *Atlantic*"—indeed, as *defined* by the *Atlantic*—Howells, knowingly or not, expressed his intense desire for no intercalated "Sabbath Reflections" in the remarks that Twain was about to make from his "soundest of hearts and clearest of heads," so that there should be no cause to "blush . . . at the cost of anything honestly high or good."

What guidelines to public expectations might have been in Twain's mind? Did he have any sense of acceptable limits beyond which polite speakers ought not to wander? For what might be considered an appropriate sort of humor for such an occasion, Twain had only to consult his own memory of the 1874 *Atlantic* dinner, the only previous time he had been present. There, Oliver Wendell Holmes had delivered "At the 'Atlantic' Dinner, December 15, 1874."[12] Holmes's light verse included some play on the words *"felis"* and *"felicitous,"* along with mention of "the Cochituate" and drilling (or "boring," in both senses) for Boston's new water supply. The assumption is not only that we know our Latin but that we're also New Englanders together—and, more to the point, Bostonians, at least by adoption. A sophisticated verbal cleverness is something we can all enjoy, and we can even poke a little bit of fun at the magazine's—and our own—pretensions to be cultivating the masses:

> May the monthly grow yearly, till all we are groping for
> Has reached the fulfillment we're all of us hoping for;
>
> . . . .
>
> Till abstinent, all-go-to-meeting society
> Has forgotten the sense of the word inebriety;
> Till the work that poor Hannah and Bridget and Phillis do
> The humanized, civilized female gorillas do;
> Till the roughs, as we call them, grown loving and dutiful,

12. George F. Whicher, ed., *Poetry of the New England Renaissance, 1790–1890,* 303–5.

Shall worship the true and the pure and the beautiful,
And, preying no longer as tiger and vulture do,
All read the "Atlantic" as persons of culture do!

The context and the polysyllabic rhymes make clear that "we" are right and the (probably uneducable) masses always and forever wrong. Indeed, it's hard not to equate the (mostly Irish) lower classes with the "gorillas" who may, in some happy future, do the work of today's "Hannah and Bridget and Phillis." To be so arch, to look downward so cleverly, one must be in total control, although no one was going to take very seriously any pretensions to abstinence voiced after a seven-course dinner, with a different wine at each course. Somewhat snobbish and self-satisfied, the verses reflect the urbanity and felicity that one might expect to lighten solemn festivities.

And festivities were supposed to be solemn. In 1877, no one chuckled during Emerson's recitation of Whittier's "Ichabod." Whittier's poem represented a morally serious voice, and such high moral seriousness carried with it the obligation of reverence, reverence for the forces of cultural—that is, literary and moral—order, and for the figures who embodied them. In 1861, Josiah Holland as Timothy Titcomb had spoken— almost in despair—of the "growing lack of reverence" from which the American character was beginning to suffer. He complained that we even "nickname our Presidents; and 'old Buck' and 'Old Abe' are spoken of as familiarly as if they were a pair of old oxen we were in the habit of driving." Holland, kept from the 1877 *Atlantic* dinner by his duties as editor of *Scribner's Magazine* in New York City, wrote of his fears for this new America. His letter, read by Howells with no apparent irony despite its tone of cloying adoration, reprises his earlier sense that what the country most needed was a revitalization of its almost defunct sense of reverence. Clearly, the idea had considerable importance to Holland, for he later reprinted his 1861 essay, "The Poetic Test," in all later editions of *Lessons in Life*, with no changes. Here is part of the 1877 letter that Howells read aloud before introducing Twain:

> I wonder if these old poets of ours—Mr. Dana, Mr. Bryant, Mr. Emerson, Mr. Longfellow, and Mr. Whittier [all present, please remember]— appreciate the benefit they confer upon their fellow citizens by simply consenting to live among them as old men? Do they know how they help to save the American nation from the total wreck and destruction of the sentiment of reverence? Why, if they will only live and move and have their being among us from seventy years of age to 100, and consent to be loved and venerated and worshipped and petted, they will be the most useful men we have in the development of the better elements in the American character . . . . The influence which these beloved and venerated poets exercise upon the public mind and character, simply by being lovely and

venerable, is, in the highest and sweetest degree, salutary and salvatory. May heaven bless them and spare them to us these many, many years.

Nobody was about to speak of "Old Greeny [Whittier]" or "Old Waddy [Longfellow]" or "Old Wally [Emerson]." Not only did reverence and humor fail to mix: even to attribute vernacular attributes to dignities, or dignitaries, was infra dig., was, in effect, to inflict an *in*-dignity. This, then, was the emotional, intellectual, and social context when Twain stood up to deliver his famous address.

Today, as modern Americans read the speech, it seems funny, splendidly witty. The skill with which Twain blends the well-known lines of his putative "Mr. Longfellow, Mr. Emerson, and Mr. Oliver Wendell Holmes—dad fetch the lot!" into the unlikely context of the conversation between a Western miner and his three unwelcome cabin-guests continues to please and even to amaze. Passing around the jug of humble hospitality, the simple, but very well-meaning, miner can't help but get "kind of worked up" when "Mr. Holmes looks at it and then fires up all of a sudden and yells—

> Flash out a stream of blood-red wine!
> For I would drink to other days."[13]

By having the miner barefooted when welcoming him into the cabin, Twain sets up the last, and perhaps the most telling, quotation of all: at the end of his tale of woe, the miner recounts that when he finally

> "woke at seven, they were leaving, thank goodness, and Mr. Longfellow had my only boots on, and his own under his arm. Says I, 'Hold on there, Evangeline, what are you a-going to do with *them*?' He says, 'Going to make tracks with 'em, because—

> > Lives of great men all remind us
> > We can make our lives sublime:
> > And, departing, leave behind us
> > Footprints on the sands of Time.'"

Twain's twisted, allusive use of Longfellow's "A Psalm of Life, or *What the Heart of the Young Man Said to the Psalmist*," one of the most popular, and one of the most solemnly didactic, poems of the genteel tradition, immediately precedes the conclusion's punch lines, in which first Twain assures the miner that " '*these* were not the gracious singers to whom we and the world pay loving reverence and homage; these were impostors,' " and then receives the miner's jolting riposte: " 'Ah! impostors, were they? are you?' " Twain then tidied up his "frame," separating

---

13. This and all other quotations from "The Whittier Birthday Speech" are from *Selected Shorter Writings of Mark Twain*, 151–55.

himself from his miner and from the Western context of his yarn, and sat down. Probably we will never know what most of his auditors thought. In Twain's traumatized memory, the question of who really was the "impostor" hung in the air: Twain recalled stunned silence, followed by one nervous laugh, followed by shame.

The story of Twain's overreaction to the perceived failure of this speech has become fairly common knowledge.[14] It now appears, however, that the failure lay primarily in the minds of William Dean Howells and Mark Twain, although the public reaction seems to have been increasingly negative the farther from Boston it is traced (except for the California newspapers). Still, Twain's guilt was real enough, and its immediate cause clear enough. The stylistic aggression of putting rude vernacular into the mouth of someone addressing even impersonators of "the gracious singers to whom we and the world pay loving reverence"— to say nothing of describing them as "seedy" and "fat" and "built like a prize-fighter" and then of scrambling their verse and demeaning its applications—passed the bounds of the permitted. Finally, revealingly, the attack turns back on itself, simultaneously reaching ignoble heights and dissolving into weak, though surprising, ambivalence when the question of who is and who is not an "impostor" hangs unresolved at the very end. With Howells's mortification and embarrassment on top of his own to spur him on, ten days later Twain wrote a letter of abject apology "To Mr. Emerson, Mr. Longfellow, & Dr. Holmes" that begins: "Gentlemen: I come before you, now, with the mien & posture of the guilty—not to excuse, gloss, or extenuate, but only to offer my repentance."[15] The genteel level of his language—"mien"; "extenuate"— complements the depths of his servility.

As we know, Twain in time came to see the speech as one of his very best efforts, and to wonder at the lack of appreciation shown by the audience as well as by the principals there present. But that was much later. In December 1877, the American way of speaking had blown up in his face, and he himself was not innocent. He had long known the literary and the public meaning of vernacular, as his habitual and successful manipulation of contrasting dictions makes obvious. His use of sanitizing, distancing quotation marks around various Southwesternisms delivered by the narrative voice of *The Adventures of Tom Sawyer* (e.g., "style" and "jimpson" within the first two pages) establishes that just a year before the *Atlantic* dinner, Mark Twain knew perfectly well how

14. Especially illuminating interpretations appear in Smith, *Mark Twain*, and in Kaplan, *Mr. Clemens and Mark Twain*.

15. This quotation, and subsequent ones concerning the speech, are from Smith's account in chap. 5, *Mark Twain*.

a genteel audience would evaluate vernacular speech. It was low, and, as others were quick to say, it appealed only to the low and vile parts of its auditors, if it appealed at all. For most people, violations of taste, by their very nature, precluded discussion. They caused an unspeakable problem.

3. RESPONSES, AND INTIMATIONS OF CROSSING OVER

On that December evening in Boston, Francis James Child, secure in his Harvard professorship and sophisticated as a collector of folk ballads, had found the speech totally delightful. He was one of the exceptions. Most of the rest were mildly amused, perhaps, or indifferent, or annoyed. The more widespread response found its full expression in the pages of the *Springfield Republican*, for which Josiah Holland was no longer writing, but which still preserved his perspective in good working order. The *Republican*'s report of the dinner refers to the "Nevada delirium tremens of Mark Twain" as an insult to the company: "It must have been very much as if the Nevada beverage itself had been slyly substituted in their glasses for the delicate wines that should have been there, and they had quaffed it unaware of the change." An unsigned letter to the editor (surely not Holland's: he would have been but too glad to claim the credit) so epitomizes the language of the genteel tradition in horrific recoil that it deserves to be savored in full:

MARK TWAIN'S MISTAKE AT THE WHITTIER DINNER

To the Editor of The Republican:—

No one caring in the least for the 'fitness of things' can read without a sense of pain the words of 'Mark Twain' at the late Atlantic-Whittier dinner. Imagine the scene, the really brilliant company, bright in the best sense of that suggestive word—'shedding much light, opposed to dark,' as Webster has it [the writer is already stacking his moral deck, you'll notice]—gathered to celebrate with sober joy and good cheer the 70th anniversary of a man of the most singular delicacy and refinement, combined with a strength, simplicity and sturdiness not always found with so much gentleness! Fit combination of events, the celebration of the progress of a life, which has had for its object the making of to-morrow better than today; and the speeding of an enterprise, which having passed its teens, looks forward to an earnest, ever broadening life. Gathered around the charming board with the gentle poet and the friend whose skill and enterprise enable them to sing to the whole round world [a compliment to publisher Houghton], we see him who thinks that "life is not an empty dream" [Longfellow, again], but that it holds high and holy, bright and gladsome things, of which he who has clean hands and a pure heart may taste. Beside him sits the philosopher [this will be Emerson, who apparently heard most of Twain's contribution in a pleasant, senile trance] who has dug deep and brought to light much that makes us think and hope, even if the mines *have* encroached on what are sometimes considered pre-empted claims. [Christians of the more conventional sort were still unhappy about "The Divinity School Address" of 1838.] Then, also, if wit and fun were wanted, and keen thrusts at sham and pretense, accompanied with a sincere reverence [AH!!!] for the beautiful and true, he who sits at the left is able and willing [Dr. Holmes, the third of Twain's "impostors"], and there are two others, who, were quiet, delicately delicious humor cared for, could bring it forth. Into this China shop bursts a wild Californian bull. True gentlemen bear insult in silence, and let such things dash on to their own destruction. But there is food for reflection in the incident. The songs, the literature, the wit and humor of a land tell tales, and when a bright, clever man, who does possess genuine humor, and has really discovered a new and curious vein [this is a phrase to remember], instead of fitting it to something that will amuse and relax the mind, without polluting it, finds his greatest glory in embellishing with his gift the low, poor, weak parts of our nature, and dressing in the garb of bar-room habitués the men who stand at the other end of life,—is it not well to enquire whether the popularity of this man ought not to have already reached its climax? Literary men in America, where so much is tolerated, ought to aim higher than the gutter, no matter what they have of talent, or even genius. American social life, upon which, with God's aid, must be built the mighty fabric of the future state, is in the formative period, and, jealous as we might have been of our political honor, a thousand times more jealous must we be of that most precious possession—reverence [again!] for that which is truly high. According to England's laureate, the good things of time are ours:—

> "To shape and use; arise and fly
>   The reeling Faun, the sensual feast!
>   Move upward, working out the beast,
> And let the ape and tiger die!"
Springfield, December 19, 1877.[16]

Not only must literature be didactic, moralistic, as allusion to "A Psalm of Life" and quotation from Tennyson's *In Memoriam* insist; but in his vernacular extravagance, Mark Twain has polluted us by "embellishing with his gift the low, poor, weak parts of our nature." He has encouraged us to bring to the surface our suppressed, or repressed, objections to propriety and to ideality (and, of course, to reverence). Twain stands accused: he has attempted to demolish our commitment to an ideal vision of life.

The culture's insistence upon the value of ideal constructions, no matter what the observable facts, makes understandable that impassioned rejection of Twain's after-dinner yarn for having dared to attribute the vulgarity of the uncouth miners of Twain's young manhood to figures

---

16. See Smith, *Mark Twain*, chap. 5.

bearing the hallowed names of venerated cultural icons. That the revered language of Emerson, Longfellow, Holmes, et al., should leak so inappropriately from the mouths of "impostors" threatened the legitimacy of a whole tradition. That the ears of the gentlemen themselves should be subjected to the uncouth vernacular appropriate to a boorish, uneducated Western miner exemplified so vile a rudeness that we can understand why Twain wondered if he himself were not an "impostor" in the court of high culture. But Twain, as well as others, had begun, and had acquired a method with which, to question the didactic ideality of a polite literature that kept on trying to see, as Holland and his kindred spirits wanted people to see, "that the poet's ideal is the embodiment of God's will," no matter who may have the moral or psychological measles.

Not until May 25, 1906, did Mark Twain come around to his final evaluation of that 1877 speech, seeing it as one of his funniest efforts: "Unless I am an idiot," he concludes, "it hasn't a single defect." He found it "saturated with humor," with no "suggestion of coarseness or vulgarity in it anywhere." By 1906, although Twain had won the battle, he still thought about it. His mind kept on returning to the event, rather like the way one probes an old wound or a newly drilled tooth. Back in 1877, guilt, shame, and self-disgust had been his lot. He had proven to himself and to Livy how worthless a creature he was, how out of tune with the ideal, how shabby and awkward a fugitive from the non-culture of the Wild West. However we may laugh today at the pretensions of traditional gentility, when we look back upon that complex, threatening encounter between Mark Twain and the Eastern literary establishment, we must remember that not much over one hundred years ago, the question about which was the impostor was by no means settled. Nor should we in our current, putative wisdom be too quick to award the palm of victory to the "real": although we now would smile forbearingly at any suggestion that we degrade ourselves when we applaud literary uses of the American way of speaking, Mark Twain himself, particularly in the stories of his last years, found increasing fascination with purely mental states—that is, ideal states—of being. Many of Twain's late manuscripts suggest that life is but a dream. The dream-state of existence often achieves in his work a reality more persuasive than that of any waking state; "The Thirty-Thousand Dollar Bequest" is but one example. In setting aside the easy idealism of the genteel tradition, Mark Twain nevertheless offers us versions of the ideal. To be sure, his nonmaterial realities cannot be mistaken for a to-be-wished-for embodiment of a "plan" by any "God" whom a sane person would care to revere. Still, what exists only in the mind can have (often does have, as Twain shows us) ultimate "reality," the power to shape actions as well as feelings.

However, just as Twain, seeming champion of material reality, ends by affirming the realm of the ideal, so the anonymous letter-writer of 1877, for all his genteel propriety in objecting to vernacular trampling upon the ideal, has objected in metaphors drawn directly from vernacular, even vulgar, experience: Emerson *is* a Western miner, after all; he becomes, however metaphorically, even a crooked trespasser upon Christian theology's "pre-empted claims." Not even Twain had gone so far as to say such a thing as that. And Twain himself is to be valued for having "really discovered a new and curious vein," although a vein merely of humor. Each side appears to be expressing a certain ambivalence, however unexpected, however unconscious. In the case of the anonymous letter-writer, this ambivalence would be, no doubt, very unconscious indeed. His talk of "pre-empted claims" and of "a new and curious vein" co-opt the language of the Western experience in order to assert allegiance to Eastern propriety. But his metaphors reveal an unintended demonstration of the powerful attraction exerted on the refined East by the raw West.

In Twain's case, intention is often hard to determine. Twain's preference for the vernacular perspective emerges with exceptional clarity as early as "The Celebrated Jumping Frog of Calaveras County" (1865), wherein, as I have briefly noted, the pompous speaker of standard English, seeking information for his "friend from the East" about one "Reverend *Leonidas* W. Smiley," expresses boredom, confusion, and disappointment upon being inundated by Simon Wheeler's vernacular yarn about a compulsive gambler by the name of *Jim* Smiley. The reader, entranced by the charm of Wheeler's way with words, can only shake a pitying head toward the officious speaker of proper English, too busy to waste his time simply enjoying lingo unproductive of solid information. But the creator of Simon Wheeler—and of Huckleberry Finn—also invented the narrator of *Roughing It* (1872). This latter commends with patronizing elegance the conversion to Christian belief and practice of Scotty Briggs, condescendingly observing—complete with exclamation-marks—that neither Scotty nor "his little learners" noticed any "violence . . . to the sacred proprieties!" in Scotty's slang version of "the beautiful story of Joseph," told to "his pioneer small-fry in a language they understood!" (end of chapter 47).[17] In context, it seems to me difficult, extremely forced, to attribute irony to Scotty's reminiscent eulogizer. It is, of course, possible that Twain is here inviting the reader to laugh at the propriety-driven narrator; but if he is, he is doing so with

---

17. References to well-known texts, readily available in many editions, are to title and (where relevant) chapter, and are not to be found in the bibliography.

a subtlety beyond the responsive capacities of all readers to date, myself included.

The question of Mark Twain may never be settled, but that is precisely my point. Even this most stalwart nineteenth-century exponent of the vernacular found in the apparently "other" cadences and vocabulary of the genteel culture a comforting retreat from the demands of intellectual and psychological independence. In reciprocal fashion, Josiah Holland's intellectual avatar, the anonymous writer of that letter to the *Springfield Republican*, found enjoyment in the lingo of the Western experience, with his "veins" and "claims." Similarly, but with considerably more vitality, George Washington Harris, creator of Sut Lovingood, the most vulgarly unrepressed of all the Southwestern scalawags I have encountered, offers up his creation as a self-satisfied, and even envied, example of a stratum of society in which "[m]en wer made a-purpus jis' tu eat, drink, an' fur stayin awake in the yearly part ove the nites: an' wimen wer made tu cook the vittils, mix the sperits, an' help the men du the stayin awake" (88).[18] Sut's triumphant vulgarity articulates and expresses, over and over again, the forbidden joys of sexuality, of overindulgence generally, and of recognizing the undersides of human motivation. But Harris, as his recent biographer, Milton Rickels, demonstrates, longed, and laid the groundwork, for a thoroughly "genteel" existence.[19]

At the same time, while presenting Sut as the wildly free but intensely disreputable boor, deluded as well as decadent, whom Harris himself would scorn to find in his church pew (228), Harris holds up his own ornately genteel language as an object for ridicule when measured against Sut's vigorous vernacular. "Eaves-Dropping a Lodge of Masons," in *Sut Lovingood: Yarns Spun by a "Nat'ral Born Durn'd Fool["*], begins with "George's" tear-stained imitation of sentimental literature. George evokes a past so far removed from material reality that he exhausts the patience of even the most convention-bound reader before Harris finally has Sut interrupt in an explosion of vernacular contempt: " 'Oh, komplicated durnashun! that haint hit,' " complains Sut. George must either be " 'drunk, ur yure sham'd tu tell hit, an' so yu tries tu put us all asleep wif a mess ove durn'd nonsince. . . . I'll talk hit all off in English, an' yu jis' watch an' an see ef I say, "echo," ur "grapes," ur "graveyard" onst' " (227–28).

Harris and his readers enjoy the irreverent virtuosity of Sut's way of telling, but over and over again, Harris uses Sut's narrow perspective and even narrower understanding to confirm the social and intellectual implications of his rude language: Sut is to be humored "for the sake of

18. Page numbers will be to Harris's *Sut Lovingood.*
19. Rickels, *George Washington Harris,* 22 et passim.

a joke" (49), but not respected, not taken seriously as a human being. As a momentary release from the demands of high culture, Sut's escapades provide a delightful alternative. As representing a permanent state of being, Sut remains beyond the pale. Similarly, Twain's vernacular denigration of Emerson, Longfellow, and Holmes, however liberating and enchanting on the evening of December 17, 1877, and long after, left Twain—along with a significant number of others significant to him— with the feeling that Western vernacular expression had no place amid the solemnities of Eastern literary high seriousness. Having criticized gentility, having rejected reverence both for the past and for foreign models of thought and speech, Twain found himself longing for both. The ideal, so often a target for vernacular scorn, turns out (as we will see) to beckon seductively even to Mark Twain, even to Sut Lovingood.

4. AMERICAN SELF-RELIANCE? THE CASE OF HAWTHORNE'S ROBIN

Mark Twain's cultural self-consciousness and self-distrust have analogs in a far more widely human context. In the process of attaining personal independence, individuals, no matter what their nationality, have long found a complex ambivalence in, rather than a straightforward congruence between, learned expectations and achieved desires. Most modern industrial societies have striven to break the old human patterns of holding on to the parents emotionally, financially, or socially. Even before the mobility—for jobs and therefore of homes—fostered by industrialization, the ethos of the frontier put a high value on individual self-sufficiency. Without recapitulating fairly familiar ideas, I'll simply recognize the truth of some generalizations and accept the geographical, economic, and organizational facts that have seemed to account for the condition. I'll be talking about Emerson later on, but, for now, let us simply remember that the title of his essay "Self-Reliance" spoke to generations of Americans, even if the complex essay itself puzzled or eluded more readers than it reached.

Americans were supposed to be—that is, were both expected to be and thought to be—independent. Nathaniel Hawthorne's Robin, in "My Kinsman, Major Molineux," seems at the story's start the epitome of such expectation: young, strong, tough, and modest, both in means and in demeanor, he enters "the little metropolis of a New England colony," after his day's trek of over thirty miles, "with as eager an eye as if he were entering London city." Here, one might anticipate, comes a young man who will show us what it means to be a young American. But the allusion to "entering London city" will turn out to be loaded: although Robin appears to embody a simple, sturdy self-reliance nine years before Emerson's essay, we soon see that he doesn't at all.

Repeatedly reminding himself, and us, that he has the reputation of being "a shrewd youth," Robin comes into the city from the country in order to "profit by his kinsman's generous intentions." That is, Major Molineux, a wealthy and respected cousin of Robin's father (a farming minister), has promised to set Robin up in life so that he can bypass all the troublesome steps to independence. Robin has only to find his kinsman in order to be taken care of. Here is one young American perfectly content to rely upon family influence to make his way in the new world. The two-edgedness of Hawthorne's words commands attention:

> The Major, having inherited riches, and acquired civil and military rank, had visited his cousin, in great pomp, a year or two before; had manifested much interest in Robin and an elder brother, and, being childless himself, had thrown out hints respecting the future establishment of one of them, in life. The elder brother was destined to succeed to the farm which his father cultivated in the interval of sacred duties; it was therefore determined that Robin should profit by his kinsman's generous intentions . . . .

"It was therefore determined": however vigorous and active Robin may be physically, the vague passivity of the verb puts Robin in the same class as his predestinated brother. And Robin happily goes forth to encounter his destiny. Arrived in town, he asks various people where he can find his kinsman. He keeps on being surprised and annoyed by their rude refusals to help him. He misunderstands their curtness as ignorance, or else as discourteous disrespect for his own homespun appearance. After a dreamlike sequence in which the discouraged Robin imagines himself back home with his family, he encounters a gentleman who offers to assist him, and who stays with Robin on a street corner to await the Major's promised appearance. When the Major finally does appear, however, he is in a cart, tarred and feathered and hooted at by an angry mob, many of whose members Robin has earlier asked for help in finding his kinsman. The procession comes to a halt; "Robin's knees shook, and his hair bristled, with a mixture of pity and terror." Then the ensuing hush is broken by "a voice of sluggish merriment." One after another of those whom Robin has previously encountered join in the laughter, "enjoying the lad's amazement." At last all are laughing, and "Robin's shout was the loudest there." Then Robin, in great embarrassment, decides to return to the country, but the helpful gentleman won't show him the way just yet, asking Robin to wait a while before making up his mind.

Take away Robin's vociferous laughter, and we have the story of a hick from the sticks who fails to understand city ways, and who ends up disappointed in his expectation that all he has to do to succeed is to appear under the auspices of his well-established relative. He makes mistakes about everything, under the illusion that his native shrewdness more than suffices for city success, and then wants only to retreat to whence he came. The last words of the helpful gentleman, which conclude the story, remain ambiguous: refusing to show Robin the way to the ferry "tonight," he suggests the possibility for future growth on Robin's part. " 'Some few days hence, if you wish it, I will speed you on your journey. Or, if you prefer to remain with us, perhaps, as you are a shrewd youth, you may rise in the world without the help of your kinsman, Major Molineux.' " This is the eighth appearance of the syllable "shrewd" in the story. Previously, its use—by the narrative voice or by Robin—has signified either authorial or dramatic irony. Although some readers take the helpful gentleman to be one of Hawthorne's devil-figures, playing on Robin's still-inflated sense of self to tempt him into worldly disregard of his roots,[20] Robin's laughter calls for a different reading. Because he has laughed, Robin shows that his point of view has changed: the gentleman's words certainly pick up on Robin's earlier, unfounded optimism concerning dependence upon the Major, as well as on Robin's over-estimation of his own capacity to understand; but, in addition, Robin has indeed changed, has shown himself to have arrived at a much "shrewder" sense of self than he possessed at the story's start.

This may seem an unwarranted burden to place upon the mere fact that Robin laughs. Laughter, after all, is contagious, and has echoed all through the story, with Robin's naïveté as its target. Robin wants his turn, too. " 'I have laughed very little since I left home, sir,' " he says to the helpful gentleman when he hears shouts, music, and "a wild and con-fused laughter," all of which signal the approach of the grisly procession that celebrates the Major's disgrace, " 'and should be sorry to lose an opportunity. Shall we step around the corner by that darkish house, and take our share of the fun?' " So Robin is certainly prepared to laugh. Then Hawthorne, in two long and extremely careful paragraphs, dramatizes first the obstacles to laughter and then the process of overcoming them. Recognizing his kinsman "in those circumstances of overwhelming hu-miliation," witnessing "the foul disgrace of a head grown grey in honor," Robin experiences a classic catharsis, "a mixture of pity and terror." As he and his kinsman stare at each other in wordless recognition, a desire for mere "fun" has no place in Robin's consciousness.

> Soon, however, a bewildering excitement began to seize upon his mind; the preceding adventures of the night, the unexpected appearance of the crowd, the torches, the confused din and the hush that followed, the spectre of his kinsman reviled by that great multitude,—all this, and more than all, a perception of tremendous ridicule in the whole scene, affected him with

20. See, e.g., Neal B. Houston and Fred A. Rodewald, " 'My Kinsman, Major Molineux': A Re-Evaluation."

a sort of mental inebriety. At that moment a voice of sluggish merriment
saluted Robin's ears; he turned instinctively . . .

and sees one of his earlier tormentors "drowsily enjoying the lad's
amazement." Before the paragraph ends, three of those who earlier had
laughed at Robin are laughing now. The next paragraph begins with a
lengthy description of one of these, who

> supported himself on his polished cane in a convulsive fit of merriment,
> which manifested itself on his solemn old features like a funny inscription
> on a tombstone. Then Robin seemed to hear the voices of the barber, of the
> guests at the inn, and of all who had made sport of him that night. The
> contagion was spreading among the multitude, when all at once, it seized
> upon Robin, and he sent forth a shout of laughter that echoed through
> the street,—every man shook his sides, every man emptied his lungs, but
> Robin's shout was the loudest there.

The scene ends as the procession moves off "in counterfeited pomp, in
senseless uproar, in frenzied merriment, trampling all on an old man's
heart. On swept the tumult, leaving a silent street behind." Half a page
then concludes the tale, as Robin, no longer naïve, no longer pretentious,
with his "cheek . . . somewhat pale, and his eye not quite as lively as in
the earlier part of the evening," requests twice to be shown the way to
the ferry that will take him back where he came from, but meets instead
with the helpful gentleman's ambiguously tentative encouragement.

Hawthorne attaches this laughter if not to the cosmos, then at least to
the whole world: "The cloud-spirits peeped from their silvery islands,
as the congregated mirth went roaring up the sky! The Man in the Moon
heard the far bellow. 'Oho,' quoth he, 'the old earth is frolicsome tonight!'" When Robin laughs, that is, Hawthorne steps back and inter-
poses some cosmic distance between laugher and laughed-at. At this
point, a reader separates Robin's laughter from that of the rest: they laugh
at Robin for being so mistaken about the status of his kinsman, and they
laugh in thoughtless cruelty. "On they went, like fiends that throng in
mockery around some dead potentate, mighty no more, but majestic still
in his agony. On they went, in counterfeited pomp, in senseless uproar, in
frenzied merriment, trampling all on an old man's heart." Hawthorne's
presentation makes the heartless mob appear odious in the extreme: their
laughter is a "tuneless bray, the antipodes of music"; he uses such phrases
as "increasing din," "confusion of heavier sounds," "shrill voices of mirth
or terror," "instruments of discord," "wild and confused laughter," and
"the uproar." The laughter of the mob, of the masses, has no rational
component to it that one can see.

Later, near the end of chapter 9 of *The Scarlet Letter* (1850), Hawthorne
will distinguish between the "eyes" of "the uninstructed multitude" and

"the intuitions of its great and warm heart," finding the former "exceedingly apt to be deceived," the latter "often so profound and so unerring, as to possess the character of truths supernaturally revealed." Here, almost twenty years earlier, he emphasizes the irrational cruelty of the mob emanating from its failure to make necessary distinctions. The public unrest that erupts on Robin's first night in eighteenth-century Boston (identified only as "the little metropolis of a New England colony") has nothing to recommend it. The lot of the colonial governors appointed by the king was not an happy one, as both history and Hawthorne tell us. Although "softening their instructions from beyond the sea," they still appeared to "the people" to exercise too imperious an authority, so "that of six governors in the space of about forty years from the surrender of the old charter, under James II," three were driven out of office, a fourth aggravated into an early grave, "and the remaining two, as well as their successors, till the Revolution, were favored with few and brief periods of peaceful sway. The inferior members of the court party, in times of high political excitement, led scarcely a more desirable life."

Major Molineux, apparently one of those privileged, genteel, royalist functionaries, becomes the convenient victim of the enraged mob, but Hawthorne asks his readers "to dispense with an account of the train of circumstances that had caused much temporary inflammation of the popular mind." That is, although political issues lie behind the mob's actions, Hawthorne explicitly sets them to one side. The humanly individual results, not the politically communal, have center stage. Old Molineux, whatever his authoritarian or royalist biases, has served honorably, at least by his own best lights. Without specification, Hawthorne suggests that whatever has led the Major to his present disgrace has to do primarily with the people's irrational reactions, not with any act of betrayal on the Major's part. The mob, in "trampling all on an old man's heart," might be said to be breaking one of the British eggs from which the American Revolutionary omelet will be made, but political expediency is simply not the issue in this story. Robin's self-centered ignorance of political reality, however, will turn out to cost him dearly, though "only" in a psychological way. Because Robin expects for himself something very like unearned Old World inherited position and comfort, he has indeed entered the colonial "little town" as if it were "London city." He has in his head no thought of young Ben Franklin's entrance into Philadelphia and of its aftermath of hard work.

Because Robin encounters puzzling deflection or mysterious rejection each time he mentions the name of his kinsman, a reader might be expected to infer that the political background so fuzzily drawn in that first paragraph will turn out to be precisely the part of the picture that Robin has been missing. Hawthorne here compresses a small bit of historical raw material into even smaller compass, and then presses it into service under the guise of explaining that he isn't going to explain it at all. The sympathy he squeezes out of a reader for heartbroken Major Molineux becomes part of the emotional energy that he uses to shift the weight of one's involvement with Robin from shared disappointment to a new sort of hope. Disappointed or confused by the frustration of Robin's hopes for patronage, a reader moves on to impatience at the persistence of those immature hopes, and then to the fresh hope that Robin will be able to act on the very American sentiment of the friendly gentleman, the hope that Robin " 'may rise in the world without the help of [his] kinsman, Major Molineux.' " Material rising, although the issue in Robin's consciousness, here gives way in the reader's mind to thoughts of a psychological progression with strong ethical overtones: Robin, one feels, "ought" to grow up. He should "earn" his success.

Robin's laughter has in it an element that the laughter of the mob lacks: although both laughters bear out Nietzsche's aphorism that "to laugh is to be malicious but with a good conscience," Hawthorne has situated that "good conscience" in different domains. The mob, despite its heartless brutality, its raw malice, sees itself as justified by political reality. Hawthorne suggests that they have acted wrongly, but he suggests with equal force that they feel justified, that their collective conscience is "good," because they have been taking action against what they perceive to be an unjust government's oppression. Robin's laughter, on the other hand, has no political component to it at all. The malice behind it stems, in part, from his disappointed expectations of worldly assistance; his conscience is "good," however, because another part of that malice is directed toward himself, and draws its force from his sudden understanding of, and disgust with, his own earlier, naïve, and dependent posture.

He may well be expected to feel malice toward his kinsman: the Major fails to play his expected role of hospitably welcoming country cousin Robin to the big city. Instead of meeting a powerful patron able to confer future favors, Robin finds a suffering victim of the very society he had been dominating; his kinsman turns out to be a tormented outcast instead of a source of social and economic power. The "good conscience" that supports Robin's laughter has its less obvious basis in feelings that Hawthorne implies but, as is so often the case in his work, does not state. Robin's sense of betrayal comes to seem to Robin— not just to the reader—in large part Robin's own fault. Robin's much-vaunted "shrewdness" has taken a beating, as if from Robin's own stout country cudgel. Robin sees for himself how wide of the mark have been his "shrewd" accountings for the disrespect he was shown all through the first part of the story. In retrospect, the other Americans seem to have been almost indulgent toward his naïveté. Hawthorne has made unambiguous the irony in each reiteration of the word "shrewd" in every scene in which it appears.

But Robin's laughter, in its brutal and malicious detachment, signifies more than this. Robin has come to a still larger self-understanding. Up until actually encountering his kinsman, Robin has taken it as his right that he should be spared the pains of rising in the world simply by his own exertions. In several pages of regressive reverie, Robin torments himself with fantasies of desolation, of loneliness, and, finally, of rejection. Peering through the window frame of an empty church, he feels a disquieting isolation; and then, as he sits at the doorway, the churchyard graves lead him to "an uneasy thought": "What if the object of his search . . . were all the time mouldering in his shroud?" He even frightens himself with the fancy that the Major's ghost might "glide through yonder gate, and nod and smile to him in dimly passing." Then he conjures up a vision of home, with outdoor religious service beneath the family oak, and prayers and tears for the absent loved one.

This orgy of self-pity leads to other reveries, and almost to sleep, but Robin starts to alertness "at the sound of footsteps along the opposite pavement." In a "loud, peevish, and lamentable cry," Robin sings out: " 'Hallo, friend! must I wait here all night for my kinsman, Major Molineux?' " This petulance reveals his unarticulated sense that he has the right to expect the world to take care of him. For the first time, instead of polite request, Robin expresses his wish in the manner of a spoiled child, thereby dramatizing its infantile nature: imperious, demanding, he sounds like a three-year-old, angry at the delay of dinner. And instead of the rebukes that his earlier, more maturely couched, requests have received, Robin for the first time receives a patient, disinterested response, "in a tone of real kindness, which had become strange to Robin's ears. 'Well, my good lad, . . . Can I be of service to you in any way?' "

Readers find Robin's laughter persuasive—"in character," as we used to say—not only, not even primarily, because they see Robin's disillusion with his own "shrewdness," but because they sense Robin's sudden recognition of what, consciously or unconsciously, they have already recognized: Robin's suddenly disappointed expectation rested on a false basis from the beginning. Old World patronage and dependence, so appropriate to Old World social, economic, and political modes, take on new meanings in the context of the New World. By sanctioning the reliance of the younger upon the established position of the older, the stratified society of Europe offered hierarchical as well as hereditary security, to be sure. Along with that security, however, went the imprisonments of place and position, and the limiting necessity of reckoning with the wishes and whims of the patron.

In pre-Revolutionary New England, as in Hawthorne's nineteenth century, such dependence (or security) means not a necessary acceptance of things-as-they-are but, rather, a servile, degrading, and, finally, infantile arrest of personal development. Robin's laughter, I suggest, rings true not only because Robin can be seen to have changed his self-conception about being "a shrewd youth," but also—and more important—because Robin sees in a New World light the dependence upon his kinsman that he has hitherto seen only through eyes shaded by a cloth of very European cut. Robin sees—and I believe that Hawthorne wants readers to understand that Robin sees—nothing new about himself, but he sees in a new light what he has always been. Suddenly, and though laughing partly in bitter disappointment as well as in malicious anger at the sight of his disgraced kinsman (who now, alas, will be forever unable to help him as he had wanted to be helped), he laughs also in frank recognition of his own absurdity in expecting that the burden of growing up to make his own way in the world would, should, and could be made to pass from him. He has brought London expectations to Boston, where New World realities require their disappointment. The psychological moment of the American Revolution has arrived.

Because Hawthorne, that great writer of romance, is also a great realist of the human heart, he leaves open, unresolved, the use that Robin may make of his new understanding. He shows us that desire for independence does not rule out a deeper desire for its opposite. His acute sense of history, as well as of the reality of ambivalence and of the ambiguity of most things human, leads Hawthorne to place in opposition elements that popular conscience, and consciousness, tended to find compatible, even mutually supportive. If Robin is going to make his way unaided by his kinsman, he will do so not on the frontier, not by striking out into the wilderness, but in the labyrinthine city. Further, the achievement of independence promises separation from the religious observations of the ministerial father as well as separation from the soil. Hawthorne here relegates both the Jeffersonian fantasy of agrarian self-sufficiency and the Puritan ideal of quiet piety to a past that will no longer be accessible to Robin if he evinces the "self-reliance" of the archetypal American. Even more strikingly subversive, independence—political independence, in any case, and by implication elements of psychological independence as well—here implies at least a period of transition during which the excesses of mob rule must sully members of the nobility because nobility suppresses democracy. Hawthorne, ardent Jacksonian Democrat though he was, writes with a surprisingly Hamiltonian sense of the people's beastliness. As delineated in this story, the psychological and social costs of independence turn out to be great.

Hawthorne-as-historian presents a series of images that encapsulates ambivalence toward American independence. Babies do sometimes get thrown out with bathwater. The honorable services of an old man retain their honorableness even when they stand in the way of history. Just as Hawthorne will begin *The Scarlet Letter* with an ambiguous rose-bush, perhaps an aboriginal survivor from "the stern old wilderness" and perhaps a new birth from the spirit of liberty represented by "the footsteps of the sainted Anne Hutchinson," so do many of his works look beyond simplicity to the complexity of historical and psychological reality. Readers will remember "The Maypole of Merrymount" and numerous other examples, too. The fact of American rejection of Britain, of American political independence, has its reverberations. But how do we conceptualize the results of that rejection? In what ways do we see ourselves as different, uniquely American and not just colonial?

5. Melville, the American Difference, and Richard Chase

Few writers have been more astute at putting before us a fully imagined sense of the differences, and of their consequences, than that bluff sailor from New York, Herman Melville. I want to bypass the major works, even *Mardi*, with its clear-eyed chapters on Britain's political and economic practice, and turn to two short pieces, a pair with a single title, "The Paradise of Bachelors and the Tartarus of Maids." By the time he wrote this, Melville was far, in time, distance, and psychology, from *Typee* and the wonderful island of Nuka Heva, with the naked Fayaway on the one hand and the cannibals and the unexplained injury that almost "unmanned" his narrator on the other. His interest seems more public, more societal. No longer is he fantasizing about his bachelor days as a sailor in the South Pacific and at the same time exploring his complicated guilt about sexuality, as Newton Arvin has suggested he did in *Typee*. Almost ten years after his first novel, Melville sets up two antithetical worlds that can come together only in the narrator's, and then in the reader's, imagination. In contrast to his friend Hawthorne, Melville insists upon American difference from, not connection to, England. Not accidentally, but significantly, in *Moby-Dick*, the British Captain Boomer of the British *Samuel Enderby* accepted things as they were in marked and deliberate contrast to the American captain of the American *Pequod*.

In "The Paradise of Bachelors," Melville offers us an image of comfortably irresponsible bliss: "nothing loud, nothing unmannerly, nothing turbulent," the narrator assures us, just first-rate dining, with first-rate wines, somewhat in excess of moderation, but only enjoyably so, partaken of in company with "nine gentlemen, all bachelors," in the

chambers of a "right bluff, care-free, right comfortable, and most com-
panionable Englishman" at "No. ——, Elm Court, Temple." Convivi-
alities of the board and of the tongue mark the evening, so that the
narrator's conclusion has a certain persuasiveness: " 'Sir,' said I, with a
burst of admiring candor—'Sir, this is the very Paradise of Bachelors!' "
But paradise, like bachelorhood, has its limitations, and Melville has
been careful to heighten a reader's awareness of them. These bachelors
tend toward the legal profession, a sad falling off for those who inhabit
the quarters and have usurped the name of the old "Knights-Templars":
" . . . the vowed opener and clearer of all highways leading to the Holy
Sepulchre, now has it in particular charge to check, to clog, to hinder, and
embarrass all the courts and avenues of Law. . . ." More directly in the
matter of bachelorhood, Melville's narrator takes us to "the quiet cloisters
of the Paradise of Bachelors" from "the mud of Fleet Street—where
the Benedick tradesmen are hurrying by, with ledger-lines ruled along
their brows, thinking upon the rise of bread and fall of babies—. . . ."
This "Paradise" is very like the womblike London that Robin has been
anticipating: comfort and security, insulated from the hectic struggle for
existence that roars in the streets beyond.

The Benedicks keep on marking Melville's contrast between bachelors
and husbands, three times in the story's first five pages. Shakespeare's
Benedick, in the first scene of *Much Ado About Nothing*, insists to his
friend Pedro, "I will live a bachelor," and counters Pedro's "In time the
savage bull doth bear the yoke" with considerable violence: "The savage
bull may; but if ever the sensible Benedick bear it, pluck off the bull's
horns and set them in my forehead, and let me be vilely painted, and in
such great letters as they write 'Here is a good horse to hire,' let them
signify under my sign 'Here you may see Benedick the married man.' "
By the play's last scene, Benedick has won, or lost, his way to Beatrice,
and Pedro twits him cruelly: "How dost Benedick, the married man?"
By referring to his married men as Benedicks, then, Melville underlines
the husband's status as defeated bachelor, while also calling attention
to the cares associated with putting bread on the table for the mouths of
the babes whose births keep complicating a husband's finances.

"But fine though they be, bachelors' dinners, like bachelors' lives, can
not endure forever." True it is that the dining bachelors in their paradise
"had no wives or children to give an anxious thought. Almost all of
them were travelers, too; for bachelors can travel freely, and without
any twinges of their consciences touching desertion of the fireside." This
happy state has its strong appeal. But lives do end; how deeply have
these happy bachelors experienced their own? "The thing called pain,
the bugbear styled trouble—those two legends seemed preposterous
to their bachelor imaginations." Delightful, perhaps, but limited. An

entire range of human experience remains unknown, unknowable, to Melville's bachelors.

Why did Melville so carefully set his paradise of bachelors in London, England? Plenty of images for jollity existed in Knickerbocker's New York, the city of Melville's friend and editor Evert Duyckinck and his convivial acquaintanceship. Why England? And turning to "The Tartarus of Maids," why so specifically New England? London and Liverpool, to Melville's firsthand knowledge, could furnish forth raw materials for any number of pictures of cold, confined misery. Why does Melville— even beyond his acute sensitivity to names—put his paper mill "not far from Woedolor Mountain in New England"? The mill, to be sure, has sexual reasons for being close by "the Mad Maid's Bellows-pipe" and "the Black Notch" and "Blood River" and "the Devil's Dungeon": by the time the narrator has come to understand the process by which paper is made, he probably—and the reader certainly—has come to recognize the analogy with human gestation. Beginning with "white, wet, woolly-looking stuff, not unlike the albuminous part of an egg," and passing on to a "room, stifling with a strange, blood-like, abdominal heat, as if here, true enough, were being finally developed the germinous particles lately seen," the process, taking " 'only nine minutes,' " " 'nine minutes to a second,' " ends as "a scissory sound smote my ear, as of some cord being snapped; and down dropped an unfolded sheet of perfect foolscap . . . still moist and warm," a blank sheet of paper, John Locke's tabula rasa indeed.

When we consider that the narrator is in "the seedsman's business" and therefore in need of envelopes for dispensing his wares, we may want to think of Melville the writer, with intellectual seeds to distribute, as well as of Melville the husband and father. But a reader's attention, with the narrator's, focuses on the "girls," "all maids," whose faces "mournfully, beseechingly, yet unresistingly, . . . gleamed along, their agony dimly outlined on the imperfect paper, like the print of the tormented face on the handkerchief of Saint Veronica." The principal proprietor, "an old bachelor," and one Cupid, "a lively lad," are the only males visible in the fecund sterility of the mill. Both belong to the managerial class, and both exude vitality. The girls are worse off than even those "Benedick tradesmen" at the start of "The Paradise" who are "hurrying by, with ledger-lines ruled along their brows." Physically imprisoned by both the cold and their twelve-hour workday, " 'day after day, through the three hundred and sixty-five days, excepting Sundays, Thanksgiving, and Fast-days,' " the "girls" seem as predestined as the paper they so mechanically make. The narrator watches two workers performing separate operations. "I looked upon the first girl's brow, and saw it was young and fair; I looked upon the second girl's brow, and saw it was ruled and wrinkled. Then as I still looked, the two—for some small variety to the monotony—changed places; and where had stood the young fair brow, now stood the ruled and wrinkled one." And above all, the machinery strikes the narrator: not only do the girls "not so much seem accessory wheels to the general machinery as mere cogs in the wheels," but "machinery of this ponderous, elaborate sort strikes, in some moods, strange dread into the human heart, as some living, panting Behemoth might. But what made the thing I saw so specially terrible to me, was the metallic necessity, the unbudging fatality which governed it."

These are wonderfully rich stories. Melville suggests that the "girls," having no sexual experience at all, somehow become the victims of an impersonal baby factory, or paper factory, and therefore grow lines on their foreheads just the way those Benedicks of married men do. The elderly "principal proprietor" spells out for the narrator the virginal quality of his help: " 'We will not have married women; they are apt to be off-and-on too much,' " says he; and Narrator reports that "some pained homage to their pale virginity made me involuntarily bow." The narrator reports that these women are always referred to as "the girls." They suffer the agonies of a process likened to gestation, but experience no rewards that a reader can discern. The bachelor-Templars have degenerated into lawyers, producing nothing valuable, but live comfortably and painlessly, whereas the exploited mill girls of New England produce the great essential for writers and readers (and lawyers), meanwhile living lives of quiet desperation.

But why in New England so explicitly? Dark, satanic mills abounded, as Melville well knew, in the same England that housed his jolly bachelors. Something in the manner of these stories—the contrasting manners of the two parts of the one set, to be more accurate—seems at least as suggestive as the direct social commentary. It puts me in mind of Richard Chase's insight in *The American Novel and Its Tradition*. Chase contended that many American novels, even some that seem contentiously realistic, might better be called American romances because our fictions differ so noticeably from what F. R. Leavis called "The Great Tradition," by which Leavis meant the English novel. Leavis called Emily Brontë's *Wuthering Heights* "a kind of sport," a hint that Chase expands: "Of course Mr. Leavis is right; in relation to the great tradition of the English novel, *Wuthering Heights* is indeed a sport. But suppose it were discovered that *Wuthering Heights* was written by an American of New England Calvinist or Southern Presbyterian background."[21] Although he saw that the book

---

21. Richard Chase, *The American Novel and Its Tradition*, 4.

would be unique whoever wrote it, Chase asserted that "if it were an American novel it would not be a sport." He distinguished between an American and a British (Leavis's "Great") tradition as between a unifying presentation of the surfaces of life, especially social life, with a resolution of whatever thematic interests the novel has raised, and a presentation of the extremes of experience and feeling, with no special concern to resolve contradictions and differences. Chase used the words "massive, temperate, moralistic" to refer to the rendering of life and thought in the British tradition, and "alienation, contradiction, and disorder" to speak of the American commentary upon life. Again: Ahab's metaphysical rage, Ahab's behavior generally, seems in this context to belong to American romance in the same way that Captain Boomer's accommodating acceptance of things-as-they-are smacks of the British novel.

One way to think about this contrast would be to consider Ishmael as he writes *Moby-Dick*, or Huck Finn at the end of his *Adventures*. Huck, clearly, is alienated, about "to light out for the territory ahead of the others" so as to escape Aunt Sally's efforts to adopt and civilize him. But this is no more a resolution of Huck's problem of finding a place for himself than is the miraculously unbelievable freeing of Jim by Miss Watson in her will a resolution of a self-styled Christian society's problem in reconciling the immorality of slavery with the morality of Christianity. Twain ends Huck's book with no resolution at all for the tension between Huck's satisfactory life with Jim, isolated on that magical raft, and Jim's poignantly expressed need to reunite his own family, chained to and by a white society whose cruel constraints even Huck cannot tolerate. This tension is not so different from one in James Fenimore Cooper's *The Prairie*: Natty Bumppo rejects civilization as embodying all the engines of the devil for the corruption of mankind. The authorial voice, however, assures us that civilization refines and generally improves the character of Paul Hover, one of the personages of whom Natty (as well as readers) generally approves. No resolution occurs: civilization is terrible; civilization is desirable. Both feelings are real, and both feelings are large, deep, and abstract.

Ishmael illuminates the issue in a slightly different way. As a young man who encounters Captain Ahab and the rest of the *Pequod*'s voyagers, he is attracted to the water and haunted—as he tells us in the first chapter, even unto his inmost soul—by the image of "one grand hooded phantom, like a snow hill in the air." But old Ishmael, who writes the story, has learned that "in pursuit of those far mysteries we dream of, or in tormented chase of that demon phantom that, some time or other, swims before all human hearts; while chasing such over the round globe, they either lead us in barren mazes or midway leave us whelmed." Trying to get hold of "the ungraspable phantom of life" leads to death, or, if one is lucky, merely to disappointment. Ishmael, by the time he sits down to write, has learned that accommodation beats romantic questing. "For now," says he as he looks back on the voyage that almost cost him his life, "For now, since by many prolonged, related experiences, I have perceived that in all cases man must eventually lower, or at least shift, his conceit of attainable felicity; not placing it anywhere in the intellect or the fancy; but in the wife, the heart, the bed, the table, the saddle, the fire-side, the country; now" he is ready to settle for the felicity of human fellowship and renounce all efforts at metaphysical enlightenment. That is, Ishmael concludes where Dickens's John Jarndyce, Esther Summerson, and David Copperfield, where the characters of George Eliot and Henry Fielding, and of all the rest of the Great Tradition, begin: they prize, as he finally comes to prize, the commonplace, as in Wordsworth's "unremembered acts / Of kindness and of love,"[22] that they must labor to attain, that he has ignored and taken for granted.

The lure of abstract truth that Ishmael talks about and finally renounces, of an intellectual apprehension that will somehow allow one to feel at home in the universe, exerts its grip on Puritans of all persuasions, and also manifests itself in a great deal of American literature. Melville's settings for his "Paradise" and "Tartarus" have a rightness that goes far beyond the author's humanitarian recoil from the exploitative mills of Massachusetts, and nineteenth-century democratic condemnation of the cloistered exclusivity of British upper-class jollity. The different ways in which Melville's single narrator tells the two stories anticipate Chase just as if Melville had deliberately set out to conform to the paradigm.

"Paradise" is real. The foods and drinks and furniture and buildings are solid, even historically tangible, in the case of the Temple. The conversation, summarized, though not transcribed, suggests the jovial materiality of the diners' lives as well as a total lack of concern with social problems and issues of the moment. Anecdotes about the Iron Duke and about student days at Oxford, wines, scenery, rare books, the translation of a comic poem: these topics have a material superficiality and a solidity that represent the selfish self-satisfaction of the bachelors in their enviably comfortable, if emotionally vacuous, lives. If Melville could have known Robert Frost's "Provide, Provide," he might have had his Templars mistake its irony for straight advice: they have provided well for themselves, with no apparent awareness that less fortunate lives might be any of their concern, or that comfort as an end in itself finally cloys. Melville's moral judgments emerge from the surface realism of the

22. "Lines Composed a Few Miles above Tintern Abbey . . . ," ll. 34–35.

story. Its English setting reflects its English mode of operation, as Chase explicated that mode.

When we turn to "The Tartarus of Maids," we enter not merely a different landscape, New England hills instead of London streets, but a different wordscape, too. The Devil's Dungeon paper mill, where "Machinery—that vaunted slave of humanity—here stood menially served by human beings, who served mutely and cringingly as the slave serves the Sultan," is aptly named. And so is Woedolor Mountain and the Mad Maid's Bellows and the Black Notch and Blood River. By the time we have absorbed the aptness of all these names, their geographical flimsiness, coupled with their allegorical utility, lets us know that we are among abstractions, and that the story will be an exploration of internal states even more than of social realities. Reading "Paradise," one can imagine easily how the bachelors spend their time when they're not feasting in each other's chambers. But there is no imagining at all how the maidens of "Tartarus" interact with each other offstage. The details of their lives, their lives themselves, have no reality for a reader. They embody meaning, not mimesis. What comes to life in the story is a set of feelings—primarily the narrator's and, through his, a reader's—in response to a kind of cerebral psychodrama involving industrialism and parturition without sexuality, as in the ironic reference to the "girls" as slaves of "the Sultan." Industrialism indeed becomes parturition, a mechanical necessity imposed on female human beings. The tortured existence of the "girls" has its analogies to the pains of childbirth, the aftermath of sexual experience, the penalty for fallen womankind in a world suffering from post-Adamic trauma.

Not that the two parts constitute an "argument" for one side of the Atlantic against the other. The jollity of the bachelors is no less sterile than the gloomy parody of parturition enacted by the maids. In neither case can there be a next generation. In both cases, Melville reminds us of the presence of death. When, at the very end, the narrator exclaims, "Oh! Paradise of Bachelors! and oh! Tartarus of Maids!" he makes us recall that his "burst of admiring candor" in praise of the "Paradise" followed immediately his observation that "bachelors' dinners, like bachelors' lives, cannot endure forever." The deathly pallor, the frost-filled cold, of the "Tartarus" paper mill contrasts cruelly with the fire-warmed bachelor chambers, but the narrator awakens more than a sense of contrast alone: learning that the cloth in the rag room comes from all over the world, even from "Leghorn and London," he suggests that " 'among these heaps of rags may be some old shirts, gathered from the dormitories of the Paradise of Bachelors.' " His query about bachelors' buttons elicits from young Cupid the information that flowers by that name cannot " 'grow in this part of the country,' " and then a query about " 'the gold bosom-buttons of our boss, Old Bach,' " as the principal proprietor is called. America, too, has its bachelors.

The deliberate tenuousness of these associations calls attention to the gap between the narrator's words and the author's meaning. This somewhat sentimental narrator sighs over the hard lot of the "Maids" in contrast to " 'the very Paradise of Bachelors!' " He also laments, however, the emptiness of mere pleasure as experienced by the bachelors. Neither way of life represents an acceptable social or psychological order. Whence can emerge a next generation? What has happened to familial warmth? The broad irony of the paradise contrasts pointedly with the atmosphere of claustrophobic self-scrutiny in the Tartarus, as the narrator examines his own reactions as intently as he does the process of making paper.

This latter internal drama fits perfectly with the expectations Richard Chase leads one to have of American fiction. But the same Herman Melville creates in "Paradise" a fictive world that conforms to Chase's discussion of the British novel. It's as if Melville had gone out of his way to set in New England a story embodying peculiarly American qualities of sensibility and, in Old England, its very British antithesis. Melville gives the British social order a solidity and a permanence that convey its physical tangibility, but at the expense of psychological meaning. Readers may infer a womblike effect of the environment upon the diners, but nothing suggests any congruent emotional experience on their part. In the "American" story, however, the despair embodied in the impersonal processes of manufacturing goes beyond the material surfaces of lives, pointing to a psychological reality experienced by the characters rather than to the materially realized details of their ordinary existence.

Most of Melville's writing emphasizes the nontangible. Ishmael, for example, though at times immersed in blubber, cares much more for the metaphysical suggestiveness of whales in general, and of the not yet seen Moby Dick in particular, than for the available, actual whales he must chase, kill, and convert into salable substance. The "Paradise" and "Tartarus" stories not only encompass the two different worldviews of the comfort-seeking bachelors and of the significance-seeking American narrator, but also illustrate two different modes of fiction that turn out to adumbrate contrasting qualities of British and American ways of imagining. The teller of the "Paradise" points to material artifacts, as if to emphasize the characters' freely chosen preoccupations. But the same narrator, describing "Tartarus," stresses feelings and processes, as if to point to a communal psyche in the process of being shaped.

If Chase were discussing religions instead of literatures, the "massive, temperate, moralistic" vision, which he attributes to British fiction,

would pretty well sum up the accommodating spirit of the Great Anglican Compromise as it gradually worked itself out over the years: " . . .
it gives the impression of absorbing all extremes, all maladjustments
and contradictions, into a normative view of life." Here, Chase on the
British novel uses concepts and words that might just as well have
been describing the Anglican Church. Similarly, his evocation of "the
Manichaean quality of New England Puritanism . . . with . . . its opposition of the kingdom of light and the kingdom of darkness"[23] comes from
a discussion of Puritan religion but also forms part of his examination
of American fiction. Without insisting on a strict connection of cause
and effect, I want to assert a resonance of temperament, of spirit, of
perspective, that may help to clarify lines of descent and dissent in the
American literary commentary upon experience as it both echoes and
argues with its British cousin.

Chase's concern with the psychological implications, the practical
Manichaeanism, of American Puritan Calvinism points the way to real
and illuminating insights. But I want to look for the effects of the ideas
and structures of thought pounded repeatedly into the heads of people
over the years. Commentators tend to hurry over the dusty, dull, doctrinal surface so as to get to the good, red, psychical meat below. I want, now,
to think about the shaping effects upon our cultural atmosphere of the
haze, the motes and dust, represented by sermons preached on recurring
themes over time. We will find that the connections and differences
between Anglican and Puritan have a great deal to do with the shape
and texture of American literature, including American humor.

To paraphrase Chase on Emily Brontë, what if Archbishop Laud had
been representing the Massachusetts Bay Colony during those same
years when he was head of the Church of England? He'd have fit right in,
wouldn't he? His treatment of the Puritans harmonized precisely with
what Puritans wanted to do—and, when they got the power, did indeed
themselves do—to dissenters from what became the New England Way.
The Church of Laud appears no more to embody the spirit of accommodation in the face of social reality than the Massachusetts Bay Colony
appears to anticipate the spirit of religious toleration, an attitude with
which it used to be so mistakenly credited. Nathaniel Ward's *The Simple
Cobler of Aggawam* represents Puritan thinking in this respect. In 1647,
before Charles I's beheading but after Parliament had taken effective
control, Ward feared that the people back home would allow political
exigency to lead to a relaxation of principle. Such a turn he protested
with all his force:

23. Chase, *The American Novel*, 11.

I would willingly hope that no member of the Parliament has skillfully ingratiated himself into the hearts of the House that he might watch a time to midwife out some ungracious toleration for his own turn; . . . He that is willing to tolerate any religion, or discrepant way of religion, besides his own, unless it be in matters merely indifferent, either doubts his own or is not sincere in it. . . . God does nowhere in His word tolerate Christian states to give toleration to such adversaries of His truth, if they have power in their hands to suppress them.

This statement pretty well embodies the intolerant Puritan position, immediately recognizable as such, that led to exile for Roger Williams, for Anne Hutchinson, and for numerous others less well known to us. It suggests not accommodation, not acceptance, but an intolerant insistence upon the one proper process for developing true Christians, God-oriented spiritual beings. It also seems indistinguishable from the many examples of Anglican Laud and his adherents. Anglican accommodation came slowly, or at least unevenly. The early-seventeenth-century impulse toward metaphysical certainty gripped both Anglicans and Puritans. This similarity seems never to have caused any problem for the scholarly community: unflattering as it is, at least to modern eyes, our recognition of its truth goes hand in hand with our pride that we have gone well beyond our forefathers in our tolerant respect for the rights of others to hold to their own beliefs. The commonplace view has been that Jefferson, Franklin, and others of their independent kidney, themselves having no strong commitment to a specific theological persuasion, had no trouble accepting the right of all to believe as they preferred. We will later notice the stance of Roger Williams, who was equally tolerant but for quite different reasons.

For now, it is enough to go forward with three notions firmly in mind: first, the implications of Melville's two stories suggest that British and American literary sensibilities differ significantly, the British developing into what will in time be seen as a "realistic" mode, the American trying to "strike through the mask" of material appearances to whatever transcendental meaning may lie concealed. The realm of the ideal, with its emphasis on the meaning behind the appearance, has its basis here. Second, the words of Nathaniel Ward, representative in substance although unique in vigor, indicate both a contrast between Puritans in Massachusetts and those across the Atlantic and an eventually embarrassing community between American Puritans and British Anglicans. And third, Mark Twain's language at the *Atlantic* dinner of 1877 and Hawthorne's story of Robin suggest, in their different ways, an uneasy blending of disparate elements: rejection of reverence for the past and a striving for independence of various sorts. These impulses, however violent in their turning away from comfortable, although potentially repressive, patterns, imply by their very violence the attractiveness and power of that from which they turn. From discontinuities, let us make out continuities. Scholars have always recognized the continuity between Anglican and Puritan intolerance, although it may have become obscure to the popular imagination, wherein strict Puritans and very tolerant Pilgrims have long been indistinguishable. We turn, now, to a different, and a surprising, continuity, one that at all levels of national awareness we Americans have done our best to repress.

II
God's Chosen People
The Anglican Perspective

1. Megalomaniacal Fantasies . . .

The Puritans thought that they knew perfectly well why they crossed the ocean. In part because their various situations were less extreme than the pressures facing the explicitly separatist Pilgrims, the Puritans kept up the politically astute fiction that they had no intention of separating themselves from the true Established Church. Technically, verbally, Puritans presented themselves as wanting not to leave but to reform. Accordingly, they condemned all Separatists in a way that twentieth-century observers consider disingenuous. Still, three thousand miles, especially in those days, signified a major decision. The Puritans' break from the Anglican establishment has meant to subsequent Americans, especially to subsequent New Englanders, a declaration of specialness, a sense that they saw themselves as something, if not new, at least different under the sun.

This fantasy of being special has haunted us since before we became a nation. Not that being separate always meant being better: differences between colonial life and life in the Old Country seemed all too clear and all too disadvantageous to William Byrd of Westover, in Virginia. His pretensions to urbanity and his longings for London stir our sympathies as well as our condescending smiles. But to the north, these perceptions of difference became a perpetual cause for celebration. Students of the American Puritans take as a given the strength and persistence of the

Massachusetts Bay colonists' claims to be a new Israel, to be God's new chosen people, creating and inhabiting His City on a Hill. Consequently, these Puritans felt that the eyes of the world were to be riveted upon them and their efforts, both as models to be emulated by Protestants generally and as deserters to be scorned by the stay-at-homes. From John Winthrop on board the *Arbella* through Thomas Shepard, William Stoughton, and the Mathers, and including numerous well-known, unknown, and partly known others, a distinguishing mark of New England's early mind-set was the ministerial insistence upon New England's "typological identification with Israel." Harry S. Stout, whose 1986 work I am here quoting, goes on to say—as Norman Pettit notices in his December 1987 review in *The New England Quarterly*—that "Israel remained as crucial to New England's self-identity in 1760 as it had been a century earlier."[1]

This late word confirms what has never, so far as I know, been a matter for doubt. But behind this assumption lies another one, related, but different: we Americans have assumed a uniquely American thrust to such claims. Study after study suggests wide agreement that one of the things that distinguished seventeenth-century Massachusetts Bay Colonials from their Anglican brothers-in-opposition back in England was that, while the Puritans knew that they were God's chosen people in the immediate now, in exactly the same way that the Israelites had been in the days of the Old Testament, the Anglicans had no such pretensions.[2] Andrew Delbanco, in his introduction to *The Puritans in America: A Narrative Anthology*, quotes Sacvan Bercovitch's comment that "no English patriot could confuse his country per se with the Heavenly City."[3] Not that any New Englander saw the Massachusetts Bay Colony as heaven on earth. Indeed, while some anticipated that the New Jerusalem would begin in America at some inferred future time, many, as Reiner Smolinski has recently shown, did not.[4] In context, the issue is whether a given

1. Norman Pettit, 606, review of *The New England Soul*; Stout, *The New England Soul*, 252.

2. Theodore Dwight Bozeman's *To Live Ancient Lives: The Primitivist Dimension in Puritanism* is a recent exception. I did my research for this chapter before Bozeman's excellent book was published. In the process of explicating the Puritan drive toward the "primitive" rather than the "modern," and providing full documentation for a reading of Winthrop's "Model" that emphasizes an imitation of ancient ways rather than an example for the rest of the world, Bozeman mentions, tangentially to his central argument, that "[l]ong before the 1620s, men had begun to think of England as joined in covenantal relation with the Lord" (98), and that "[i]n identification with biblical Israel, England was pledged to a Deuteronomic pact with God" (291). His documentation for "English jeremiads of the later seventeenth century" (320), however, refers only to works by Puritans.

3. Alan Heimert and Andrew Delbanco, *The Puritans in America*, iv.

4. Reiner Smolinski, "*Israel Redivivus*: The Eschatological Limits of Puritan Typology in New England."

"modern" earthly polity saw itself as the focus of divine concern in the same way as ancient Israel had done. Bercovitch asserts that his "English patriot" had no such vision. Delbanco, in agreement, goes on to point out that the far different view from New England "played an important part in the development of a distinctively New England mind." Thence came the naming of Canaan and New Canaan, Salem and New Salem, and so on. That southern colonists, most of them Anglicans, indulged in the same sort of place naming seems to have gone unremarked.

Doctrinally, little distinguished Anglicans from Puritans. We have always known about the vestment disputes, but we also understand that Calvinism was very close to Anglicanism, at least through the early seventeenth century, although not later. Church polity, not essential theology, differentiated Anglican from Puritan, as it differentiated Presbyterian from Congregationalist. This difference reflected credit upon our forebears: John Wise showed, in the very text and texture of Congregational church polity, a nascent democracy that would burgeon into the political climate of 1776. Over the centuries, both critics and supporters of the American national self-image agreed that we Americans, for worse or for better, saw our land as God's new Israel. The new Jerusalem promised in the Book of Revelation might or might not begin its actual, its political, existence on our side of the Atlantic (opinion was divided on this thorny issue), but the Massachusetts Bay Colony, and then the nation itself, benefited—sometimes suffered—from God's rewards or punishments in precisely the same way as did His chosen people of the Old Testament.

Although more and more observers subsequently came to see in this assurance a particularly virulent form of chauvinism, one thing we could know in our hearts and could use as at least partial justification: Old and New England, Anglican and Puritan, differed in their degree of pretentiousness when it came to certainty about their place as God's chosen people. We were, regrettably but understandably, the victims of our Puritan heritage. Our nineteenth- and twentieth-century national efforts to impose either democracy or a Pax Americana on the rest of the world might be misguided, but at least they made sense in the light of our own unique past. Being what we were from our beginnings, we had at last come of age, economically and militarily. To a gradually increasing minority, our participation in the new colonialism meant that we were still the victims of a uniquely vicious, however well-intentioned and sincerely believed, insistence that we, and we only, were God's new chosen people, picked out by Him for His own purposes, just as the ancient Jews of the Old Testament had been. Our independence from England meant being able to do God's will in our own unique way as God's uniquely protected modern nation.

Not only were our ancestors—psychological, intellectual, political—told all this, but they were told it, so it seemed, while their more civilized, urbane, relaxed British Anglican cousins heard no such thing. American true believers thought that they, and no other earthly polity, were indeed God's chosen people; those few Americans who were skeptical believed that we labored under the misapprehension that this was the case, and that we, and only we, were being told such nonsense by our ministers. The statements of other students of American literature repeatedly confirm my own, previously unexamined, assumption: seventeenth- and eighteenth-century Anglicans were not told, as their American Puritan counterparts were, that God had picked out their geographical nation as His own. Britain's writers sang a patriotically different tune, especially in epic and drama, but the Anglican pulpits of Britain, we thought, never burdened auditors with the serious proposition that they occupied precisely the position of Israel in the Old Testament. They never had to cope with the glory and the weight of such a divine choosing.

John Milton had said that God would be sure to inform first of all "his Englishmen"[5] of any new truth, but Milton was, after all, a Puritan. Winthrop's City on a Hill might expand temporarily to include Cromwell's Commonwealth. Still, before and after the Puritan aberration, however much a demi-Eden, however close to paradise, England, however favored by God, remained merely an earthly kingdom, spiritually special to the English, of course, but not to be paralleled in specific ways with ancient Israel. Andrew Marvell, in "To His Coy Mistress," could allude to "the conversion of the Jews"; but between 1290 and 1656, no Jews had been officially allowed to live in England. Cromwell changed Edward I's law in this regard in order to make more probable the Puritan sense of England's special status with the Lord. Anglicans, I (and, I believe, others) had always assumed, never publicized any such sense. But this assumption turns out to be contrary to actual Anglican preachment.[6]

The American fantasy of being special seems to have worked in two ways. On the one hand, as a literal belief among New Englanders, and then among Americans generally, it served to unite and to flatter. Among later skeptics, it served to organize crushing denunciations of a uniquely American megalomania. Either way, America remains special. "You are his familiar people: and if he lose his honour in you also, he loseth it altogether. Therefore consider you the works of the Lord, and his intent in them. Stirre up your hearts, and frame your lives to

---

5. John Milton, *Areopagitica* (1644).
6. For even more extensive documentation than follows, see my "God's Chosen People: Anglican Views, 1607–1807."

a real thankfulnesse."[7] Doesn't this British Anglican exhortation have a fine New England ring to it? Consider this one: "If ever any people under heaven felt the royall presence, the particular providence, or stable promise of their GOD in familiar sort, it is, and hath been, this British Nation."[8] Or, preaching on Psalm 126:3, and after a catalogue of some of the Old Testament special providences that God provided for the benefit of his first chosen people: "These and the like great works the Lord has done for his Church ["of the Jews"]." But consider, the speaker tells his auditors, what God has done for us, here and now, in England, by the miraculous discovery of the Gunpowder Plot: "The manner or meanes of our deliverance was altogether wonderful. Therefore let us rejoyce in this great work of God, as his ancient people in this place."[9] Over and over, Anglicans pontificate, "God hath singled us out to be his People";[10]

> we have had as many of the distinguishing characters of the jewish Nation upon us, both in the blessings that we received from God on the one hand, and in our ingratitude to him on the other [the accusation of popular ingratitude as part of a New England jeremiad needs no explication after, inter alia, Perry Miller and Sacvan Bercovitch], . . . we have had such a series of Deliverances as perhaps cannot be matched in History, since that of the Israelites coming out of Egypt.[11]

"We have the very same obligation to Thanksgiving, with David and the men of Judah in my text [2 Samuel 18:28]. The truth is, our case seems to be so much of the same with theirs, almost in every particular, that I cannot but wonder, that I even stand amazed at the exactness of the parallel."[12] And one more, for now:

> I do not believe that he has shown the like care of his Providence over any other Christian Nation: Nay, scarce over them in the Jewish Church. What should be the meaning of our most gracious God in all this? Is it his meaning to set us up like a Light on a Hill, that we should be a pattern to

7. Thomas Taylor, *The Romish Furnace*. Preached November 5, 1612. London, 1619; reprinted in 1634, with a preface by William Jemmat, "To all that wish well to our syon . . . ." (I have given bibliographical information for this and other sermons in the notes rather than expand the bibliography unduly.)

8. William Leigh, no title. Preached November 5, 1609. London, 1609.

9. Thomas Taylor, no title. Preached November 5, 1615. London, 1619; reprinted in 1634.

10. Anon ("A Country Conformist"), *Advice to English Protestants*. Preached November 5, 1689. London, 1689.

11. Gilbert Burnet (Bishop of Sarum [Salisbury], 1689–1715), no title. Preached November 5, 1689, to the House of Lords. London, 1689.

12. John Hinton, *Thanksgiving for the Defeat of Monmouth*. Preached July 26, 1685. London, 1685.

all other Nations? Is it his meaning that we should be his instruments to help others?[13]

As in my quotation from William Leigh (footnote 8), it is "this British Nation" that God treats with in so "familiar" a manner. The rhetorical questions in the last quotation may remind one of John Winthrop, or of any Massachusetts Bay Colony minister. But they were raised, let us be sure to note, before the Queen at Whitehall in 1692 by William Lloyd, appointed Bishop of St. Asaph in 1680, toward the end of Charles II's reign. The Anglican sermons that I shall be quoting go back to 1607. The British Nation, the British Anglicans (not just the Puritans), before there ever was a Massachusetts Bay Colony, had plenty of public exposure to the notion that they were the new chosen of God, with the obligations as well as the benefits appertaining thereto. Only a small sampling of the evidence for what I find to be this fascinating truth appears in my text and notes, but the experience by which I came to it is easily replicated, perhaps most easily by leafing through the Thomason Collection of tracts and sermons in the British Library. In striking out so bravely, so independently, one thing the Puritans did not do was to develop their own sense of God's choosing of a people for special care. They simply appropriated that of their Anglican contemporaries.

Now as Harry Stout's *The New England Soul* shows, the sermons preached on election days, and on days of public fasting and humiliation, or of public thanksgiving, tended to insist upon the parallels between God's regard for the people of the Massachusetts Bay Colony and for the people of ancient Israel. Ordinary sermons, the sermons preached on Sundays, and the lessons delivered at Thursday lecture, occupied themselves with the holy concerns of individual souls. That is, whereas the sermons preached on special occasions focused on the society at large and on its special relationship with the Lord, the sermons most often heard did reflect the concern for individual salvation that is at the heart of Protestantism.

The citizens of the Bay thus heard a mixed message: although God had long ago determined where each one of them would spend eternity, it remained their own responsibility to watch and pray and hope, and to seize hold of any opportunity the Lord might offer them to accept him into their sinful hearts. The confusions in the chronicle have been often enough spelled out: somehow, intriguingly, Calvinistic predestination and self-reliant individual responsibility managed to coexist, both in the hearts of the people and in scores of sermons. Perry Miller, in 1935,

13. William Lloyd (Bishop of St. Asaph, 1680–1692; of Lichfield, 1692–1699; of Worcester, 1699–1717), no title. Preached May 29, 1692, to the Queen at Whitehall. London, 1692.

summed up this paradox, this anomaly, this "central problem of the seventeenth century as it was confronted by the Puritan mind," as a "striving on the one hand to maintain the subordination of humanity to God without unduly abasing human values, and on the other hand to vaunt the powers of the human intellect without losing the sense of divine transcendence."[14] This dilemma was confusing enough in its contradictory insistences upon the individual's obligation to assist in his or her being born again and also upon the gratuitous nature of the Lord's dispensation of his predestined grace, in aid of which no human act could exert any force at all. The message becomes even more mixed when we add to Stout's thorough explication of the individually salvational tenor of "ordinary" sermons what has been so well known and documented concerning those "occasional" sermons: although individuals cannot by their behavior oblige the Lord to grant them salvation, their behavior as individuals nevertheless influences mightily the Lord's treatment of their community. If indeed they have a community in the Lord's keeping, as the Puritans assured themselves that they did, then their corporate relationship to the Lord is analogous to Israel's. But let us look at the state of affairs in Anglican Britain.

2. MEGALOMANIA . . . WITH A BRITISH ACCENT

The Anglican sermons that insist upon Britain as God's new Israel, and upon the Church of England as His Church and the British as His chosen people, had, like comparable New England sermons, communal occasions for their delivery. In New England, most such days varied in the calendar from year to year. Election days occurred with a predictable regularity, but no one could anticipate when days of thanksgiving, or days of public humiliation and repentance, would be required. Conditions determined the occasion. In Old England, the emphasis on regularity was reversed. Although an occasional fire, flood, famine, or military venture could call forth national responses from the pulpit, and certainly local responses to local events, assertions that the British nation was peculiarly God's came especially with the anniversaries of particular national events.

More specifically, three annual occasions above all others called forth the celebratory, or condemnatory, reminder that although God may only probably reward His people on earth when they obey His commandments, He most surely delivers them over to earthly punishment for their communal misdeeds. Furthermore, if gratitude for past blessings slackens unduly, then punishment, simply on the grounds of that

14. Perry Miller, "The Marrow of Puritan Divinity," 74.

ingratitude, will follow. First came November 5, 1605, Guy Fawkes Day, and the commemoration of the Lord's protection of Britain in the face of Gunpowder Treason. Parliament ordered memorial sermons preached upon every ensuing November 5, a custom later augmented, although also wonderfully complicated, by the addition of November 5, 1688, the anniversary of William III's landing at Torbay despite winds believed to have required divine aid in their overcoming. In each, the hand of the Lord was seen to be instrumental in rescuing his people from the dangers of Roman Catholicism, although the difference between 1605 and 1688 had significant political impact. But let us stay for a while with the general outline and ignore (for the moment) the fascinating details.

Second, on January 30, 1649 (1648, Old Style, and therefore "1648" in the original documents),[15] Charles I suffered his "decollation," as it was sometimes called. In 1661, a year after the Stuart monarchy had been restored, January 30 became a day of repentance, of fasting and public humiliation, unless the thirtieth fell on a Sunday, in which case Monday the thirty-first became the day for sermons and grief. Third, in the same year of 1661, the Restoration itself, celebrated on May 29, Charles II's birthday, joined November 5 and January 30 (or 31) as fixed days of public acknowledgment for divine favors or divine chastisement. Despite the extremely divisive nature of much of this sermonizing, the acts of Parliament requiring the observance of all three dates in all Anglican cathedrals and churches remained in force until 1859.

As one might expect, these observances fell out of favor by the end of the eighteenth century, but the Napoleonic crisis led to vigorous reinstitution in 1807. "National sins are visited by great national calamities," proclaimed Thomas Burgess, Bishop of St. David's, on January 30, 1807. He did so because, as a footnote to the published text proclaimed, "[t]he Sermon appointed to be preached before the House of Lords on the 30th of January, which had been discontinued for some years, it was His Majesty's pleasure should be revived this year."[16] Burgess both comforted and corrected his audience of Lords and his more general readership. However threatened his fellow Britons might at present feel, the citizens of France have much more to fear because of "the example of violated and insulted justice which was there set. The nation, which was loudest in its censures and execration of our regicide, has followed

15. The Calendar (New Style) Act of 1750 changed the new year's start from March 25 to January 1. This, along with some other changes, went into effect at the beginning of 1752. Dates in my text and notes that include two consecutive years separated by a slash (e.g., January 30, 1709/1710) should, then, be understood to signify the more recent year in our present system, although documents of the time will refer to the earlier year.

16. Thomas Burgess (Bishop of St. David's, 1803–1825; of Salisbury, 1825–1837), no title. Preached January 30, 1807, to the House of Lords. London, 1807.

the example, . . . fill[ing] the Continent with disaster and dismay." But the British have been neglecting their own duty "of repentance and amendment" and, in consequence, "we have been 'treasuring up wrath against . . . the righteous judgment of God' (Rom 2:4–5.)."

In a spectacular equation of religious with patriotic duty, Burgess reminded his hearers that "Every one may contribute something to the stock of public good, and therefore to the national safety, by the faithful discharge of his duties." And then he adds this footnote: "We cannot too often . . . press on the public attention that pregnant and ever-memorable order of our great naval Hero: 'England EXPECTS EVERY MAN TO DO HIS DUTY.' " These duties include both a thorough repentance for an earlier generation's treatment of that anointed king, Charles I, and a complete obedience to the will of the present monarch, George III. Burgess knows that "[T]he sins of past generations and the present have brought Europe to a crisis, from which nothing but the aid of Divine Providence can extricate us. And we have no room to hope for God's protection, but by following his earnest invitations to repentance and obedience."

The bishop's rhetoric has little, if any, force, and one wonders how seriously the House of Lords (including even those members who were also bishops) was able to regard the duties of repentance and obedience in the face of the Napoleonic blockade, to say nothing of Burgess's conflating Nelson's idea of duty with that of the Church. This is beside the point: the occasional sermons, impotent forms by the end of the eighteenth century, had retained their power in England at least as long as their colonial American counterparts. That the king in 1807 specifically requested a revival of the January 30 sermon may reveal little more than a formulaic grasping at straws in the midst of the French threat. Even so, it indicates that even so recently as the start of the last century, the public, if not the Lord, might be expected to pay some attention to so venerable a custom.

These three sorts of occasional sermons had the power to attract public attention well into the eighteenth century. After oral delivery, the texts themselves were frequently printed and then reprinted. One of the most celebrated political fracases of the period received its impetus from the November 5, 1709, sermon preached at St. Paul's by Dr. Henry Sacheverell and then reprinted at such a rate that about 100,000 copies were in circulation by the time of Sacheverell's trial the following February and March. Geoffrey Holmes in *The Trial of Dr. Sacheverell* wrote: "As a short-term best-seller *The Perils of False Brethren* had no equal in the early eighteenth century."[17]

17. Geoffrey Holmes, *The Trial of Dr. Sacheverell*, 75.

No less striking in their own rhetorical extremes, numerous other occasional sermons seized upon their particular occasion to emphasize the importance of Britain in the divine scheme of things. In 1714, for instance, Thomas Bisse told the House of Commons on May 29 that "God said, Let there be a Restoration of my Church [in 1660], and it was so. . . . [T]here cannot be given to the numerous scoffers of this Nation a greater sign, than that wondrous and ever memorable work of the Restoration."[18] As late as 1748, the May 29 preacher to the Lord Mayor and Aldermen of London, at a packed St. Paul's, marvels at how clearly "we of this Nation . . . are able to trace out the Footsteps of divine Providence in this our land."[19] After a quick reminder of the double blessing celebrated on November 5th, he turns to the business of the day, evoking the dark sufferings of Charles I and the even darker plight of the nation under the Commonwealth. "Then did God say, Let there be Light, and there was Light." The affairs of Britain and the creation of the world might thereby be seen to have equal importance. In any case, God has been keeping his special eye upon the British. Therefore, "As no Kingdom under heaven can boast a better Constitution, or a more pure Religion, let us testify our Gratitude by a virtuous and peaceable Conduct." Despite the concluding sentiment, the tone comes uncannily close to the bragging of a Western teller of tall tales.

Thomas Comber, Dean of Durham Cathedral, even spells out in his lengthy discussion of *The Offices for the Vth of November, the XXXth of January, and the XXIX of May* (1696), that Psalm 118 "was composed originally for David's Coronation, after . . . Exile. . . ."[20] Its use, therefore, on each May 29 has special propriety, for the case of David and the Jews forms "almost an exact parallel to our case" vis à vis Charles II and his return under the special care of "the God of our Salvation." Over the years, Charles II repeatedly turns out to have corresponded to David, almost as anti-type to type.[21] Even a 1661 sermon by Peter Heylyn who, as Laud's creature and then hagiographical biographer, repudiated all Puritan-like modes of thought and of speech, makes the point.[22] I have

18. Thomas Bisse, no title. London, 1714.

19. Peter Pinnell (A.M., Rector of St. Mary Magdalen, Bermondsey, Surrey), no title. Preached May 29, 1748. London, 1748.

20. Thomas Comber, *A Discourse*, 193.

21. E.g., Peter Heylyn, May 29, 1661; D. H. Killigrew, May 29, 1668, preached before the King at Whitehall; John Lake, May 29, 1670; George Stradling, January 30, 1674/1675; John Horden, May 29, 1676; William Smith, preached at Norwich Cathedral, May 29, 1677; Richard Burd, May 29, 1684; William Lloyd, May 29, 1692; Nicholas Brady, preached at Richmond, Surrey, May 29, 1715. (Each was published in London the year in which it was preached.)

22. See John Huber Walker, "A Descriptive Bibliography of the Early Printed Works of Peter Heylyn."

found one sermon in which an Anglican priest (Richard Burd) goes even so far as to equate Charles II with Jesus: "This happy day hath given us a blessed resurrection to life again" (see footnote 21), so the British had better "learn the lesson of obedience" lest "our own exceeding guilt and sinfulness that destroyed the nation, and plunged us into such an abyss of misery and confusion" once more bring chaos to the realm. Five years later, the Glorious Revolution occurred—that much-praised exercise in overt *dis*obedience—but that's a strictly political part of the story.

Often whole sermons for May 29 developed the ideas latent in, "The stone which the builders refused is become the head stone of the corner. This is the Lord's doing; it is marvelous in our eyes" (Psalm 118:22–23). David and the Jews, Charles II and the British: the parallels are part of God's historical design. Who runs may read: the pattern so clearly woven by the Lord into the carpet of history reveals at every turn that the English and their Church are God's new chosen people, his latter-day Israel. No Puritan minister could have stated the case more plainly than numerous Anglican priests and bishops so repeatedly did.

3. Ossa upon Pelion Concluded
And Then?

Perhaps the point can be taken as read, but I shall pile on just a few more illustrative quotations. John King, in 1607 (November 5), traces for his learned Oxford audience Latin etymologies and the derivations of Hebrew words, but primarily moves from the blessed "faith [of the Jews] when they made . . . the Lord of the world . . . their proper and peculiar God" to "[t]hat Popish Sodome, full of Jesuits," from whence sprang the Powder Plot: "There never was example in the world of so sacinorous [not in the *O.E.D.*] a fact, a sin so exceedingly sinful." Because, says King, we are who we are, God saved us, "himselfe fighteth for us; and Deus Jacobi of whom I trust he hath sworne by his holinesse, that he will never faile him, and hath made an everlasting covenant with his whole seed, his image our hopeful Prince, and his whole happy race (si custodierint if they will keep his testimonies, and walk after his laws) this God of Jacobi is our defense." The God of Jacob: of James I, to be sure, but who could miss the play on Jacob-who-became-Israel, one of the eponymous names of the Old Testament? Hatred and fear of the Roman Church receive the expected attention, but King emphasizes the certainty that God protects His People, who, in the seventeenth century, are the English nation.

A year later, he makes the same point in a way even more strikingly anticipatory of the way in which New England's major spokesman apostrophized leaders: "Most Gracious Sovereign. You are yet a living

Lion. And the lion of the tribe of Judah graunt you may long and long so be." So Cotton Mather later found John Winthrop to have been an American Nehemiah. King also paraphrases Psalm 124 in a way once thought of as exclusively Puritan-like: "If the Lord had not been on our side (May England now saie) if the Lord had not been on our side what then? Our foundation had been cast downe, and theirs had been reared up." King's substitution of "England" for the Bible's "Israel" would have been calculated to comfort, not to startle, his auditors. In similar fashion, Cotton Mather concluded his "Life of John Winthrop"[23] by paraphrasing "the words of Josephus about Nehemiah, the Governour of Israel," so that what in the original Greek of Josephus was "the walls of Jerusalem" becomes in Mather's Latin the eternal memorial, the walls of New England ("ETERNAM . . . MONUMENTUM, *Novanglorum* MOENIA").

Not only do the sermons of British Anglicans spell out England's favored position in the eyes of the Lord; they also extrapolate from that position in a way that Americanists have learned to identify as belonging to the New England jeremiad, that sermon form that drew its strength from two related assumptions: God delivers His People from disaster; but, like any good parent, he also punishes them when they transgress. Indeed, as by now needs no saying, the fact of the punishment indicates the depth of the caring. So Thomas Westfeild, in 1630, offers his congratulations, so to speak, because "if any Nation may call god their Saviour next this people [the Israelites]; surely, I think, we may do it," the self-congratulation being in the evidence: "Consider how God saved us in 88. Was not that a great work? Remember how God saved us in the gun-powder treason: was not that a wonderful work? Remember how God saved our lives from death five years since, in that same great and heavy plague [of 1625]: Was not that plague a terrible work?" But he also delivers the threat, the warning: "Yet surely, brethren, have not wee forgotten God? . . . God may charge us as truly he charged this people, we have forgot God our Saviour, that hath done so great things, so wondrous things, and so terrible things for us."[24]

The most quoted biblical text for this view of God as both loving and punitive was Amos 3:2: "You only have I known of all the families of the earth; therefore I will punish you for all your iniquities." On April 16, 1648—about eight-and-one-half months before the beheading of Charles I—a particularly interesting Anglican preached on this text; the title page from the 1681 London reprint will suffice for my purposes:

Israel and England paralleled: in a sermon preached before the hon. society of Grayes Inn, upon Sunday in the afternoon, April the 16th 1648. Being

23. Cotton Mather, *Magnalia Christi Americana*, Book 2, chap. 4.
24. Thomas Westfeild, no title. London, 1630; reprinted in 1656.

now very seasonable and useful for all such as retain the principles of the people in those times. By Paul Knell, master of arts of Clare Hall in Cambridge, and sometimes chaplain to a regiment of cuiras[s]iers in his late majesties army.[25]

The *DNB*'s entry on Knell mentions his savage attack upon Cromwell's army and the Independents in "A looking-glasse for Levellers, held out in a sermon preached at St. Peter's, Paul's Wharf, 24 Sept., 1648," anathematizing in some detail the conduct of Fairfax and his "bloodhounds" at Colchester: an outspoken man he must have been, and no sympathizer with non-conformist ways of speaking.

These "parallelings" of Israel and England go on and on. England, her sermonizers see, suffers, and will continue to suffer, because God, just as Amos had said, punishes His children when they sin. England, clearly, finds herself in the position of ancient Israel. In his November 5th sermon for 1716, the "Vicar of Hanslope in the County of Buckinghamshire" did the usual job of raking the Papists over the coals—e.g., "[L]et the Good-Nature of a Papist be what it will, it is in danger to be spoiled by his religion."—but his primary concern is to establish some facts and the inevitable conclusion:

> Public judgments or Deliverances are the mighty voice of God calling upon a Nation or People to return to him. . . . [T]hat God doth concern himself for the Good and Welfare of whole Nations and Kingdoms, considered as such, as well as for that of his particular servants, is both rational to believe, and is confirmed by Intimations of Scripture in the case of Israel.[26]

And also in the case of England:

> God hath not been wanting to mark us out a People unto himself by Chastisement . . . Rebellion and Civil Wars, Tyrannies, . . . and Fire, and Pestilence. . . . But the heaviest Burden that ever we labored under . . . was Cromwell's Usurpation. . . . [T]o reduce us again under the Roman Yoke, it were endless to reckon up all the Plots and Conspiracies. . . .

And, as has been the case up until now, eventually He has saved the English, as the celebration of this day attests. "Not to be wrought upon by such . . . Calls, argues a most desperate Temper, and is a mighty aggravation to the sins of any People." Hence, as say so many other sermons on both sides of the ocean, and in parish church and Anglican

25. Paul Knell, *Israel and England Paralleled*. London, 1681.
26. Sh. Garmston, ("Vicar of Hanslope in the County of Buckinghamshire"), *Proper Thoughts for the 5th of November . . . for the Happy Deliverance of this Nation (1.) From the Powder-Plot, and (2.) From Popery and Arbitrary Power, by the Blessed arrival of His late Majesty King William, of immortal memory, as on this Day 1688.* "Preached in the Parish-Church of Hanslope." London, 1716.

cathedral as well as in Congregational meeting house, it would be best that we repent and change our ways.

Garmston's reference to the Plague of 1665 and the Fire of 1666 as among the Lord's chastisements of His people, even so late as 1716, would have come as no surprise to a British congregation, any more than the assumption that God's punishments indicate God's care. So said Luke Milbourne:

> That dreadful Plague . . . was a terrible Memorandum to us of our duty; those devouring Flames which laid this unreformed, unthankful City in ashes, were a loud call to Repentance and Amendment; but they have had very little effect: . . . are not those long and destructive wars which we have been for many years involved in . . . perpetual evidences of God's anger? . . . . [27]

Like Israel, we were punished (repeatedly) and (repeatedly) we, like Israel, repented and were "restored" by God. Recently, however, our repentance has had more of seeming than of reality: "But, alas! we turned aside too soon, like a broken bow; we acted only as if we had been delivered, that we might commit greater abominations." And then Milbourne goes on to hold out to his hearers the straw so familiar to so many New Englanders:

> The greatest comfort we have, is . . . that by those convulsions we still feel, it seems God has not yet said of us, Why should ye be stricken any more, ye will revolt more and more? God, it may be, has not given us over as wholly incorrigible, but allows us a Time and Space for Repentance. When we have once taken this Care, . . . even this City may be called, and be the City of Righteousness, the Faithful City. To which, let all these Nations say, Amen. FINIS.

The point, as American Puritans knew so well, is that "The Lord by bringing dayes of trouble upon his Servants, aimeth at their Instruction. . . . Israel was Gods son . . . ; now the Caldeans were a Rod, whereby God scourged that son of his." Further, although "personal afflictions often times come only or chiefly in a way of Trial," Increase Mather, as in "The Day of Trouble is Near" (1674), echoed (deliberately? inadvertently?) his Anglican predecessors and contemporaries, and anticipated his Anglican successors, in their knowledge that "public Calamities are wont to come as Corrections and just Punishment for sin." Precisely because the Lord "dwells in this place, . . . we may conclude that he will scourge us for our backslidings. So doth he say, Rev. 3:19. *As many as I love, I may rebuke and chasten.*" For Anglicans, as for Puritans,

---

27. Luke Milbourne, *Good Princes and Faithful Counselors, the Blessings of a Repenting Nation*. Preached May 29, 1716, at St. Ethelburga's, London. London, 1716.

God's sendings of disaster in response to human failure to live by His law indicated that "God has not yet said of us, Why should ye be stricken any more, ye will revolt more and more?" No chastisement for disobedience would indicate not God's mercy but his deserved indifference, His turning of the divine back upon His New Israel prior to His selecting another Chosen People with whom to stand in loco parentis.

By now, it should be more than clear enough that only bibliographical citation will allow a reader to distinguish British Anglican from American Puritan sermons that have to do with the preacher's concern for land and people as explicitly the Lord's. But however surprising the similitude, two striking differences must now claim our attention. One of them will be obvious enough, perhaps so obvious that only the importance of not ignoring the obvious emboldens me to spell out the two ways of understanding the final disposition (and position) of the soul, the British Arminian and the Colonial almost-antinomian. The other difference concerns assumptions about history and material reality drummed into heads over time by sermonic insistence. That is, consequences followed from Parliament's having established the annual reminders of November 5, January 30, and May 29. Mostly, these will have to wait until the next chapter; before going on to the matter of souls, however, I shall briefly suggest some of these consequences.

As so many American Puritan ministers from year to year on the occasion of the annual election sermon, and as other special occasions offered, so Luke Milbourne, year after year after year, made a special effort on January 30. His posthumously published *The Royal Martyr Lamented, in 14 sermons, . . .* (London, 1724) ends with one of his stronger insistences on the parallels between Israel and England. This sermon of 1719/1720 was just as vigorous as the first in the volume (1706/1707) that, published by itself in 1707, had run to five editions in three years. Milbourne's last, "Royal and Innocent Blood expiated: or, God justified in punishing a wicked people," goes on for thirty-seven pages. The first twenty-one-and-one-half of them recount God's gracious dealings with Israel, Israel's ungrateful responses, God's punitive repostes, and the reasons for them. The remaining pages explore British history in order to establish England's special place in God's present scheme. As with Israel, God has visited Britain to punish the whole people for "the wickedness of schism," as we should expect Him to do. Although the text around which Milbourne organizes this particular sermon is Nehemiah 9:33, " . . . thou art just in all that is brought upon us; for . . . we have done wickedly," Milbourne never gets very far from the first verses of Romans 13, from which, over the years, he had quoted with remarkable frequency, especially 13:1, " . . . there is no power but of God: the powers that be are ordained of God."

Milbourne's sermons equal in vituperative strength any January 30 efforts I have seen. Their interest lies not simply in the extremes to which Milbourne carried the old grudge against king-killing Puritans and their Romanist principle but at least equally in the systematic (and very representative) way in which he communicated the relationship between historical and religious concerns. Along with his many hundreds of fellow sermonizers over the decades, he made clear to his auditors and readers that matters of historical concern to Britons were also matters for concern to the Lord God. That these matters were complex, that they required careful explicating, even tedious unraveling, might also be true. So much the fuller field for sermonizers to till.

Even the Glorious Revolution of 1688 left him uneasy; as for the beheading of Charles, a few months after Milbourne's own birth, Milbourne spent all his professional life searching for language strong enough to convey his condemnation. Indeed, he found himself singled out by name in the anonymous *High-Church Politicks: or the abuse of the 30th of January considered. With remarks on Mr. Luke Milbourne's railing sermons, and on the observation of that Day* (London, 1709/1710), which took issue—almost as Roger Williams might have done with the people of the Massachusetts Bay Colony—with Milbourne's apparent unawareness that "Christ says, his Kingdom is not of this world." "Israel," that is, is not a literal earthly polity, but a spiritual community of individual souls known only by God. Mr. Anonymous, however, no more represented the main steam of Anglican belief than Roger Williams had represented New England Congregationalism. Perhaps that was part of his reason for remaining anonymous. In any case, one year after the "remarks," Milbourne, in a January 30 sermon by one Edmond Archer, received all the defense he could have wished:

> 'Tis said, indeed, that this Day, and the zealous manner of observing it, do keep up differences and perpetuate Divisions, which seems to be inconsistent with the Piety, devotion, and humility of a Fast. But then it is not considered, that these differences and distinctions are of absolute necessity, and must be preserved as long as the world shall last, for they are founded upon the necessary difference between Good and Evil.[28]

Because the inflammatory tenor of many of these specifically Occasional sermons led to periodic doubtings, in public, of the wisdom and utility in continuing the practice, its defense found expression in a large number of the sermons preached on the three Days. And all of this added to the public sense that vital and complex issues were being addressed.

28. Edmond Archer, no title. Preached January 30, 1710/1711, before the Lower House of Convocation. London, 1710/1711.

Mostly, however, the equation of seventeeth- and eighteenth-century England with Old Testament Israel occupied most of the attention of most of those preaching such sermons on all special occasions for public thanksgiving or humiliation, even apart from the usual November 5, January 30 (or 31), and May 29. Through the decades and across the centuries, this process continued in a literal and unsophisticated fashion. Psalm 124 ("If it had not been the Lord who was on our side, now may Israel [or, as it might be, England] say . . . they had swallowed us up quick . . .") keeps on reappearing in hermeneutic contexts that point to our duty to maintain "the integrity of our future conduct" now that God has saved us, even though "we had the greatest reason to apprehend the Execution of Judgment from an Angry God, whom the sins of a Nation, abandoned to iniquity, had so industriously incensed against it."[29] Because the Anglican congregations of Old England were so often told that they in their polity were God's new chosen people, preachers could expect even sophisticated auditors in St. Paul's to accept as a matter of course the inferences about punishments and obligations that we associate instead with the Old South Church at Boston and its fellows. So, as late as 1750, the Great Fire of London (1666) clearly had been "kindled by Divine Permission . . . Divine Displeasure . . . against . . . [t]he Usurper [Cromwell, who] had prostituted religion. . . . We had . . . hurried into intemperance and excesses of all kinds . . . forgot God. . . ." And then the crusher: "If we persevere in our Follies, God's threatening, and method of dealing with his favorite People the Jews, may instruct us what we (I had almost said no less favorites) may expect at his hands."[30] So Thomas Fothergill, M.A. and Fellow of Queen's College, Oxford, traces parallels between Israel's legislation of annual national mourning for Josiah and England's observance of the anniversary of the death of Charles I. "There is no Person we read of in sacred History, whose death occasioned so universal and lasting a Sorrow, as that of the Prince [Josiah], whose funeral obsequies are here recorded. . . . How far our own case may resemble this of the chosen People, will best appear from a consideration of the Person and Circumstances which occasioned the respective observances."[31]

29. Robert Pool-Finch, . . . *On occasion of the glorious victory obtained by his royal highness the duke of Cumberland over the rebel-army, near Culloden-House, April 16.* Preached Sunday, May 4, 1746, "in the parish church of Greenwich in Kent." London, 1746.

30. William Meades, *A sermon . . . the day . . . as a public fast for the dreadful fire, which happened in London, in the Year 1666.* Preached September 3, 1750, at St. Paul's. London, 1750.

31. Thomas Fothergill, (M.A., Fellow of Queen's College, Oxford), no title. Preached January 30, 1753, at St. Mary's, Oxford. London, 1753.

After a detailed, self-confident, and (to one less admiring of Charles than Mr. Fothergill) forced exposition, he urges us to "consider the advantages, which may accrue to us from . . . [observing] this Day . . ." (by this time, more than Luke Milbourne's Mr. Anonymous have concluded that such observation foments faction rather than encouraging piety): "Restoration to the Divine Favour," a general sort of benefit; and then to help bring about that restoration, a much-needed return to obedience, if not passive and political (no longer the issue it had remained through the first part of the century), then social; for "we see Men getting every day nearer to a level with one another, and growing more familiar and bold with sacred Characters."

Not that his contemporaries would go so far as to kill a king: he simply wants the sorts of proper observation and obedience—a century later, the American Josiah Holland (that genteel reverer of elderly American poets) will be calling for "reverence"—that might be expected to "stay the Divine Wrath; and ever keep us from being as our Fathers, a stubborn and rebellious Generation. . . ." Psalm 126 reminds us of "[t]he great mercy which God wrought for his people [by ending the Babylonian Captivity]," and of the gratitude expressed by the Jews upon their restoration. We, too, must remember that "1. God in his displeasure doth give up his own people, his dear Sion into captivity, being highly and long provoked with their heinous sins. Here is Sions captivity. 2. God nevertheless in his wrath, remembering mercy, doth in his appointed time turn again her captivity."

The parallels between ancient Israel and seventeenth-century England so strike the soul as well as the eye as to compel us to learn what the Jews learned too late: no matter how much God loves a nation, "it is not safe for any nation, whose sins are very great, . . . to presume upon the favour or patience of God, though his special Love-tokens to them have been very great."[32] As was said of the miraculous discovery of the 1605 Gunpowder Plot, we must keep in mind

> that it was the deliverance of God's own People, that have abandoned the corruption of his Religion, and that have embraced the truth . . . considering all this, the deliverance was wonderful and a good work, and from God it came. . . . as God hath delivered us, so he will deliver us still, if we still hold his Truth without corruption, and keep ourselves in innocence.[33]

32. James Warwell, *Votiva tabula; or, a solemn thanksgiving offered up to God the mighty protector of Kings, for the wonderful protection, and happy restauration of . . . Charles the Second . . . .* Preached May 24 and June 28, 1660, and "a little enlarged" (88 pages) for publication. London, 1660.

33. Thomas Wilson, *A sermon on the Gunpowder Treason, with reflections on the late plot* [of Titus Oates], using Psalm 124 ("If it had not been the Lord who was on our side, now may Israel say; . . .") as text. London, 1678.

"Pardon me if I say that God Almighty seems to have a great inclination to save this Nation, and make us happy, if so we would but yield to be such our selves. He hath not done so to other People; nay, what could he have done more to oblige and reclaim us?" We are obligated to the Lord for, among other signs of his caring, "a long Civil War, a devouring Plague, and a Consuming Fire. . . . If after all these various trials and means used by God, we still go on in our sins, this mightily aggravates the guilt, heightens the provocation, will certainly increase our punishment."[34] By "punishment," he means calamities that will afflict a nation under God's particular care, and the evidence that we are God's people he finds overwhelming. From the time of the Spanish Armada through the Restoration, "[t]hese Great and Continual Deliverances" offer living proof.

Although—as is painfully clear—I do enjoy piling up the illustrations, surely the main points that I would infer from them must by now be apparent. Although the British Anglicans were every bit as sure as the American Puritans that they were the Lord's particular people in just the same way as the ancient Israelites had been, their certainty led them to no speculations about their possible role in any approaching millennium, in any immediately expected Second Coming. Rather, their attention was focused on the occasions of this world, of their own history, and on the ways in which the Lord could be seen to have dealt and to be dealing with them on the basis of their behavior. Not transcendent mystery but practical matters of war and politics and plague and prosperity, of obedience and duty and freedom and obligation, held their interest. British preachments accented implications for proper conduct, both personal and political, in this world. Whether Charles I was being compared with Jesus or with Josiah, the point of the comparison had less to do with the typological significance of the murdered king than with the undeniable fact that his murder led to prompt and proper divine retribution against a guilty people.

Even the Cromwell years could be seen to have served Britain well, for God "made us whole and sound again, if happily we would be taught by that severe judgment, to sin no more."[35] Just as the Jews wandered forty years in the wilderness, so England was for forty years punished (counting both Cromwell and James II) for "what you have this Day in your public prayers to almighty God confessed it to be; 'The Barbarous Murder of an Excellent Prince:' " as was the case with Israel, "National Sins bring down National Judgments, which all men

34. Benjamin Calamy, no title. Preached May 29, 1682. London, 1682.
35. Edward Pelling, no title. Preached November 5, 1683. London, 1683.

will more or less feel, till they are removed by a National Repentance and Humiliation."[36]

That Charles I, in one of the great whitewash jobs of all recorded history, often comes out sounding like Jesus Christ returned to earth was in part the Dissenters' own fault because, as Anglican sermonizers upon January 30 never tired of pointing out, the Lesson of the day was the account in the Gospel of St. Matthew of Christ's death. The typologically aware Puritans certainly dropped a stitch in this case. In a way, they paid for their indifference to nonbiblical history, or to the Anglican way of dealing with dates in the Book of Common Prayer. As Henry Leslie made clear in his benchmark sermon preached to the royal family at Breda in the spring of 1649, the Puritans might have done better to execute the king on another day. His *The Martyrdom of King Charles the First or His Conformity with Christ in His Sufferings* set the tone for what followed. "And indeed," said he,

> the providence of God gave me first occasion to institute this parallel: for that day that our gracious Sovereign was murdered, . . . the Chapter that was read to him, was the seven and twentieth of Saint Matthews Gospel, which contains the Passion of Christ; and the chapter was read, not by choice, but by direction of the Rubrick, it being the Lesson appointed for that day, so that we could not but conceive that the Murther then to be acted, was like unto that which in the chapter is described. And indeed you will find it very like unto it . . . in the dignity of the person murdered, the kind of death that he suffered, and the quality of the murderers.[37]

Leslie instituted the similitude of Charles as crucified between two thieves, the Presbyterians and the Independents; but the details would make a long story indeed.

Leslie's point—and the point of his successors—was to glorify Charles, condemn his slayers, and keep before his auditors and readers the historical realities of their common past. This world, not the next, was the point of focus. At the Restoration, "our Nation received a blessing from Heaven," for which we owe more than mere gratitude: "And now what return can we make? . . . Why, the text [Isaiah 1:26] here points out our duty to us, which is really to become the City of Righteousness, the Faithful City." And duty must be done, or "what can we expect less than the same punishment should attend the same sins? . . . we have experienced the indulgence of Heaven, and our prevarication now, will

---

36. William Sherlock, no title. Preached January 30, 1691/1692, before the House of Commons. London, 1691/1692.

37. Henry Leslie, *The Martyrdom of King Charles the First or His Conformity with Christ in His Sufferings.* Preached in Breda June 3 and 13. First printed "at the Hage," 1649; London, 1660.

much aggravate our guilt, since the abuse of mercy is the most provoking of affronts." And then follows the Jeremiad-like climax: the people had better change their ways, above all "because we now seem to be upon our last time of probation."[38]

That Britons give national thanks or make national repentance upon the anniversary of specific occasions in itself underscores their sense of similarity to the ancient Jews. Just as God commanded the Sabbath as a weekly celebration of the creation, so, after special acts, "He still required that the Time wherein he did so, should be religiously observed every year, in memory of what he then did. . . . [T]he Passover . . . Pentecost . . . The Feast of Tabernacles," and other specific memorials mentioned in the Old Testament were especially for the Jews. "[T]hree only . . . are peculiar to our Church and Nation, the 30th of January, the 29th of May, and that which we now celebrate [November 5th], all settled by Act of Parliament. . . ." January 30 has its "Precedent of Divine Authority" in Jewish lamentation for "Josiah's Death" (2 Chronicles 35:24, 25). Likewise, people should find

> a precedent in the Jewish Church . . . for celebrating the 29th of May (1 Maccab 4:36, 52, 59. 2 Maccab 10:5, 6, 8. John 10:22, 23). . . . And so we come to . . . the fifth of November. Which was such a conspiracy, and such a Deliverance, that the like is scarce to be met with in any History, sacred or prophane, except in this Book of Esther [9:27–28]. . . . And certainly we have as much Reason to keep the fifth of November, as they had for their Feast of Purim.[39]

Puritans, as has often enough been said, took no stock in anniversary observances: days of thanksgiving and of repentance in one year might bear little or no calendric correspondence to similar occasions in another. Except for the political, the secular, occasion of election day, they left the determination of days for communal joy or sorrow to the circumstances that the Lord brought to pass. If the same date in two different years turned out to have a similar special significance, the Puritans appear to have made nothing of the fact.

Not so the Anglicans. Not only did "Almighty God . . . inspir[e] the King's most excellent Majesty with a Divine Spirit" in 1605, but he went so far as "to Deliver us again from the same sort of Enemies" on the same date in 1688. Bishop Beveridge shakes his head in pious wonder: "They who do not see the hand of God in all this, it is because they

---

38. Leopold William Finch, "Warden of All-Souls College in Oxon.," no title. Preached May 29, 1701, before the Lower House of Convocation meeting at Oxford. London, 1701.

39. William Beveridge (Bishop of St. Asaph, 1704–1708), no title. Preached November 5, 1704, before the House of Lords. London, 1704.

will not: they who do, cannot but highly esteem that Church, which Almighty God hath so mercifully delivered from such imminent and apparent dangers." The devil assails the nation, with the pope leading the forces of Antichrist. Clearly, the nation must be God's to be so assaulted, and so delivered. November 5, both 1605 and 1688, provides not only excellent reminders that England is the new Israel, as do the punishment of January 30 and the reward of May 29, but that the conduct of subjects affects the fate of the nation.

4. BRITAIN VERSUS THE BAY COLONY? YES . . . AND NO

Anyone even vaguely familiar with the thought and form of those New England sermons called "jeremiads" by Perry Miller, Sacvan Bercovitch, and others cannot miss the force of the parallels. Important differences, however, appear in the context of what I would call "practical Calvinism," or practical religion generally. They concern individual souls rather than national (or colonial) covenants. While the election and fast-day sermons of Massachusetts Bay were differing from the almost antinomian individualism of the usual Sunday and Thursday fare, with its insistence on the need for a new birth for the grace-filled parishioner and its repeated assertion of the mystery shrouding the final disposition of the soul of even the best-behaved churchgoer, the occasional sermons of Old England, with their very New England-like emphasis upon the connection between behavior of individuals and God's treatment of the corporate entity, supply a practically Arminian echo of Sunday calls to all good Anglicans to behave well in order to merit and receive eternal salvation.

By the end of the seventeenth century, predestination and election seem to be receiving no emphasis whatever in the Anglican pulpits of England. This omission seems especially surprising because the doctrine kept its place in the seventeenth of the Thirty-nine Articles of Anglican faith. In occasional sermon after occasional sermon, the bishops and priests of England insisted upon the differentiation between God's treatment of individuals and His treatment of communities and nations: individuals receive their primary rewards and punishments in the next world, whereas communal desserts can be dished out only here, below. Charles I, as scores of sermons insisted, suffered on earth, not because he himself deserved punishment, but because he, as prince of a kingdom gone wrong, suffered for the sins of his people, who, in turn, were punished here for their own corporate, and therefore necessarily earthly, failures. But Charles most certainly received his reward in the next world, just as did and would individual Britons. In just the same, rather than in a contradictory, spirit, "regular" sermons exhorted the congregations of Anglican churches and cathedrals to live good lives here and now in order to earn the reward of heaven.

Paradoxically, what we have in Old England seems to my twentieth-century eyes a great deal closer to traditional Old Testament piety than the curious shifts of New England covenant theology within a context of Calvinism. Of course there must have been some Calvinistic Anglicans who took seriously the predestination of Article 17. Speaking generally, however, it seems safe to say that if one discounts the Christian addition of rewards and punishments in a next world, most later-seventeenth-century Anglicans confronted an Old Testament-like insistence that human behavior, here and now, calls forth God's responses. For these Anglicans, the Christian belief in heaven and hell means not only that there are final rewards and punishments for human behavior, but that these, though not totally revealed here below, conform pretty much to the moral expectations of human beings. Bad things do indeed happen to good people, and the wicked do indeed partake of the corporate prosperity, but final justice will in time be done. The problem of the Book of Job need trouble us no more.

"Goodness," said John Tillotson as early as 1678, has "secret charms" in contrast to "miracles." Among the

> things, which justly recommend . . . our [Anglican] religion, . . . miracles are the great external evidence and confirmation of its truth and Divinity; but the morality of its Doctrines and Precepts, so agreeable to the best Reason, and wisest apprehensions of mankind, so admirably fitted for the perfecting of our natures, and the sweetening of the spirits and tempers of men, so friendly to human society, and every way so well calculated for the peace and order of the world: These are the things which our Religion glories in as her crown and excellency. . . . Among many other things, which may justly recommend the Christian Religion . . . goodness [counts for more than] . . . miracles.[40]

This high valuation of morality rather than faith we can regard as centrist and influential: Tillotson, one remembers, became Archbishop of Canterbury in 1691. In context, Tillotson was contrasting the miracle-heavy papists with the common-sense Anglicans, whose religion was presumed to foster the basic decencies. Equally, one sees in his emphasis on "friendly" behavior and human "morality," all within the context of "the best Reason," a humanistic and social sort of exhortation far different from the spiritual and individualistic tenor of most sermons ordinarily preached in the Massachusetts Bay Colony. No mystery surrounds the soul's journey in Anglican Britain.

40. John Tillotson, no title. Preached November 5, 1678, before the House of Commons. London, 1678.

The contradictory thrusts now seem different from what earlier interpretations have suggested. For the Anglicans, for Old England, decent—that is, socially considerate—behavior benefits the nation in this world and the citizen in the next. This emphasis on "morality" and "goodness" (à la Tillotson) found support in most usual Sunday preachings. Definitions of obligation to the community and to the self were in close harmony: rewards and punishments for behavior accrued to communities in this world, to individuals in the next. Dependence on the Lord included the Arminian ability to influence his judgments, both here and hereafter.

But not so in New England. John Winthrop, in his famous "Model," called for a loving and cooperative community, whose members would recognize their communal covenant with the Lord by selflessly assisting each other and by refraining from putting material gain ahead of spiritual probity. "If," said Winthrop, "we . . . shall fall to embrace this present world and prosecute our carnal intentions, seeking great things for ourselves and our posterity, the Lord will surely break out in wrath against us, be revenged of such a perjured people, and make us know the price of the breach of such a covenant."[41] But it would not have occurred to Winthrop to suggest that behavior in this world in any way obligated the Lord to find a place in heaven for anyone, or that "the breach of such a covenant" would result in anyone's eternal damnation. However much Anne Hutchinson insisted that most of the Massachusetts Bay Colony ministers were preaching a gospel of works, very like unto the Anglicans whom they had crossed the ocean to avoid, Winthrop and those ministers knew that she was wrong. Sanctification might—or might not—be a sign of justification, but no one achieved justification as a result of behavior. Although the nation (or the colony) would prosper in proportion as its citizens conformed to divine will, salvation of individuals depended upon what in God-determined essence those individuals were, not upon the deeds that marked their existence. Individuals could record, ponder, and analyze their own deeds, but their essence was known only to the Lord.

This distinction—essentially one of theological doctrine—gradually softened into an ever-increasing Arminianism, echoing somewhat later in America what had happened in England during the seventeenth century. But Calvinist mystery left its mark. The kind of spiritual roller-coaster ride described in so many Puritan journals, whereby assurance of salvation and grave doubts succeeded each other ceaselessly, made for special fascination in the study of the self. Alexis de Toqueville's anticipation that individuals in the American democracy would find themselves

41. John Winthrop, "A Model of Christian Charity," 90–91.

self-preoccupied has long, and justly, been seen as an anticipation of both Emerson and Whitman. De Toqueville's insight, however, might just as plausibly have referred to Puritan denigration as to romantic (Emersonian; Whitmanesque) celebration of self.

In any case, both England and New England, Anglican and Independent, saw communal success in worldly matters, or communal disaster, as resulting from divine approbation, or condemnation, of human behavior. But our differences from Britain matter at least as much as our commonalties. In matters of high art and of low comedy, of local interest and of international politics, the complexities of being American stem, at least in part, from this curious mingling of the predestined antinomian, eager to discover her or his standing with an arbitrary Lord but powerless to affect it, and the self-reliant Arminian, capable of assisting communal prosperity because the community is under the special authority of a moral Lord. British Anglicanism, in its strident occasional sermons, proclaims a clarity and a certainty about connections between both individual and community behavior and the responses of God, His rewardings and His punishings. American Puritanism, equally clear about communal matters, preserves a sense of mystery in the matter of individual salvation.

In our apparently never-ending engagement with self-knowledge, we may find illumination, even benefit, from contemplating the implications of this real difference and this real similarity. Our chauvinism has British roots that nourish an infantile megalomania concerning our nation's part in a divine plan. At the same time, our Puritan anxieties, feeding as they do our self-important sense of our individually predestinated place in God's drama concerning salvation, may lie behind the wild oscillations between our concern for communal security and insistence on individual freedoms that have characterized past and present American difficulty in balancing the needs of society and the liberties of citizens. It may well be that the shifting emphasis between personal salvation on Sundays and communal well-being on special occasions has served to complement the God-dependent antinomian (or is it really self-reliant Arminian?) individualism usually associated with the American frontier.

In any case, distinguishing the will of God from the wills of human beings remained (remains?) a complicating confusion, one that chastened maturity, not infantile megalomania, may possibly sort out. Insisting on their own otherness from Anglican Arminianism, the American Puritans were, no doubt, correct. When we, however, insist on the unique nature of their sense of themselves as the Lord's Chosen People, we put them, and by extension ourselves, in a false position, as the words of so many hundreds of Anglican sermons attest. The consequences of this false position may never come clear in terms acceptable to all generations and factions. (Was World War I an effort to make the world safe for democracy, an effort to protect cartels and access to raw materials, neither, both, what?) Still, the practical results of considering the possibility that one may be deluded probably differ from those that follow from proceeding on the assumption, e.g., that because the Lord is one's Shepherd, one should not want for oil.

From Anglican equations of Israel with Britannia, a series of perfectly logical steps led to empire and the "white man's burden." The legacy of similar Puritan equations between Israel and America seems to include our present sense that somehow we are responsible for the rest of the world, and that the rest of the world owes us respect and even obedience. Because we are indeed by no means unique in the self-flattering of our old nomination, perhaps we can allow ourselves to learn from the descendants of Anglican ancestors. At least we might say that although we have "more," what we have may not be exactly the same as a divine blessing and a divine mandate.

Equally, we might gain something from recognizing—perhaps even with a view to overcoming them, although this seems extremely problematic—how deep our uncertainties, our insecurities, do lie. As we will see, the Anglican articles of belief, in a fine phrase not often quoted, summed up an important part of the Calvinist mind-set as all too likely to bring about a state of "wretchlessness . . . no less perilous than desperation." Even with increasingly rationalistic ways of looking at things, however, the terror that Edgar Allan Poe knew was "not of Germany, but of the soul" defied, in America, all genteel efforts to bury it, to render it powerless. But before coming home to our own roosted pigeons, we must spend a little more time on the far side of the Atlantic.

III

Certainty: Divine or Human?
BISHOP BURNET AND THE MATTER OF CHOICE

1. RELIGIOUSLY POLITICAL, POLITICALLY RELIGIOUS

If New England represents a polity that is, in a biblical sense, God's Chosen People, His New Israel, then that fact might seem to call for a declaration of independence from the Anglican establishment. We know that New England Congregationalists declared no such religious independence, differing sharply from the Plymouth Pilgrims, who from the beginning insisted upon their status as out-and-out Separatists from the non-church that miscalled itself the Established Church of England. As has many times been said, and wondered at, the Congregationalists of the Bay Colony kept up the practical fiction that they themselves represented the true Church of England and had never separated themselves from that true Church, only from its perversions. That Anglicans also called themselves God's chosen raised no necessary problems for Puritans: they believed that some Anglicans used that phrase correctly because they represented the true church of which Congregationalists in New England formed the center. As for the majority of Anglican bishops and priests who presented the false claim to divine favor, history would, sooner rather than later, catch up with them. Anglican claims that the British nation itself was "chosen" could be taken as including reference to its American colonies, at least of the Massachusetts Bay sort.

"Independence," then, was at most a latent, not a lively, issue. Another, and more immediately significant, aspect of Puritan echoes of the Anglican commonplace worked its way out in a respect for human freedom and human choice. This respect was not widespread; but, as we shall see, it was gaining clarity and intensity by the end of the eighteenth century, and on both sides of the ocean. Its primary articulators would be an Anglican bishop and a Massachusetts Bay country minister. To see how this came about, we need to look beyond the specific nature of the claims to be God's chosen and note the general conclusion to be inferred from the very fact that they could be made in the first place. So long as God's will stands clear and unambiguous, intolerance of what runs counter to God's revealed word remains an obligation. To speak of the Anglican sources of some Puritan assumptions involves more than the idea that God watches over His particular people on this earth and that we—whether British Anglicans or colonial Congregationalists—are those people in "today's" world.

The Puritans assumed, and said, that religious toleration indicated either powerlessness or inadequate belief. We find Anglican analogs in the "Thorough" policies and practices of Archbishop Laud, policies and practices intended to make the Anglican Church "thoroughly" Anglican, purged completely of Puritan opposition. Also, the Calvinism that originally underlay Anglican theological thought—the backbone of Puritan belief about God's dealings with individual human souls—led to an articulation of multiple interpretations (and therefore of the utility of toleration) that in England antedates an expression of principle usually attributed to American patriots—especially to Thomas Jefferson—in their efforts to cast off the chains that bound them to the Crown. Now—at the very end of the twentieth century—to rehash even some of the complex doctrines of Calvinist theology may well encourage even hardy readers to skip. Please don't. On the one hand, fantasies of being special lie just beneath the surface, and, on the other, solid foundations for religious toleration lie there, too, a fact that may not be so obvious.

I do not propose to alter the historical outlines of the growth of practical toleration. The English Puritans themselves, under Cromwell, had both psychological justification and political necessity for allowing varieties of religious belief and practice, despite strong advisements from Massachusetts Bay colonials not to do so. Roger Williams, thrown out of the colony in 1635, very quickly became a popular figure in Cromwell's England. He insisted that God's truths finally could not be known by mere human beings and that therefore to persecute anyone for believing unpopular doctrine or finding solace in unconventional (so long as socially harmless) ritual might well be to banish truth and to confirm error. The Anglicans, once they regained control after 1660, at first saw less political necessity for toleration, as witness the various repressive acts of 1662. Also, to speak more subjectively, they knew they were God's chosen. To know that one's religion is a reflection of God's will might well mean not only that one believes correctly but that other beliefs are just flat wrong. Therefore, why tolerate them? Surely that wild colonial, Nathaniel Ward, was correct: to tolerate differences of religious belief is to kill true religion. The large-scale shift from the intolerance of Laud's pre-1640 days to the practical toleration that marked eighteenth-century England is far beyond the scope and concern of this study. A few of the symptoms of that shift will suffice for my purposes.

2. OF TOLERANCE, INTOLERANCE, AND BISHOP FLEETWOOD'S COUNTRY CURATE

Although I shall focus on Gilbert Burnet's 1699 exposition of Article 17 of the Anglican confession of faith, I begin by returning to a combination of politics and religion that had been festering for years, the reaction to the specific nature of the sermons preached in memory of the killing of Charles I on January 30, 1648 (Old Style). Let us go back to the first sermons preached upon the event of January 30. Delivered to the royal family in Breda in the spring of 1649, June 3 and 13, and printed "at the Hage" that same year (then in post-Restoration London, 1660), they provided the Anglican model for one sort of January 30 sermon that became increasingly distasteful to increasingly more listeners. Henry Leslie's title, *The Martyrdom of King Charles the First or His Conformity with Christ in His Sufferings,* we remember, said it all: "And indeed, you will find it [the killing of Charles] very like unto it [the crucifixion] . . . in the dignity of the person murdered, the kind of death that he suffered, and the quality of the murderers." This sermon announced one significant thread that ran through many—not all, to be sure—of the sermons preached in response to parliamentary and royal decree. (As we have seen, the decree held from 1660 until 1859, although, as we have also seen, it did not always receive full obedience.)[1] After a while, even some of Charles's most ardent defenders began to acknowledge that perhaps likening him to Jesus was going a bit far, but others found no exaggeration in that similitude.

A related thread reveals more directly the sense of Anglican self-satisfaction. Thinking of Charles I as another Jesus put his execution into an especially evil, and extremely small, class of earthly crimes. Even without this addition to the bare facts, that Charles had the title of

---

1. Thomas Burgess (Bishop of St. David's, 1803–1825; of Salisbury, 1825–1837), no title. Preached January 30, 1807, to the House of Lords. London, 1807. "The Sermon appointed to be preached before the House of Lords on the 30th of January, *which had been discontinued for some years,* it was His Majesty's pleasure should be revived this year." (Emphasis mine.)

king made his death serious enough. Over and over, those who killed him received epithets that stressed their participation in the king-killing principles of the papists. Just as Queen Elizabeth of blessed memory had had to cope with Roman Catholic perfidy, threats, and plots, and just as James I and the royal family, along with Parliament, almost found themselves at the mercy of Roman-inspired Gunpowder Treason, so also even the avowedly anti-Roman Catholic Dissenters could be seen—often were seen—as traitors not only to the Crown but also to Protestantism. Through the last four decades of the seventeenth century, and well into the eighteenth, January 30 (or Mondays, January 31) came in many a cathedral and parish church to signify a time for the freshening of old wounds. Irritating though the occasion might be, however, it also served to keep fresh in people's minds some of the political and religious issues that shaped daily British experience.

Among ministers notorious for their penchant for condemning in the strongest possible language both those guilty of Charles's death and all of their literal, philosophical, and religious descendants, Luke Milbourne stands out. He preached for many years at St. Ethelburga's, in London. He stood out to such a degree that that anonymous pamphlet, published in late February or early March of 1709/1710, referred to him by name in its title: *High-Church Politics; or the abuse of the 30th of January considered. With remarks on Mr. Luke Milbourne's railing sermons, and on the observation of that day.* Mr. Anonymous represents a growing number of Anglicans—clerical as well as secular—who had been attempting to combine political and religious interests in the cause of stability and harmony. The first part of his effort, as a loyal citizen of post-1688 Britain and subject of Queen Anne, elaborates on the contradiction inherent in celebrating the changes of administration signified by May 29 (1660) and November 5 (1688)—with specific reference to the military defeat of James II at the Battle of the Boyne—while on January 30 condemning all resistance to rulers, "which in effect is declaring King William's [and therefore Queen Anne's] possessing the Throne as usurpation." Then he goes on to the effects of toleration, as practiced in Britain and perceived by the rest of the world: "The Church of England has found the glorious effects of Toleration and Condescension to Dissenters, and they have so far triumphed over our heats and animosities, as has been a fatal disappointment to our enemies. . . ." But the way in which Luke Milbourne (and too many others like him) observe January 30 and celebrate Charles I is, "perhaps, one considerable reason of the general contempt of the Clergy of this Age. . . . Though the King was a great Prince, yet sure we must allow he came infinitely short of Divinity." To assert otherwise is to forget, or ignore, that "Christ says, his Kingdom is not of this world. . . ."[2] This world, not the next, is the one to cope with. Its complexities make it challenging, to be sure, but very, very interesting, very much worth the trouble. This is the message I find implicit in the hundreds, the thousands, of occasional sermons—and reactions to them—delivered and published in Britain through two centuries.

The notion that the phrase "the Kingdom of God" has a spiritual dimension only, and not a worldly one, had lacked the currency of another phrase, "Primitive Purity," which denoted the doctrine and worship of the Established Church of England (along with such variations as "Primitive Simplicity," "Primitive Religion," and "Primitive Christianity"). In 1636, one Herbert Thorndike (1598–1672) was installed as "prebendary of Layton Ecclesia in the Cathedral of Lincoln, just vacated by the death of his personal friend, George Herbert."[3] In 1670, he completed and published a book (reprinted in 1680) of over 180 pages unpromisingly titled "A Discourse of the Forbearance or the Penalties . . . Which a Due Reformation Requires." He intended to outline "the means to restore Unity in this Church." Primarily, he looks at the behavior of New England Independents, who "have not only banished Antinomians, and put Quakers to death; But have imposed a Penalty of five shillings a Lordsday, upon all that come not to hear their sermons . . ." (160).

He finds such intolerance unconscionable. Thorndike, and other Anglicans equally outspoken, insists that his Church, the Church of England, imitates the Primitive Church, as neither the Roman Catholic nor the Independent Churches come close to doing. "[T]he world knows that there never was any such Religion in the World, as that of Independents, before the planting of New England" (159). Over and over, neither the Independents nor the Church of Rome adhere to "the Canons and Customs of the Primitive Church" (23, et passim).

Thorndike in 1670 was not able—or not ready—to recognize any logical similarity between the attitude of Massachusetts Bay Independents and his own in labeling them "misbelieving fellow-subjects." This failure seems the result of no particular policy; rather, it marks simply one instance of a kind of deliberate blindness whereby one notices most clearly the mote in the eye of the other person while ignoring the beam in one's own. We know the phenomenon well by now, and we use such words as "projection" and "repression" when we talk about it. As Henry David Thoreau (among others) said in the nineteenth century, and many psychiatrists in the twentieth, we find ourselves shocked only when

2. Anonymous ("A Country Conformist"), *Advice to English Protestants*. Preached November 5, 1689. London, 1689.
    3. *DNB*.

we contemplate behavior repugnant to our conscious selves that strikes chords of sympathy in our buried selves. A writer "can communicate to us no experience [that we have not imagined for ourselves], and if we are shocked, whose experience is it that we are reminded of?"[4] This sort of repression—of information, of feelings, of perceptions—can manifest itself in what to the outsider appears to be a most perplexing paralysis of will or confusion of intellect. So Thorndike, finding that "the greater part of His Majesties Subjects in that Plantation [Massachusetts]" were having "their souls . . . murdered, by the tyranny of their misbelieving fellow-subjects," (160) expresses his shocked horror at New England's doing unto Anglicans what the Anglican establishment was doing to Dissenters.

In this context, Luke Milbourne's "railing sermons" suggest an imperviousness to changing times almost wonderful to behold. In January of 1682/1683, Milbourne insists that the king-killing principles of Jesuits and Separatists mark an unsuspected harmony between the two groups: the Roman Catholics of November 5 cannot be distinguished from the Puritans of January 30. In his last published January 30 sermon—1719/1720—the Romish principles of king-killing, having been taken over by the Puritans, furnish him with his main reason for insisting on a policy of nontoleration, or, rather, for lamenting the mistaken policy of toleration then in force. Truth in 1682 remained true thirty-seven years later, although the definitions of tyranny and of loyalty depended upon which side one was on.

Meanwhile, some people had changed with the times, apparently possessing the ability to perceive the effect upon others of established self-righteousness; that is, they were able to perceive self-righteousness as such. Significantly, Milbourne never achieved the office of bishop. One William Fleetwood, bishop of St. Asaph from 1708 until 1714, and then of Ely until his death in 1723, addressed the House of Lords on January 30, 1709/1710, offering a perspective that differed markedly from Milbourne's. Although he expressed the usual concern about the "everlasting stain laid on the honour of the English Nation, by adjudging their King to Death, against all Reason, all Law, and all example of our ancestors," and even found Charles to have been an exemplary king, the main thrust of his sermon has to do with the political landmines confronting those who preach in observation of the day.

> This Day is, through the excessive partiality of some of both sides, become a Day of Great Trial to the Preachers: Talk of the Duty, Honour, and Obedience of the Subject to the Prince, and you are thought, by some,

4. Henry David Thoreau, "Letter to Harrison Blake," 369.

to preach away the People's Liberties and make them slaves; Talk of
the People's Liberties, and you are opening, presently, a door to mutiny,
disloyalty, and flat rebellion, with some others. They are both of them, God
be thanked, in the wrong. . . .

This double sense is not so terribly complicated, but it is not for
the simple-minded, either. Similarly, just as Anglican vituperation on
November 5 rubs contemporary British Roman Catholics the wrong way,

> so the Observation of this Day is become (like the Vth of November to the
> Papists) exceedingly grievous and distastful to all Dissenters . . . for the
> license that (they say) is taken, upon it, of inveighing against them. . . . It
> was not, certainly, appointed to become a Day of wrath, and Provocation
> of our fellow subjects.

And Fleetwood further suggests that "more men have been shamed by
gentle usage, than reviled into repentance." Therefore, the biting certainties of a Luke Milbourne, apart from being un-Christian, are ineffective.
This is true not only because of human nature but also because the facts
of history have more facets to them than straightforward propagandists
can allow.

Bishop Fleetwood, apparently not compelled to repeat endlessly the
old tune now so discordant to so many, focuses instead upon the two
issues whose opposing emphases foment unrest. The people's liberties
and obedience to the prince, both important, both controversial, depend
for their meaning so much upon individual conscience and individual understanding that to handle them from the pulpit cannot help
but alienate, and even arouse the passions of, valued members of the
congregation. Aware of the buried explosives, Fleetwood deliberately
chooses to suppress mention of them. I'll return to the terms of his choice
in a moment. First, I want to contrast that deliberate suppression with
something else.

Exactly ten years earlier, also before the House of Lords, John Sharp,
Archbishop of York, had demonstrated (unconsciously, one assumes) the
dangers of repression. Taking as his text Paul's advice to Titus as, in effect,
Bishop of Crete, "Put them in mind to be subject to principalities and
powers, to obey magistrates," Sharp acknowledged that some people
now insist that preachers should confine themselves to questions of
holiness and sin, and leave politics out of their sermons. "But," Sharp
said to the lords—who included his fellow bishops—"my job is to make
good Christians, who must be good subjects for conscience sake." Those
who preach, to be sure, must never "side with party or faction"; the
point, however, is that they have an obligation to support the established
government. Politics and religion strike him as inseparable—as, in a
nation with an established church, they well might.

Suddenly, and to his surprise, Sharp finds himself skating on thin ice: the Bible, he says, makes perfectly clear who are "principalities and magistrates," and equally so "what are subjection and obedience." Subjects must "honour, respect, and reverence" their magistrates, "pray for them, defend them, be peaceable." But all this obedience, it turns out, is owed only to "the standing laws of the country," and "not to the will of the prince. The subject is answerable for everything he doth against the law, even when he doth it by the King's command." God, that is, "has supreme dominion over our consciences." So what are we actually to do? If Sharp were really distinguishing between a merely autocratic and arbitrary "will of the prince" and "the standing laws of the country," as at first he seems to be doing, the answer would be clear. But he shifts from this relatively constricted arena to the real source of conflict in his time. If we merely "doubt the lawfulness of laws," we must obey. But when there is no doubt—that is, no doubt in the individual's mind—that the law as written by human beings is wrong, "man must not obey. Always obey God, not man." But this obedience to God must embody both nonresistance to, and passive obedience of, the magistrate: the subject must never go so far as "tumult, insurrection, or rebellion." Jesus offers the perfect example of nonresistance, which, however, is

> not to be expressed in the same way in all places. . . . To speak as plainly as I can: As the laws of the land are the measures of Active Obedience; so are also the same laws the measure of our submission. And as we are not bound to obey but where the Laws and Constitution require our Obedience; so neither are we bound to submit but as the Laws and Constitution do require our submission.

Let me try to put Sharp into more modern and more direct English. People have to obey the law of the land. At the same time, they have to obey the law of God. The law of God takes precedence over the law of man, but the law of man tells us what laws we are to obey. When the law of the land contradicts the law of God, we are to obey God. How can we know when the law of the land does indeed run counter to what God commands? We consult the law of the land. One might expect Sharp to allude to the Bible, here. Instead, his solution comes down to paying closer attention to human legal writ than to divine revelation.

The effect of such double-talk might well have been a gradual awareness on the part of increasing numbers of people that the text of the Bible offers a great deal less certainty than they had been led to expect. This, however, by no means corresponds to what Sharp explicitly stated. He stepped right over the gaping incoherence in his argument as if it didn't exist, and closed his turn-of-the-century sermon with what to him made incontestable common sense: the laws of England make "the King's person sacred and inviolable. To attempt his life is high treason." Therefore, what happened in 1648/1649 remains both a "scandal to Protestant Religion" and a "reproach to the people of England." Admitting that he's "sensible how uneasy some are at the mentioning of this; and how gladly they would have both the thing, and the memorial of it, forgot among us," Sharp claims that he "would so too, provided God has forgotten it and provided too that factions among us were forgot. So long as we have apprehensions, we must remember this Day," using it to "implore the mercy of God."

Simply by defending the observance of the day, Sharp reminds his hearers, however inadvertently, that at least some respectable members of the Established Church, not simply Dissenters, were calling for an end to the flagellations of January 30 sermonizing. When William Stephens blasted forth his "Animadversions on the last two 30th of January Sermons" (London: February, 1701/1702), he decried the "ill nature and uncharitableness" of "a certain Doctor upon the same occasion," who offered up as paraphrase " 'Father, forgive them not, for they knew what they did.' " Rather, said Stephens, we ought to say, "From envy, hatred and malice, and all uncharitableness, good Lord deliver us."

Now the doctrines of passive obedience and nonresistance, understandably central to the restored government and the restored church after 1660, made very difficult reading after 1688 and the Glorious Revolution. The first verses of Romans 13 suddenly became difficult, too. Between 1660 and 1688, the second verse—"And they that resist shall receive unto themselves damnation"—served as the text for countless May 29 and January 30 sermons. Along with the first verse, which in apparently unequivocal fashion established God as the source of "the powers that be," it formed the basis for both Anglican and Puritan, both British and colonial, thinking about government. Less than four years before the Puritans in England cut off the head of Charles I, John Winthrop reminded some of his cantankerous fellows in Hingham that his authority as a magistrate came from the Almighty, even though the electors of Massachusetts had called him into office. Not being a clergyman, he didn't refer to the text; but his basic premise was a commonplace of Puritan as well as of Anglican thought. Both agreed: "Whosoever therefore resisteth the power, resisteth the ordinance of God: and they that resist shall receive to themselves damnation." Therefore, how could one justify blatant opposition to Winthrop, to say nothing of the killing of King Charles I or the rejection of King James II?

The Puritan stance of 1648/1649 anticipated that taken by many Anglicans following 1688. Concretely, the trick became to read the first part of verse four in a new way, as if unrelated to verse three: "For he is the minister of God to thee for good" took on an independent life of its own. Instead of being read as referring exclusively to the behavior of subjects, which a ruler would, on God's authority, either praise and reward if good or censure and punish if not, the significance of the sentence lost the causal "For" and came to refer to the behavior of the ruler rather than to that only of the ruled. Similarly, the subsequent, "But if thou do that which is evil," in condemning evil in subjects, no longer excused rulers who themselves broke the law. So long as rulers command what is good, what is within the law of the land, they remain God's ministers, with their authority from Him. The fifth verse—"Wherefore ye must needs be subject, not only for wrath, but also for conscience sake."— thereby took on a more limited meaning than it had been seen to have. Absolute obedience to rulers? Absolutely, but only so long as those rulers themselves obeyed the law.

The post-1688 context, although wonderfully complex, seems to me to be well understood by now. Bishop Fleetwood understood it very well indeed back then. One of the anomalies—at least to twentieth-century Americans unfamiliar with the era—lies in the positions taken by supporters of the various factions. Those most loyal to Queen Anne and to the House of Hanover insisted on the insidiousness of passive obedience and nonresistance, and upon the folly of demanding unquestioning obedience to the ruler as God's anointed. Those with Jacobite leanings, on the other hand, based their sense of the illegitimacy of the new government upon the "rebellion" of 1688, indistinguishable in their eyes, so they said, from what had happened in 1648/1649. That is, after 1688, those most committed to the ruling monarch insisted that the ruling monarch ought not to receive unquestioning obedience. Those most disaffected—those loyal to the king over the water—kept insisting upon the absolute necessity for absolute obedience. Geoffrey Holmes, and others, have worked out the approximate nature of the correlations between High Church, Tory, and Jacobite sympathies on the one hand, and Low Church, Whig, and Hanoverian ones on the other.

J. P. Kenyon's *Revolution Principles: The Politics of Party, 1689–1720* shows at length and in detail how the obligation to preach sermons for November 5, taking into account 1688 as well as 1605, pushed many of the Anglican clergy into voicing positions that today seem at best equivocal. They wanted, of course, to give thanks for God's miraculous assistance in saving His nation from the Roman Catholic "menace." King-killing principles, clearly ascribable to Guy Fawkes and the other Gunpowder Treason people, had by God's miraculous intervention been prevented from devastating the royal family, Parliament, and the realm. God, in His goodness, in His concern for His people, had directly revealed to James I the meaning of an equivocal message casually intercepted.[5] In

5. See, e.g., William Sclater, *Papisto-Mastix, or Deborah's prayer against Gods enemies.* Preached Nov. 5, 1641, at Exeter Cathedral. London, 1641; S. A. Freeman, *The . . .*

1688, however, that Roman Catholic "menace" had no discernible "King-Killing" component in it, for James II himself was seen as the principal threat to Britain's Protestant polity. God's miraculous intervention in managing the winds around Torbay so that William could land could very easily be "mistaken" for something very like divine aid for a cause like the one that had led to the event of January 30, 1648/1649, almost exactly forty years earlier, for which the nation still humiliated itself (and scolded the Dissenters) annually. Very, very few other non-Jacobites could allow themselves to be as forthright as Daniel Defoe:

> [T]he difference lies only here; the Whigs in 41 and 48 took up arms against their king, and having conquered him, and taken him prisoner cut off his head *because they had him*. The Church of England took up arms against their king in 88 and did not cut off his head because they had him not. King Charles lost his life *because he did not run away*, and his son, King James, saved his life, because he *did* run away.[6]

The polite fiction promulgated by Parliament had it that King William, far from putting James II to flight, had merely occupied the empty throne abandoned by James in his "abdication." There had been no "rebellion" against an anointed king, simply a peaceful change of rule, a revolving of the wheels of power: a "Glorious Revolution," as we all learned in school to call it.

The full savor of the context in which Bishop Fleetwood spoke emerges only if one is familiar with the rantings and subsequent trial of Dr. Henry Sacheverell—one of the most fascinating episodes in the intermingling of church and state. I must, however, take most of it as read, or else never get back to the colonial side of the Atlantic. The curious should consult Geoffrey Holmes's *The Trial of Doctor Sacheverell* for an account not only of the trial but of all that led up to it and much of what followed. That about 100,000 copies of Sacheverell's November 5, 1709, sermon, *The Perils of False Brethren, both in Church and . . . State . . .* , were in circulation by trial-time in mid-December suggests something of the extent to which the case brought public passions to a focus.[7]

One of the Doctor's main points, coming right in the middle of the sermon, was an insistence that "[t]he Grand security of our Government . . . is founded upon the steady belief of the subject's obligation to an absolute and unconditional obedience to the Supreme Power, in all

---

happy Deliverance of King James the First and the three . . . estates of the realm, from the Gunpowder-Treason; and also for the happy arrival of his present majesty on this Day, for the Deliverance of our Church and Nation from Popery and Arbitrary Power. Preached November 5, 1690, to the House of Commons. London, 1690.

6. Daniel Defoe. *A New Test of the Church of England's Loyalty: or Whiggish Loyalty and Church Loyalty Compared*. London, 1702.

7. Holmes, *The Trial . . .* , 75.

things lawful, and the utter illegality of Resistance upon any pretense whatsoever." But instead of receiving appropriate reinforcement from the nation's pulpits, "this Fundamental Doctrine . . . is now ridiculed . . . as a dangerous tenet. . . ." Sacheverell had taken for his text a slight variation on Paul's mention in 2 Corinthians 11:26 of strictly personal "perils among false brethren": he found England itself "imperiled by false brethren." Among the various sorts of false brethren now imperiling the state, Sacheverell here pointed his finger at all those who denied the absolute duty of nonresistance, of perfect submission to earthly powers authorized by God.

On December 2, 1710—almost a year after the trial—appeared Fleetwood's satiric pamphlet, "The thirteenth chapter to the Romans, vindicated from the abusive senses put upon it. Written by a Curate of Salop; and directed to the clergy of that county, and the neighboring ones of North-Wales; to whom the author wisheth patience, Moderation, and a good understanding for half an hour." ("Moderation" was another one of the catchwords in Sacheverell's sermon, a particularly insidious quality):

> What could not be gained by Comprehension, and Toleration, must be brought about by Moderation, and Occasional Conformity; that is, what they [the nameless False Brethren of whom Sacheverell is warning us] could not do by Open Violence, they will not fail by secret Toleration to accomplish. If the Church can't be pulled down, it may be blown up; and no matter with these men how 'tis destroyed, so that it is destroyed.

Sacheverell's hysterical cry that "the Church [was] in Danger" became political grist for the Tory mill in their triumphant, though short-lived, sweep to power in 1710. Geoffrey Holmes takes delightful note of "the infectious election-chant which carried the two Tory candidates for the county of Cornwall . . . into a resounding victory over the Whigs on 1 November: 'Trevanion and Granville, sound as a bell / For the Queen, the Church, and Sacheverell.' "[8]

That Fleetwood focused on "the thirteenth chapter to the Romans" suggests just how central its first seven verses had become to a number of related issues. As far back as May 1702, Sacheverell had delivered at Oxford "The political Union. A discourse shewing the dependence of government on religion in general: and of the English monarchy on the Church of England in particular." Reprinted in London, in 1710, it combined an attack on Dissenters (as men "against whom every man that wishes its [the Church's] welfare, ought to hang out the bloody flag and banner of defiance") with reiteration of the religious as well as political duties of passive obedience and nonresistance, seeing both embodied in

8. Ibid., 252.

Romans 13. Fleetwood's exploration of that crucial text, therefore, came after several years of reckless and exacerbated passion on the subject.

We know that Fleetwood wrote it, not only because, as F. F. Madan tells us, "its authorship became an open secret,"[9] but also because it later appeared in 1737 in *A Complete Collection of . . . all . . . written by Dr. William Fleetwood*. Although Fleetwood says that he had begun shaping the piece as early as the previous winter, between Sacheverell's November sermon and the impeachment of the doctor by Parliament, the reference to Salop in his title suggests that the work was still in progress at least as late as September, 1710, when Frederick Cornewall, M.A., "vicar of Bromfield, and lecturer of Ludlow in the county of Salop," published his "Zeal for Religion recommended: in a sermon preach'd at the assizes of Salop, August 4th, 1710."[10] Perhaps the point of Fleetwood's title was that Salop desperately needed a curate if the people were being subjected to much of Cornewall's view of things. Taking as his text Paul's Epistle to the Galatians (4:18), " . . . it is good to be zealously affected in a good thing, and not only when I am present with you," Cornewall had preached zeal, not in the sense of the religious affections, but in the context of commitment to the Church, the right Church, by which he meant "A Church that inviolably maintains the rights of the Civil Power. . . ." If in this imperfect world such a thing as "a Perfect Church were to be created, the English features would be the better part of the composition," he affirmed.

Speaking from behind the unsteady mask of a naïve country curate—I call it unsteady only in part because of the title's ironically sarcastic hope that perpetrators of the absurd can achieve "a good understanding for half an hour"—Fleetwood takes steady aim at the legal, political, and moral absurdities that the "High Church and Sacheverell" faction was putting forward. Mostly, Fleetwood displays an almost Swiftian or Ben Franklinesque skill in staying within his invented character. The good curate has been to London recently and has been led to see that all in the provinces have misunderstood the Truth. "I no sooner urged that Sir S. H. [*sic*] and all the Doctors Council had defended the Revolution and the Resistance that brought it about . . . but a Bible was brought, which opened of it self at the 13th Chapter to the Romans, and I was bid to see what I could make of it." Very kindly, to save him the vexation of reading it wrongly, says he, "I was every day told, that the Doctrine of Passive Obedience and Non-Resistance was a doctrine peculiar to the Church of England. . . ." Before too long, however, his good country common sense begins to reassert itself. To be sure, he finds these big-city

9. F. F. Madan, *A Critical Bibliography of Dr. Henry Sacheverell*, 205.
10. London, 1710. Listed in Madan as item #590.

arguments compelling up to a point. "And yet," he cannot help but conclude, "it is a little absurd to say a doctrine is Peculiar to a Church, when it pretends to come from Christ, to be taught by the apostles, and by all the Primitive Writers."

Then he forgets about being a curate from Salop, and sounds very much like the learned bishop of St. Asaph, as White Kennett thought in 1715. If rational argument could have had an effect upon the passions of the time, Fleetwood's would have cooled them. "The 13th chapter to the Romans is therefore a much quieter chapter than most People imagine. . . . It left every nation to be governed by its own laws; and if they could mend those laws, they might. . . ." Acknowledging the biblical authority for the notion that "a Rebel without Repentance shall be damned," he asks,

> But does it [the Bible] tell us what Rebellion is? Or what sort of Resistance it is, that makes a man a Rebel? This innocent chapter, to my way of thinking, says nothing of the matter—it leaves us to learn from the Laws and Constitutions of each Government, what obedience is required at the Subject's Hands: what it is to be a Rebel, and [what] Resistance is adjudged Rebellion. . . . The Chapter forbids Resistance, but, truly the Laws must tell us what Resistance is, and in what case it is forbidden.

He finds Romans 13 absolutely "slandered . . . of late," and he calls on all preachers of sermons to "Let the Scriptures alone, and make them not subservient to the base and villainous Designs of wicked Men, that would enthrall their Country." What truly makes England great as a nation is that it exists under a rule of law, not of private passions. In his own preaching, he tries always to remember this:

> I seldom touch upon these Doctrines [nonresistance and passive obedi-ence] in the Pulpit. . . . And indeed I have seldom heard these Causes managed in the Pulpit, with the success that should encourage me to do the like. The Prince has generally lost more ground in the affections of the audience, than he has gained on their reason and understanding.

He invents and criticizes a hypothetical

> young Divine; . . . And I would fain learn how much the Doctrine of these Greater Men differs from that of this Young Curate, who tells us, that all Magistrates, as well the Subordinate as Supreme, are so of God, so much his Ordinance and Institution, that they are not . . . to be resisted . . . even in the most outragious violation of the Laws? [Only if] the Legislative Power [in England's case, Parliament] shall enact, that the Prince's Proclamations shall be accounted Sacred as the Roman Edicts were . . . I shall be bound by it, and . . . St. Peter and St. Paul will bind me to it. . . . The Word of God obliges all subjects . . . as the Laws of their Country have obliged them to: And has forbidden such Resistance . . . as the Laws of their Country have forbidden. Finis.

Fleetwood, a better Protestant than many, insisted upon reading the Bible for himself.

3. Toleration, Belief, and the Power(lessness) of the Will

Behind his reading lie two related but superficially extremely different sets of concerns that two other writers can help us see separately. We will also get some insight into the meaning of such phrases as "Anglican Accommodation" and the "Great Compromise." To talk of the underlying toleration of the Established Church may strike one as odd, given the example and influence of Archbishop Laud and others of his ilk. Still, even this will become possible. But first come the two concerns that I have referred to, one political and the other doctrinal. For the political, a clear example—even clearer than Fleetwood's—is in the words of Samuel Croxall, chaplain to George II, as he explores and explains to the House of Commons on January 30, 1729/1730, the implications behind the observation of the anniversaries of January 30, 1648/1649, and November 5, 1688. (For reasons that quickly become obvious, he ignores 1605.) Because of the events they memorialize, the two might well seem—indeed, have usually seemed to most people—to have been

> founded on two contradictory and incompatible principles: But, upon a cool and impartial deliberation, may be observed so mutually to correspond with and illustrate each other, as to make it appear, in a manner, necessary, that neither of the doctrines which they separately suggest, should ever be recommended, in solemn discourses to the public, but conjunctly, and at the same time. The one, is that which we are now assembled to keep, A Day of Fasting; 'To implore the Mercy of God, that neither that sacred and innocent blood, as on this Day shed, nor those other sins by which God was provoked to deliver up both us and our King into the hands of cruel and unreasonable men may, at any time, hereafter, be visited upon us or our posterity,' the other, a Day of Thanksgiving; 'For the deliverance of our Church and the nation from Popery and slavery, by the Happy arrival of his Majesty King William the III. . . .' Both which, when rightly understood, and duly applied, plainly show themselves to have been no less originally ordained than annually continued, upon wise and good grounds: being equally and jointly conducive to regulate our political behavior, by putting us in mind what we owe our King, and what our country.[11]

Our debt to our king we pay by adhering to the laws that stabilize society. What we owe our country we acknowledge by insisting upon royal recognition of the rights of free-born Englishmen.

---

11. Samuel Croxall, no title. Preached January 30, 1729/1730, to the House of Commons. London, 1729/1730.

Some, Croxall realizes, are "too weak-minded" to understand and help maintain this crucial balance, and others "so perverted [as] to keep up animosities among parties among us." Croxall's severity takes in both people and king, subjects and ruler, as well as those preachers and politicians who encourage "animosities" of any sort. All kings must realize that there is "more glory in governing a free people, than in tyrannizing over a nation of slaves"; subjects must themselves exercise vigilance, however, because if "Kings abuse, people must refuse!" Individuals, that is, have to think, if they are to be citizens as well as subjects. St. Peter, Croxall points out, distinguished between some casual "ordinance of Man," some local or temporary law that might be immediately expedient but that violated long-held principle, and "the [established] Higher Powers": in England, "[o]ur Higher power is the King, the House of Lords, and the House of Commons, jointly." It was wrong to kill Charles I, but it was also a parallel, equal wrong for Charles to violate the joint authority, the particular higher power of the land.

Although the sense of balance between the obedience that "we owe our King" and the attention to liberty and individual rights that we owe "our country" was well recognized as a goal by the early part of the eighteenth century, that goal had by no means been achieved. One William Binckes, for example, proctor for the Diocese of Lichfield and Coventry, preached before the Lower House of Convocation, one of the formal, deliberative bodies of the Established Church, on January 30, 1701/1702. Subsequently impeached for "seeming" to have equated Charles with Jesus (following the by-then hackneyed lead of Henry Leslie's 1649 sermons), he was censured by the House of Lords. A pamphlet in his defense, probably written by Binckes himself, appeared early in 1702, rehearsing the long tradition of underlining the resemblances between the two murdered men, and then blandly proclaiming that

> That foul aspersion of blasphemy, which had been cast upon his sermon by very ignorant or very malicious persons, he now looks upon as effectually wiped off by this solemn acquital. . . . Their Lordships having been pleased to resolve and declare, That in his sermon there are several expressions that give just scandal and offence to all Christian People, he thought himself bound to submit to their authority, without offering a vindication of himself; but at the same time he . . . hath not yet had the fortune to meet with any of those Christians who are scandalized and offended at the passages referred to by their Lordships.

The upshot was that, although Binckes was impeached and censured (though found innocent of absolute blasphemy) in 1702, by 1704, Binckes, then dean of Lichfield Cathedral, actually preached the November 5 sermon to the House of Commons. So, then as now, not everyone shared the developed consciousness of a Croxall.

But Gilbert Burnet did. We must at last attend to the masterfully tolerant Bishop of Sarum (Salisbury) and to at least part of his massive work, *An Exposition of the Thirty-Nine Articles of the Church of England*, first appearing in 1699, with a second edition in 1700, then hacked to bits by our Mr. Binckes in 1702,[12] only to be reissued in a third edition in 1705, and then in at least nine more after Burnet's death in 1715. The *DNB* treats Burnet at some length, calling his *Exposition*

> a laborious work, over which he spent five years. It was received with applause, except by Atterbury [a Jacobite, with leanings more Papistical than most], who wrote against it, and by the high-church Lower House of Convocation, by whom it was censured in the turbulent meeting of 1701, on the grounds that it tended to foster the very latitude which the articles were intended to avoid; that it contained many passages contrary to their true meaning; and that it was dangerous to the Church of England.

"Latitude"—that is, toleration of differences of belief as well as of ritual and of polity—became for Burnet as central a tenet as it had been for Roger Williams. He cut through all the efforts to compel people to believe what they didn't believe, all efforts to claim that persecution for belief led to change of belief instead of merely to an assertion of change in order to end the persecution. The *DNB* quotes his very words:

> In 1703 he strongly opposed the bill against occasional Conformity. "I was moved," he said, "never to be silent when toleration should be brought into debate; for I have long looked on liberty of conscience as one of the rights of human nature, antecedent to society, which no man could give up, because it was not in his own power."

Across the ocean some fifty years later, Jonathan Edwards would say something very like that in his exploration of the vexing question of the freedom of the will: we cannot will ourselves to will—to desire, to want—whatever we wish that we wanted instead of what our corrupt will was leading us to want. So with belief. But Burnet's toleration went much further than such a psychological position. Just as Croxall—along with many others—was to insist that the British constitution exhibited a necessary balance in making clear that neither duty to the king nor individual rights and freedoms could stand alone as the basis for a good society, so Burnet found that the articles of the Anglican Church also exhibited, in whole and in part, a very similar balance. I do not see that he wrote explicitly of the analogy, but precisely this analogy, conscious or unconscious, shapes his religious thought along lines that were to give shape to matters secular as well as religious.

---

12. William Binckes *A Prefatory Discourse to an Examination of a Late Book, Entitled an Exposition* . . . .

Because the *Exposition* contains almost four hundred densely written pages, I propose to look specifically only at Burnet's treatment of the seventeenth article, perhaps the most confusing, and certainly the most controversial, of them all. That even the High-Church Lower Convocation could assume a simple "true meaning" to Article 17 may come as a significant surprise to twentieth-century readers. First the article itself; then a brief and simple exposition; then Bishop Burnet.

> [Article] XVII. *Of Predestination and Election.* PREDESTINATION to Life is the everlasting purpose of God, whereby (before the foundations of the world were laid) he hath constantly decreed by his counsel secret to us, to deliver from curse and damnation those whom he hath chosen in Christ out of mankind, and to bring them by Christ to everlasting salvation, as vessels made to honour. Wherefore, they which be endued with so excellent a benefit of God, be called according to God's purpose by his Spirit working in due season: they through Grace obey the calling: they be justified freely: they be made sons of God by adoption: they be made like the image of his only-begotten Son Jesus Christ: they walk religiously in good works, and at length, by God's mercy, they attain to everlasting felicity.
>
> As the godly consideration of Predestination, and our Election in Christ, is full of sweet, pleasant, and unspeakable comfort to godly persons, and such as feel in themselves the working of the Spirit of Christ, mortifying the works of the flesh, and their earthly members, and drawing up their mind to high and heavenly things, as well because it doth greatly establish and confirm their faith of an eternal Salvation to be enjoyed through Christ, as because it doth fervently kindle their love towards God: So, for curious and carnal persons, lacking the Spirit of Christ, to have continuously before their eyes the sentence of God's Predestination, is a most dangerous downfall, whereby the Devil doth thrust them either into desperation, or into wretchlessness of most unclean living, no less perilous than desperation.
>
> Furthermore, we must receive God's promises in such wise, as they be generally set forth to us in Holy Scripture: and, in our doings, that Will of God is to be followed, which we have expressly declared unto us in the Word of God.

If you have never before actually read this article, you may be suffering from a certain shock right now. That, certainly, was its effect on me. None of the American Episcopalians with whom I have talked takes seriously the notion of predestination; indeed, most (of a very unscientific sampling, to be sure) did not at first believe that their seventeenth article and the Anglican seventeenth were the same. To believe that one will receive a just reward for one's own freely chosen actions seems much more American somehow, based as it is on an assumption of freedom so foreign both to early American Puritan Calvinists (as to all Calvinists) and to twentieth-century Freudians. To be able to do good because one has been chosen by God, beforehand, as one of His elect, rather than to be chosen by God because one has done good: an immense exercise of historical imagination, of suspension of disbelief, of negative capability, seems called for if we are to accept the notion that both Anglican and Dissenter believed this at the start of the seventeenth century. The first paragraph of the article sets forth unsparingly this central position of Calvinism.

Then the second paragraph introduces an attitude toward belief that seems to belong to Benjamin Franklin and the eighteenth century, as if the writers of the article were saying that predestation, however true, might well be not useful, as Franklin, in the *Autobiography*, will say of deism in his own time. As for the third paragraph, it appears to license either rejection of predestination, or, at the very least, an absolutely enormous "latitude": that is, how are "God's promises . . . generally set forth to us in Holy Scripture," and how do we go about making that determination? Once given the very notion that God's will may not be clearly and consistently set forth at all points in a Bible that is itself an unwavering inspiration of Holy Spirit into the minds of its transcribers, the legitimacy of intolerance falls apart; latitude seems inescapable. To twentieth-century eyes, the blatantly tortuous wording of Article 17 might seem to have signaled the emergence of such a view back in the sixteenth century; it appears, however, that the authors of the article—and believers for over a century thereafter—had eyes of a different focus. Then comes Burnet, urging toleration not simply because he anticipates the practical, political focus of a Croxall, but, in part, because (from a twentieth-century perspective) he was simply an intellectually honest man. In greater part, perhaps, he found himself, as an intellectually honest man, embroiled in the intersection of political and religious implications growing out of 1688.

He shows a sense of past and political complications implicit in the knotty doctrinal issue of predestination. Tracing the doctrines of election and predestination through the Church and through the years, he sees a sudden, marked shift toward Arminianism brought on by Laud's allegiance to Charles I and to what was widely coming to be seen as Charles's abuse of the royal prerogative. Wanting more power in the hands of an earthly potentate, Laud leaned toward a belief in a less absolute heavenly power. Burnet finds all the intolerant heat to have arisen from the secular implications rather than from the spiritual. He suggests "that this [the question of predestination], from being a Doctrinal point, became the distinction of a Party, and by that means the differences were inflamed." He shifts the controversy about predestination and election from the grounds of absolute truth as laid down by God to a matter of socio-political allegiance—"the distinction of a Party"—and then, as we'll see in a moment, to the psychological variables that shape the beliefs of imperfect human beings.

In his exposition—we might say "his reading"—of the seventeenth article, Burnet defines his context by distinguishing "Calvinist" from "Remonstrant," a use of terminology that underlines his sense that matters of belief cannot be seen as absolutes. "Calvinist," after all, signifies one holding to a system of belief associated with Geneva, a system having at its core the belief in God's arbitrary predestination of His elect. By using the term, Burnet reminds readers that a particular human being, and a Frenchman at that, read the Bible in a particular way that in late-seventeenth-century England offended more than it pleased. Yet the first paragraph of one of the very articles of faith of the Established Church articulates what to most people distinguished Calvinism from other belief. *Remonstrant*, in suggesting one who violently opposes, presents what had become the mainstream of Anglican belief as somehow a path for outsiders, for protesters, rather than for heads of that Established Church. To think of Archbishop Laud as an outsider would not have occurred to Burnet's readers, and yet that was the role to which the word *remonstrant* assigns him.

The "Calvinist" and the "Remonstrant," says Burnet, emphasize different qualities in their conceptualization of the Divine Being. For one who stresses—or insists upon—God's "Independancy, Sovereignty, and infinite Perfection," Calvinism makes sense, for the absolute sovereignty of God in choosing whom He will "as vessels made to honour" would strike such a person as irrefutably consistent and fitting. But one who made God's more "human" qualities the center of focus—"Justice, Truth, Holiness, Goodness, and Mercy," as Burnet lists them—would be more likely to see Him as a generous-spirited Englishman, in whose image humanity was made, and whose concern for fair play would prohibit His consigning us to heaven or hell on the basis simply of His sovereign whim. Burnet summarizes as follows: "Thus both sides seem zealous for God and his Glory: Both lay down general maxims that can hardly be disputed; and both argue justly from their First Principles. There are great grounds for mutual charity and forbearance in these matters."

Burnet concludes with an explicit refusal even to imply a preference:

> Thus the one side [Calvinist] argues, That the article as it lies [the first paragraph], in the plain meaning of those who conceived it, does very expressly establish their doctrine: And the other [made up of the "Remonstrants," those who see human behavior as determining God's judgment of human souls] argues from those cautions that are added to it [the second and third paragraphs], That it ought to be understood so as that it may agree with those cautions. . . . I leave the Choice as free to my Reader, as the Church has done.

By making the question one of truths that seem to conflict because of the limitations of human understanding rather than because of mutually exclusive insights into and a necessary error concerning God's ways, Burnet demonstrates why he saw "liberty of conscience" as beyond any person's ability to give up. Rather than try to compel an agreement that would be at best a meaningless acquiescence for form's sake, Burnet wanted opposing factions to listen to each other, to live and let live.

> The only possible way of a sound and lasting reconciliation, is to possess both Parties with a sense of the force of the Arguments that lie on the other side; that they may see they are no way contemptible; but are such as may prevail on wise and good men: Here is a foundation laid for charity: And if to this, men would add a just sense of the Difficulties in their own side, . . . then it would be more easy to agree on some general propositions, . . . and to maintain Communion with them, not withstanding that diversity.

The High-Church objections to Burnet's exposition of the articles go far beyond the procedural issues that occupied a seemingly disproportionate amount of space in William Binckes's *A Prefatory Discourse.* . . . Still, Binckes wrote at the express order of the Lower House of Convocation and, therefore, expressed official, not simply personal, views. The procedural issues he raised have importance for my argument because his manner of raising them reveals just how thoroughly lost the battle was before Binckes even fired his first salvo. Because Burnet purported—indeed, had excellent claim—to be writing for the illumination of William III, England's Lutheran king who, tradition insists, could not even read the Book of Common Prayer in English, his undertaking may well lead to dangerous changes, and at best sets a dangerous precedent.

> When thus the happiness of our constitution consists in a due poise and good correspondence between the Monarchy, and its Spiritual and Temporal Subjects, what could be thought of more effectually to lead to a general misunderstanding, than to go about to cast the whole into a new mould, and put things upon a new Bottom? To throw down Boundaries, and let in all sorts of Adversaries [he means the Presbyterians, Independents, and other Dissenters] into our very Bowels by a new scheme of Latitude in subscribing to the Articles, is bad enough: But to carry it so far, as to make all sorts of changes practicable, without going the round-about way of Convocational Decisions, or Acts of Parliament, is certainly much worse: . . . That a Prince . . . may call some few Divines to his assistance, whom he takes to be the most knowing and fittest Counselors; and with their Advice he may bring things to what shape he pleases, by his Regal Authority. If this be not of dangerous consequence to an Established Church, and a free People, where all things are settled and bounded by Laws, it is not easie to say what is.

With the advantage of almost two centuries of hindsight, one sees that, certainly without meaning to, Binckes here ignores the old assumption that God's absolute truth is known to some, especially to him, and in effect acknowledges that human, not Divine, fiat determines matters of truth, leaving them "settled and bounded." Given his other main points, this cannot have been his intention. Not only ought the bishop's *Exposition* have been done only after it had been regularly determined in Convocation that it needed doing, and that Gilbert Burnet was the man to do it—after all, "[i]t is very unhappy that Lower House of Convocation should at this time of day be found to complain of the writings of one of their own Bishops."—but having been done as it has, alas, been done, this troublesome exposition will give

> his Majesty a wrong State of the Case, as to our Differences in Religion in England. Such impressions to be made upon a Prince, who came a stranger amongst us, and may be supposed to have great regard to what is said by so great a man, may prove very disadvantageous to the Established Church. A great deal of blame may seem to lie at our door, were it really true, that "the wounds and breaches" made among those "who in common profess the same faith," are owing to their "being unhappily disjointed and divided by some differences that are of LESS IMPORTANCE."

That is, Binckes finds especially distasteful Burnet's general stance of toleration, of asserting that differences between the Established Church and the various dissenting sects concern matters peripheral rather than central, matters reflecting human variation of temperament, of psyche, rather than of essential truth. How can it be a trivial matter, as Burnet wrongly suggests that it is, either to "derive all Spiritual Power from the choice of the People, and a call from a Congregation in the Independent way; or change Episcopacy, though as ancient as Christianity, for Presbytery . . ."? To urge that only trivial matters separate British Protestants from each other puts the Anglican Church in a false position, making it appear to be intransigent over trifles.

Finally, Burnet has put himself, as well as the Church, doubly in the wrong: just before the end of his *Prefatory Discourse*, Binckes makes two assertions, taking them as almost self-evident truths. First of all, despite all that Burnet insists to the contrary, "the blame for Separation wholly lies at the Door of the Dissenters. . . ." Second, Burnet's *Exposition* mistakenly, dangerously, tries "to introduce a Latitude of Opinion which the Articles were form'd to avoid." By reading such "Diversity of Opinions" into articles "framed to avoid such grounds for splintering Diversities of Opinions," Burnet has struck a blow against both the Church of England and "True Religion." As he says at the end of his discussion of the seventeenth article, because conflicts concerning the nature of God remain irresolvable within the human psyche, and because these essentially human problems underlie the theological question, he "leave[s] the Choice as free to [his] reader as the Church has done." Binckes sees this as subversive nonsense: the whole point of the Thirty-nine Articles, in his view, was to provide limits, not to broaden choice. They did this by articulating God's own Truth ("True Religion," in Binckes's phrase). Because the British union of church and state increasingly politicized religious matters, what the American Puritans had feared came increasingly to pass in Old England: the secular shaped the religious, as we have been seeing in the ways in which the first verses of Romans 13 came to be read.

A final irony: it seems not too much to say that Binckes, in fighting what we can now see as a rear-guard action, often used a secular vocabulary more appropriate to political than to theological disputation. "If this be not of dangerous consequence to an Established Church, and a free People, where all things are settled and bounded by Laws, it is not easie to say what is." The idea of freedom seems to have for Binckes the same meaning as the "liberty" that John Winthrop had so traditionally defined in his address to the General Court some half-century earlier. "[N]atural [liberty] (I mean as our nature is now corrupt)" must indeed be "bounded by Laws" so that people may exercise "civil or federal" liberty, "a liberty to that only which is good, just, and honest."[13]

In a pre-Lockean era, when right reason and innate ideas seemed so obviously real, Winthrop and his auditors could accept the paradox that true liberty entailed subjection to authority. For Burnet, perceptions varied between human beings; moreover, there was no way to coerce people into acting on perceptions not their own, that is, into holding beliefs dependent upon those alien perceptions. At the same time, Binckes attributes to the British "people" a kind of psychological freedom that Burnet, a member of the Royal Society as well as a keen observer of the human condition, explicitly denies. Binckes seems to believe that a merely human fiat (whether of his beloved Convocation or of his feared king makes no matter) suffices to compel belief. Burnet, in a most Lockean sense, seems to know that belief depends upon perception. He has "long looked on liberty of conscience as one of the rights of human nature, antecedent to society, which no man could give up, because it was not in his own power." That is, no one can control the way he or she perceives. Belief being based upon one's manner of perceiving, no one can have the power to believe upon command.

Behind all these conflicting assumptions lurks a problem identical to one that American Puritans and their genteel successors also found very difficult to acknowledge, almost impossible to resolve. Binckes and his fellows could not make the transition (that for Burnet appears to have been as natural as breathing) from complacent certainty about the

13. John Winthrop, "Speech to the General Court, July 3, 1645," 92.

universal correctness of their particular beliefs and views to the sort of open-minded complexity that Burnet saw behind even the Thirty-nine Articles of the Established Church. Although the temptation arises to reduce the issue to a perennial difference between the relatively few who can tolerate complexity and the majority who appear, at least, to cling to oversimplification, too many conflicting interests exist to make plausible such a reduction to strictly psychological terms. People's beliefs do have a way of reflecting economic and social—that is, political—concerns as well as compulsions of the psyche, although I do not propose to try to distinguish one from another. From a twentieth-century perspective, the idea of the king as God's anointed, and therefore absolutely to be obeyed, seems perfectly simple, in contrast to the notion that the duty to obey magistrates depends upon the legality of what they command, legality, in turn, being determined not by biblical authority but by specific statutes established by due process. The tangledness of this complex web becomes evident in another document involving Bishop Burnet. I stress the condition of tangledness because, unlike most colonial Puritans, most British Anglicans were confronted repeatedly with the details of tangle.

One George Hickes made a statement that seems quite different from that of William Binckes, but turns out not to be. *Some Discourses upon Dr. Burnet and Dr. Tillotson* [Archbishop of Canterbury from 1691 until his death in 1694]: *Occasioned by the late Funeral Sermon of the Former Upon the Latter* was published in London, in 1695, some four years before Burnet's *Exposition* appeared. Quoting a passage from Tillotson's November 5 sermon of 1678, Hickes goes on to lambaste both Tillotson and his eulogizer, Burnet, on the grounds that his own words before the Glorious Revolution ought to have held Tillotson firmly loyal to King James ten years later. Tillotson's sermon, packed with commonplaces in favor of morality and against Roman cruelty, takes to task the religion itself:

> [W]here Religion once comes to supplant the moral righteousness, and to teach men the absurdist things in the world, to lye for the truth, and to kill men for God's sake: . . . Then surely it loses its nature and ceases to be Religion. For let any man say worse of Atheism and Infidelity, if he can.

He points, as one would expect on November 5, directly at those wicked Papists of "the church of Rome, in which are taught such Doctrines as: . . . deposing of kings . . . the horrid and bloody Design of this Day." In amazing "fairness," he goes on to add that "many papists would have been excellent persons, and very good men, if their religion had not hindered them; if the Doctrines and Principles of their Church had not perverted and spoild their Natural dispositions."

Hickes pounced hard.

I desire my reader to consider [said he in 1695], if it is not as applicable to the New as to the Old Fifth of November, and the Worthies of the Protestant, as well as the Popish Religion, who conspired against James the Second, as these did against James the First. Tell me, O ye Worthies of the Church of England, who have hazarded your lives and fortunes to preserve our religion, is it more lawful to plot and rebel for holy Church of England, than for holy Church of Rome?

Hickes's pounce has irrefutable logic behind it, unless one takes the perspective of a Sharp or a Burnet (or a Tillotson), emphasizing the laws of the land rather than the dicta of the Lord. DeFoe's 1702 explication of similarities between January 30 and the "New . . . Fifth of November," aimed at defusing animosities against Dissenters, would take the same approach, although from an opposite bias. What makes Hickes illuminating for our purposes resides in his wonderfully human blindness, his ability—shared to lesser extent by all of us, to equal extent by very few, to greater extent (I would venture to say) by no one—to impose a given logic with a masterful selectivity. On May 29, 1684, at Worcester Cathedral, preaching on Psalms 14:7 ("Oh that the salvation of Israel were come out of Zion! when the Lord bringeth back the captivity of his People, Jacob shall rejoice, and Israel shall be glad."), George Hickes had advanced two main arguments in praise of the 1660 Restoration of the Stuarts. First, looking back to "the rebellion of Absalom," he saw analogies between that "state of slavery" and the condition of the British people under the Commonwealth. Said he,

a state of slavery and captivity, consists in being obnoxious to the will and pleasure of an unlimited, absolute, and arbitrary . . . power, such as was the power of the ancient Roman emperors, of whom, as our Learned Lawyer Fortescue observes out of Justinians Institutions, the Civil Law saith, quod principi placuit legis habet naturam, that the Princes pleasure was a law. . . .

If in 1684 princes, rulers, are to be held to the law, then the "power" of James II in violating the laws forbidding Roman Catholics to serve as army officers, etc., does appear "unlimited, absolute, and arbitrary." But Hickes manages not to see this.

Second, in 1684 Hickes insisted "That the Special Providence and Assistance of God" is necessary to deliver "a people" from "such a State" and "that it is the duty of a people so brought back out of Captivity, to render Praise and thanksgiving unto God." Hickes goes on to explain how "[w]e may know, when any event is the Lords special doing. . . ." A recitation of all of his criteria would be tedious—they run to more than ten pages—but a small sampling will suggest how explicitly the "proofs" for considering May 29, 1660, miraculous could be (and by the anti-Jacobins were) brought to bear on November 5, 1688, just as they had been on November 5, 1605. The event clearly comes from God "when it is brought about by invisible means, or if by visible, yet by unlikely means." Another sign is "the strange seasonableness of it." That it benefits good people in dire straits also counts: "But of all the remarkable events in sacred or profane history, none hath been a greater blessing to any Prince or People, than the Revolution of this Day [in 1660] hath been to us, and our King." Part of the blessing—and another sign that the Divinity has indeed blessed—can be seen in "[t]he Harmony of its parts, when various accidents happily conspire, as in this Revolution, to produce the same effect. . . . this wonderful Revolution had been attended with many notable inconveniences, had it happened at any other time, or in any other manner, or by any other Instruments, than it did." Because the vocabulary sounds so similar to conventional usage later employed to evoke 1688, one may have trouble keeping in mind that the "Revolution" to which Hickes refers is that of 1660, when the Stuart monarchy replaced the Commonwealth. This sort of difficulty becomes even greater with the addition of another criterion:

> When a remarkable event happens to any, especially to public and illustrious persons, upon the same day, in which another accident, as remarkable as that, happened to them before . . . so, as our Church hath well observed, it was not without a special Providence, that on the self same day in which our sovereign was born, he should, as it were be born again, in being restored to his Triple Crown.

My purpose is not simply to have fun at the expense of George Hickes: George Hickes represents a habit of mind neither unique in nor confined to the seventeenth, or any other, century. What he said in 1684 about Charles II's 1660 often was said later on about William III's 1688, and as a result of equally cynical manipulations. That is, the date for celebrating the Restoration—May 29—became the choice because it was also Charles's birthday, not because it signaled the actual date of Charles's return to England. William III, in 1688 trying to reach Torbay on November 4—his own birthday—encountered the winds that later were seen as having marked the occasion of God's miraculous intervention. In any case, he landed not on the desired November 4 but on the even more blessed November 5: clearly, "a remarkable event" therefore occurred for the British people "upon the same day, in which another accident, as remarkable as that, happened to them before. . . ." Hickes had said, in 1684, "that they [all these marks of a special Providence] should all be visible in one event, that such a mighty Revolution should" encompass all of them, "must needs force all, but Atheists, or Epicureans, who are more absurd than Atheists, to confess with David that it was the Lord who brought back our captivity, and cry out with the Church in Ps 118: This is the Lord's doing, and it is marvelous in our eyes." If the Lord brought about the Restoration, then the Lord, by Hickes's own criteria, brought about the Glorious Revolution. If Cromwell's overturn of established law was tyranny, then so was James II's. And if James II had no right to violate the law of the land, then neither had Charles I.

None of these issues could find universally satisfying resolution through reason alone. "Is it more lawful to plot and rebel for holy Church of England, than for holy Church of Rome?" Hickes asked in 1695. Despite the context of implicit loyalty to James II, Hickes is really talking about the difficulties into which toleration will lead: once the issue becomes a matter of what a group, or an individual, thinks is "holy," rather than a matter of absolute religious truth—especially as concerns nonresistance to rulers—then we can expect a chaos of perpetual revolution to replace order. Like toleration, new-fangledness in matters of religion could lead only to this sort of chaos, a view that Hickes had made explicit in a January 30 sermon of 1681/1682. At that time, no doubt, he was not anticipating that Catholic James would so soon become king, or that the houses of Parliament, with special prodding from some of the bishops in the House of Lords, would seek to force reformation upon James. His target, as usual for the day, was the Puritans of the 1640s. The Puritans, alas, were like so many others in the unhappy history of the world: they were over-curious about religious matters, and kept on rejecting the settled answers to old questions. Seeking for truth may, in some instances, be a good thing, but "religious seekers and reformers are the worst enemies of governments."[14] History, says Hickes, shows that this is so: "Pretending a great zeal for the right God, or the right worship, . . . these seditious pretences" have obliged governments to make laws against innovations because "most governments . . . found by long and frequent experience, that Innovations in Sacred were commonly Innovations in Civil matters, and that the plausible pretense of reforming the church, did usually end in the ruine both of Church and State."

The search for "truth" demanded toleration of differences, as Roger Williams and John Milton had both known. Against such insight, Hickes, Binckes, and their like, fought in what they believed to be the vanguard of the army of the Established Church. We can see now that they were simply trying to cover their rear. Although in 1699 Bishop Burnet may have been ahead of his time, he spoke to the near as well as to the long-term future. Had he lived about two years longer than he did (he died in March 1715), he would have seen the House of Convocation adjourned indefinitely, not to meet again until 1854. His critics, and even a great

---

14. George Hickes, no title. Preached January 31, 1681/1682, to the Lord Mayor of London, et al. London, 1682.

number of his political and religious allies, shared the position that a religious interpretation of 1688 must be seen as making sense in human terms: God and his ways, as Milton had tried to show, somehow had to be commensurate to the human mind. For Burnet, an inscrutable God, whose qualities could not be comprehended within the limits of merely human understanding, allowed humanity the privilege—gave us the burden—of choice. Most appropriately, Burnet found the basis of this choice imbedded in the text of Article 17, the article of all the thirty-nine that most apparently denied choice to human beings. Those "powers of the human intellect," so threatening in the seventeenth century,[15] now emerged as essential to preserve, or at least to bolster, people's "sense of divine transcendence." The balance, however, was getting ready to swing toward reliance on the human mind. A look at colonial practice will throw some light on connections between this conflict, this "central problem of the seventeenth century," and American self-satisfaction and complacency, American self-absorption, and American uncertainty.

15. Miller, "The Marrow of Puritan Divinity," 74.

IV
Voice, Country, and Class
REAPPROACHING THE VERNACULAR

1. MATHER PROPOSES, WISE DISPOSES

William Fleetwood, when he somewhat shakily assumed the voice of that "Curate of Salop," was continuing the thrust behind much of Burnet's *Exposition* by trying to disentangle religious and political allegiances that, in the days of Archbishop Laud, had become ensnarled. Hugh Trevor-Roper persuasively argues that Laud's "Arminianism" had no necessary logical or doctrinal connection with Charles I's absolutism, any more than the accusations about Laud's "Papist sympathies" were meant as serious theological analysis rather than as expedient political hysteria to pump up the mob.[1] As Burnet had said, the rejection of predestination, of election, of Calvinism itself, "from being a Doctrinal point, became the distinction of a Party, and by that means the differences were inflamed."[2] Late-seventeenth-century discourse concerning the relatedness of church and state paid more attention to deliberate reasoning and less to divine inspiration. An increasingly rationalistic emphasis in such debate meant that even such traditionally intolerant persons as Binckes and Hickes shared with Fleetwood and Burnet the sense that human reason had a place in the discussion of matters of belief.

1. Hugh Trevor-Roper, "Laudianism and Political Power," 68, 93–98, 103.
2. Burnet, *An Exposition of the Thirty-Nine Articles. . . .*

This same persuasion had a solid foundation in Massachusetts. The very thought of an unlearned ministry had been repugnant to the American Puritans. Not only had they easily denounced Levelers, Fifth-Monarchy Men, and other antinomians who depended upon divine revelation rather than human intelligence: the American Puritans backed up their words by founding Harvard College. "Dreading to leave an illiterate ministry to the churches when our present ministers shall lie in the dust," as the famous quotation from *New England's First Fruits* (London, 1643) on the wall of the Harvard Yard still has it, they took what they considered the necessary steps. John Wise (1652–1725), a member of the class of 1673 and younger than Gilbert Burnet (1643–1715), carried the ideas of choice and of the exercise of reason perhaps further than the founders had anticipated. Even more prophetically, he struggled with approaches to vernacular argument and epithet that he never learned at Harvard. He also provides a useful handle on American, as opposed to British, ways, and on the ambivalence of colonists toward their transatlantic cousins. Finally, in the distinctive styles that he seems to have tried on and taken off to match his purposes, he offers important illustration for the notion that, as human reason comes to the fore, as intellect becomes valued along with faith, and then beyond it, the self, the individual, increasingly takes center stage. The playing of parts, so to speak, becomes almost a full-time occupation. The American self-satisfaction and complacency, self-absorption and uncertainty, to which I referred at the end of the last chapter, will be arriving upon the scene, too.

Wise's two expositions on behalf of human reason and democratic church polity (that is, New England Congregationalism) apparently had no effect at all on the dead issue of the sixteen *Proposals* of 1705 aimed at providing the Independent—some said anarchically so—churches of New England with the unifying oversight of an association. Perry Miller took this view in 1958;[3] George A. Cook was not so sure in 1966.[4] We need not deal with the complex political and theological machinations of Cotton Mather in trying both to preserve the traditions of his colonial Puritan ancestors and to establish the Church in the new but—as it was turning out—explosive communion of the United Brethren. Instead, let us notice Wise's evident delight in the malice by which in his *Quarrel* he turns some of Mather's tactics and arguments back upon the would-be autocrat of Boston: Wise, the minister of Chebacco Parish (near Ipswich), took a rural and a democratic revenge against the authoritarian city.

3. Chap. 18 in Miller, *The New England Mind: From Colony to Province*; and introduction to the facsimile edition of John Wise, *A Vindication of the Government of New England Churches*.
4. George A. Cook, introduction to John Wise, *The Churches Quarrel Espoused*.

Wise's evaluation of natural liberty and reason seems equally remarkable, not so much in the context of early-eighteenth-century thought as in its being the work of a Calvinist minister. John Winthrop had earlier articulated the traditionally orthodox view of natural liberty in his oft-quoted 1645 address: "For natural liberty (I mean as our nature is now corrupt)" Winthrop had nothing but disdain. It "cannot endure the least restraint of the most just authority"; those who strive to maintain their "natural corrupt liberties" are led to "grow more evil, and in time to be worse than brute beasts: omnes sumus licentia deteriores." (We are all made worse by [such] liberty.)[5] But Wise, confronting that same original sin and innate depravity that lay at the heart of Calvinist predestinarian doctrine, announced in 1717 that he would "wave the Consideration of Mans Moral Turpitude," asserting that "whatever has happened since his Creation [that is, the Fall], he remains at the upper-end of Nature, and as such is a creature of a very Noble Character." Instead of absolute dependency upon divine grace to read the book of nature correctly, man has been put in command of "the Lower Part of the Universe," where "his Liberty under the Conduct of Right Reason, is equal with his trust." One paragraph later, Wise considers that "the true Natural Liberty of Man"—though only "as he is Guided and Restrained by the Tyes of Reason and Laws of Nature"—means that "every Man, must be acknowledged equal to every man. . . .".

Because of the sheer audacity of his words, and because of the joy that post-1776 Americans ought to take in them, I quote Wise at length. Throughout the longest section of the *Vindication* (30–70), Wise concerns himself with a "Demonstration in Defense of our Platform, which is founded in the Light of Nature[,]" that "the Constitution of these and the Primitive Churches, is really and truly owing to the Original State and Liberty of Mankind, and founded peculiarly in the Light of Nature." Although he does also consider the example of "Antiquity," the exposition of "Holy Scripture," and the workings of "Divine Providence," he emphasizes natural reason in defense of a post-1688 sense of British liberties. This same sense, in the earlier *Churches Quarrel Espoused*, marks where Wise's argument, in an ambiguity of manner (though rarely of matter), contributes to my own.

Essentially, so far as I have been able to disentangle them, five different —in some instances contradictory, in others complementary—personae obscure the features of John Wise, the muscular minister (apparently, he was a fine wrestler) at Chebacco Parish in the township of Ipswich. But even the facts of biography turn out to be less relevant than the particular

---

5. Winthrop, "Speech to the General Court."

disguises that "J. W." changes from section to section, sometimes from paragraph to paragraph.

1. Sometimes he stands forth as the English Protestant, indignantly in opposition to, and in contrast with, continental papists. As such, he also becomes the complementary colonial Congregationalist, who sees Presbyterians as just as heretical as papists.

2. He speaks at times as a common-sense rural voice, who knows better than the theoretically minded proponents of the *Proposals*.

3. Sometimes, he calls before the bar of justice those criminal *Proposals*, speaking as a country lawyer—who, however his words may at times smack of the soil, has a solid classical education and reveres "the Judgment of the Honourable President and noble Fellows of our Famous Colledge . . ." (79).

4. Often, he appears as the freedom-loving Englishman, who shares his countrymen's respect for Parliament (12) and Crown (116), but who cherishes above all the rule of law: "All English Men are Priviledged by, and strictly Bound to the Law; that's the fruitful Reason of all good and Rule of Duty" (118).

5. But he is also the colonial, the American, who finds the unique conditions of his soil, climate, and geography essential criteria for evaluating the *Proposals*, especially in their fiscal implications.

Even such seemingly distinct stances will turn out to be far less firmly separable than they at first appear. One melts into another; they combine, recombine, and leave a modern reader wondering just where Wise does indeed take his stand. Ambiguity reigns. I propose to show that this is the case, and then to infer some of the significances that I find in its being so.

Wise called his volume "a reply in Satyre, to certain Proposals made, in answer to this question, What further steps are to be taken, that the Councils may have due constitution and efficacy in supporting, preserving and well ordering the interest of the Churches in the Country?" The title page makes no mention of the "Satyre' "s author, but the twenty-five-page "Epistle Dedicatory" ends with the initials "J. W." in very large type. (The title page of *A Vindication* . . . in 1717 credits "John Wise A.M. Pastor to a Church in Ipswich.") After quoting all sixteen of the 1705 *Proposals* against which he will be arguing, the anonymous Wise addresses "the Fraternity of the Churches in the New England Colonies" (10), by which he means not the "wise and faithful Pastors in these Churches" (10) but, rather, "the Churches over which you preside" (11), that is, the voting members of the congregations. "It is not from any Disrespect or for want of Honour to the Reverend Eldership and Pastors of your several Communities, that I apply my self more immediately and thus abruptly to your selves in this Dedication." Rather, he does so out of an immense respect for the church members as citizens. His direct appeal to them "seems most agreeable to my present Province. The Priveleges of the Fraternity being so peculiarly the theam and subject of my pains" (10). Wise's purpose in urging all the "Honourable Brethren" to "Stand in the Defence of and Maintain your Church Liberty" is to act in "the Service of my Country, and in Defence of their sacred Liberties" (11).

I shall come back to the question of "my Country" in a moment, but now I suggest that the tangle of this language points to Wise's audacity. Grammatically, "their" ought to refer to "the wise and faithful Pastors" whom Wise wishes not to offend (10–11), even "tho' I do thus Immediately address the Churches over which you preside . . ." (11). But the next paragraph (11–12) makes clear that "their sacred Liberties" are the liberties of the people, not of the Pastors. Addressing the "Honourable Brethren!" (that is, the members themselves), Wise tells them that they "have been called unto Liberty" and urges them to "know who you are" and to "Stand in the Defence of and Maintain your Church liberty . . . with Zeal, Courage and faithfulness. . . ." Quickly, he hammers home what he has called "so peculiarly the theam and subject" of his present work: "Honourable Brethren!" (15) (This phrase serves as his refrain.) "I imagine your selves to be somewhat more than ordinary; for Really you be so; . . ." (16). Because the capacities of men-in-general are said, by a few in power, to be less than they are, good men, competent men, find themselves "Buried in a Miosis [meiosis] (as is frequently Enacted by Ambition) for the sake of some inferiour Members in [the] Fraternity" (16). Too often, "we [humans] Incapassitate the Heroes of both ["the Empire and Churches"] by an Argument *a minori ad Majus, viz.* by inferring the Insufficiency of the great and wise, because of the mean and base mingled in the same Communities" (16–17). Many of those who are supposed to lack the intelligence and wisdom necessary for the post do have the makings of excellent church elders in them, and the authors of the *Proposals* wrong not only such individuals but all members of the churches by urging the creation of a supervisory body that bypasses "these New-England Liberties [that] have Cost your Progenitors" (17) so much.

When he refers to the liberties of New England, Wise at times means precisely New England, and at times a great deal more, just as "my Country," although at times the Massachusetts Bay Colony, with its peculiarities of geography and climate, most often seems instead to be the British Empire. "[T]he Parliament (that Wise and August Council of the Nation) could not have invented an Establishment in Church Order, more for the service of the Imperial Crown of the British Empire than our present Constitution, especially in such a Country and Climate as this is" (12). "My Country," with its "sacred liberties," includes "this . . . Country and Climate" of New England, certainly a loyal part of "the

British Empire." He contrasts the Independent (Congregational) system with "the Ecclesiasticks in some Kingdoms in Europe," who squeeze from ignorant and supine parishioners "a vast share of the golden Fleeces that should supply the Publick Treasuries" (12), whereas "our New England Constitution . . . leaves the whole to Empire . . ." (13). (In the context of repeated complaints from underpaid ministers, there may have been an extra turn of the screw, here.)

But Wise also distinguishes sharply between "the English" and "our New-England" constitutions and concerns. "You" (the citizens who make up the individual congregations) must "put such an Estimation and value on your Church Liberties as the English do on their Civil" (17). So who are the English? At times, "we" are among them. But at other times, they live in a particular region on the eastern shore of the Atlantic, from which tight little place they govern a mighty empire of whose need for cash "our" Church polity shows more awareness than does that of the Established Church of England, to say nothing of the Roman Catholic institutions on the continent in their relations with continental rulers.

Reading *The Churches Quarrel Espoused* with as open a mind as I can has left me in a state of considerable confusion from paragraph to paragraph, but the general effect of Wise's political references emerges with what I take to be unambiguous clarity: Wise again and again wants to "appear in Defense of my Countries Sacred Liberties" (36), and Wise takes as his country the soil that supports "the New-England Churches" and the institutions of old England as they cohere to what he sees as their core: "with veneration for the English Monarchy, I dare assert, that there is in the Constitution of our [New England Congregational] Church Government more of the English Civil Government in it, and it has a better complexion to suit the true English Spirit, than is in the English Church . . ." (54, with fuller development on 55). Wise expects his readers to agree that the Church of England shows less conformity to British principles of governance than does the Congregational establishment of Massachusetts.

Particularly as the "satyre" brings the *Proposals* to "Tryal," keeping each "Plea" of the "Process," each facet of the "Indictment," within "just Bounds" and "in a form borrowed from Sir Edward Cooke, the Kings Attorney," Wise returns again and again to his sense that "gospel Liberties" (30), "my Countries Sacred Liberties" (36), and "the antient Liberties of the English Nation" (53) all amount to the same thing. Insisting that "All English Men are Priviledged by, and strictly Bound to the Law" (118), Wise reminds readers of penalties as well as privileges attached: "English Government and Law is a Charter-Party Settled by mutual Compact between Persons of all Degrees in the Nation, and No man must start from it at his Peril" (120). ("Peril" turns out to be an allusion to the execution of Charles I and the deposition of James II.) As a culminating "Principle," Wise states, in large type, italicized: "English men hate an Arbitrary Power (Politically Considered) as they hate the Devil" (120).

So far, the presence of legal language is obvious enough, as is Wise's apparent wish to see himself and his cause as part of an old English tradition of civil liberties, rule of law, and respect for duly constituted authority. "My God, Prince and Country . . . Great ANNE, our Wise and Protestant Princes[s], New-Englands Royal Nurse and great Benefactress" (32), and many similar vocatives, appear with absolutely no flavor of irony. Also, Wise makes dramatic use of his combination of freedom-loving English and papist-hating Protestant selves. He seems to have calculated how best to heap epithets of heretical, and even of treasonous, fire on the heads of the *Proposals'* proposers. Just as Anglican preachers equated what we see as assorted and varying threats to the throne, so Wise equates the papist, the Presbyterian, and the traitor, blurring all together in a mesh of wit, humor, country invective, history, and tradition that is worth looking at for its own delightful sake as well as for what it tells us about some early shaping of an American identity.

First, a bit of the humor. Apart from his objection that the *Proposals* would trample on all those ancient English liberties that Wise had pinned down to the Cambridge Platform of 1648 in ways that I shall come back to, Wise laughs at the *Proposals* for that greatest of all American reasons: to put them into operation will cost far too much money. The *Proposals* included the perhaps inadvertent wording that "all the associations in the Country meet together, by their Respective Delegates, once in a year" (98). Wise the American, the good old country farmer with good old country sense, has a good deal to say about this. "Who-ever was the Father, the Womb of it is very fertile and bigg with Articles of Moment, it comprehends a large Territory, and a great Treasure;. . . . [J. W. will] therefore Survey it by Cosmography, and then nextly by the Laws of the Church Stock" (98). He takes a view that can be called "American" in the very broadest sense. "The Country contained in this Proposal," says he, "must extend so far as we can find any Gospel Churches Planted, or to be Planted within the English Dominion on the firm land or Continent of America," with "no Restriction made" (98). He sketches out the "Lines of Latitude" and the "Longitudes," concluding, "Now this is a noble Territory, enough for an Empire, and all English; and why may we not be thus Extensive for the good of the Churches therein planted? Other Countries have sent their Delegates near as far as this comes to, to wait upon the Conventions of his Holiness. But, the Mischief is, The Revenue won't hold out" (99).

The last two sentences are worthy of Mark Twain. Seeming sweetly to echo, to further, the aims of the proposers, Wise swiftly pulls the papistical rug from beneath the feet of unwary readers by referring to "the Conventions of his Holiness." Then, as if serenely unaware that he has said anything offensive, he follows the logic of his own irony: that Massachusetts may be in danger of following the road to Rome has no bearing on this issue at all. Simple constraints of the purse interfere with a noble plan. "But," Wise goes on in the very next sentence, "I have Thought of one way"; even if "it is some-what Chimerical, or Whimsical; Yet, tho' it be, the Proposal has no reason to repine or find fault, for that it is Its near Kins-Man." Wise uses first the rapier and then the club; then he repeats his use of both in the next paragraph. When Spain settles its present accounts with England, Wise suggests "That either the Rents of Toledo, or some good stout Gold Mine in Peru, be reserved wholly to the use of this Design," for the costs of maintaining such delegations, and of sending the delegates such distances, will be immense. "I am sure," he continues in his "survey," "your present Supplyes are not full enough for [both] your Daily Bread and these Contingent and unexpected Charges, especially seeing they were never thought of, or Provided for, in your first settlements" (100).

America is large; assembling delegates is expensive; with an implicit reminder of the money-grubbing tactics of "The Ecclesiasticks in some kingdoms in Europe" (12), to which he has contrasted the practices emanating from "our New-England Constitution" (13), Wise has begun preparations for the first resonation of his concluding blast. Next, with a nod to "the Epecurian Doctrine of Atoms" (100), he finds the *Proposals* lacking any legitimizing causative fiat. They appear to have evolved as a result of various chance events, most notably "the slaughters and depraditions committed by the Heathen," as well as "many other Afflictions," the totality of which led "the Neighbouring Ministers, in some Counties," to assemble in order "to Pray together, &c. and for no other Intent, that I ever knew or heard of" (102). But, says he, one thing led to another;

> and at last perceiving they were almost gotten into a Classical Form, before they thought of it, They began to give their Meetings the Specious Titles of *Classes Associations, and Ecclesiastical Conventions,* &c. as Securely as tho' these Titles were a Fruit naturally growing out of our own Constitution; and by Degrees began to dream that they were Really, and *De Jure,* what their new Titles and late Custom had made them only *de Facto.* . . . (103)

His argument loses much of its delight in summation, but not even my brutal treatment of it here can numb the special twist of the knife in its conclusion. Wise has repeatedly made explicit his equation of the *Proposals* with both papistical and Presbyterian practice and theory.

By infringing upon—indeed, by prohibiting—the proper functioning of church elders on grounds that too few laymen can have the necessary competence (20, et al.), and by suggesting that laymen cannot, and should not, be trusted to elect proper persons to serve as their own ministers,

> It is as much as to say, Alas! Alas! it is well known that the Churches are generally a sort of plain men, little Skilled in deep Matters. . . . Now this is much agreeing with the old Arguments, against the Laity, who were described by the Learned to be without Knowledge of the Original Languages, and other parts of Polite Learning, and so no ways fit to Interpret Scripture, therefore it is very Rationally Enacted, That the BIBLE be taken from them. . . . (91)

This ironic wit leads very logically to a perhaps heavy-handed, but extremely telling, historical blow. Roman prohibition of the Bible and imposition of a "Classes" [Classis] along with "Presbyterian Principles" (103) go together, as Wise has been trying to demonstrate. "But to make short, and Conclude my Story, when they had thus far advanc'd and Ripen'd their design, out comes these Proposals like Aarons Golden Calf, the 5th day of Novemb. 1705" (103–4). Given what we already have seen in Anglican sermons annually preached upon the occasion of November 5, we are in a position to understand what Wise was up to. He gives new life to that old equation of papist with Presbyterian with traitor, turning first to this newest golden calf, which he views with considerable alarm, "for that it is very Evident, That tho' it be But a Calf now, yet in time it may grow (being of a Thrifty Nature) to become a sturdy Ox that will know no Whoa . . ." (105), the woe being—but Wise leaves the punning, though not the point, to his reader—that "it may be past the Churches skill then to subdue it."

The next step: this new golden calf has all the marks of yet another feared beast. "For if I am not much mistaken (and Pareus too)[6] That great and Terrible Beast with Seven heads and ten Hornes, Described in the Revelations 13. was nothing else a few Ages ago but just such another Calf as this is" (105). Wise extends his metaphor in two paragraphs that sketch out the nurturing of this "Calf" by "the Great Potentates of the Earth," so "much Ravished with its Aspect and Features" that "some offered to Suckle it on the choicest Cows amongst the Herds of Royal Cattle." Having done so, "Alas, Poor men! They have paid dear for their Prodigality and Fondness," for the once frisky calf

> is now grown to be such a mad Furious and Wild Bull, that there is scarce a Christian Monarch on Earth, [(]unless the great ANNE, their Swedish and Prusian Majesties, and their High Mightinesses, with this Exception), there

---

6. David Pareus, influential early-seventeenth-century Puritan theologian.

is scarce a Potentate in the World, the Best Horse-man or Hunts-man of them all, that dare take this Beast by the Horns, when he begins to Bounce and Bellow. (105–6)

Wise turns his apparently gratuitous swipe at Rome into an immediately relevant cause for alarm. If one perceives Aaron's calf as a typological anticipation of the beast of Revelation, and if one sees the *Proposals* as a new golden calf, as Wise invites his readers to do, then those readers must perceive, as they confront, a problem. Despite the efforts of a few exceptional Christian monarchs, "the Beast generally goes at large, and does what he will. . . . Therefore to conclude, and Infer, *Obsta Principiis*! It is Wisdom to nip such growths in the Bud, and keep down by early Slaughter such a breed of Cattle" (106). Seeing in the Presbyterian-like church polity embodied in the *Proposals* a fresh manifestation of the golden calf of Aaron and therefore of the beast of Revelation, Wise makes his call for the destruction of the potentially dangerous document appear to be a matter of simple common sense, of human reason.

He then concludes his examination of the first part of the *Proposals* on a note of astrological hope. Still speaking of them as of a new-born calf, he seizes upon the fact that the Cambridge Association had presented its *Proposals* to the churches of New England on November 5, 1705, apparently—in their absent-mindedness—with no special sense of the day's significance.

> In all the Astrological Remarks I have made, I find its Nativity full of favorable Aspects to the English Churches. The 5th day of November has been as a Guardian Angel to the most Sacred Interest of the Empire: It has rescued the whole Glory of Church & State from the most fatal Arrest of Hell and Rome. That had I been of the CABAL, or Combination, which formed these *Proposals*, so soon as I had seen and perceived the date (as I imagine) my heart, with King David's would have smote me, and I should have cryed out *Miserere nostri DEUS*: The Lord have Mercy upon us; this is the Gun-Powder-Treason day; and we are Every Man Ruined, being Running Faux's Fate! Why, Gentlemen! have you forgot it? It is the day of the Gun-Powder-Treason, and a fatal day to Traytors.
>
> Our Measures Certainly intend the Blowing up the Churches, as Faux's did the Parliament; That for my own Part, I have such an Awe upon my mind of this very day, That I have made a Settled Resolution, That of all the Dayes of the whole Year, I will never Conspire Treason against my natural Prince, nor Mischief to the Churches on the 5th day of November.
>
> And so Farewell, Gentlemen, for I dare not join with you in this Conspiracy. (106–7)

Wise much earlier had planted the notion that the *Proposals* amounted to an explosive engine, a bomb that would rend "the Old Fabrick, . . . Ruin the Whole Frame," of the Church in New England, and constituted "a Bold Attempt . . . to blow up its Foundations" (43). His context, here, has to do with the importance of the Cambridge Platform of 1648 (*A Platform of Discipline Gathered Out of the Word of God*), which he sees as "the Ecclesiastical Political Charter of these Churches" (29). Just as "[i]t is very usual for many Gentlemen, . . . Landed men, and men of Estates, every man to keep his Law-Book by him, as his Bible, the Bible for the solace of his Mind, and the Law-Book for the safety of his Estate, . . . so methinks it should be with the Members of the Churches. . . ." He only half-jokingly proposes "That there should be a kind of a Penalty (if the Hazard in such a defect be not punishment enough) on such Delinquents, as live Members of Christs visible Kingdom here, and yet live without the *Platform,* the Ecclesiastical Political Charter of these Churches." The responsibility rests with every individual church member: if they are not to be tyrannized over, they must renew "the Impression of the *Platform,*" which, alas, he fears "is almost Extinct, if not quite worn out in the Country." Although each man has his Bible, "this Spear, or necessary weapon [the Cambridge Platform], in the defence of your Gospel Liberties, is scarce to be found in the hands of one in a Thousand, thro' all the host of Israel. I do therefore advise my Country, and these Churches, to furnish your selves [with a copy of the Cambridge Platform], and that you would encourage the Stationers, in this design, and they can soon Recruit you" (30).

In picturing the Cambridge Platform as a powerful weapon that, if properly used, can prevent the threatened blowing up of the churches and of the "Gospel Liberties" of New England church members, Wise twice within three pages quotes the words of the Mathers in support of his own anti-Mather position. He finds that "both our Policy and Duty" combine to persuade us "to follow the good Advice Mr. Cotton Mather leaves us in his *Golden Street,* Pag. 40. in these words, *Where we have a Plat-form left us that is According to the Word of our Gracious Lord, and the Pattern in the Mount, we shall be great Enemies to our selves if we do not keep to it*" (40). Wise wonders "Whether by comparing the proposals and our [Cambridge] Platform we don't find them Repugnant, and so Contradictory, that if one stands, the other must fall?" He answers with the assertion "that we can as soon Reconcile a Republick with an absolute Monarchy, or the best sort of free States with a Politick Tyranny," and then quotes "that Faithful and Noble Friend to these Churches, the famous and Learned Increase Mather, D. D." (42), as Mather calls attention to " 'The bold Attempts which have of late been made to unhinge and overset the Congregational Churches in New-England' " (43). For Wise's purposes the boldest attempt of all is the present one represented by the *Proposals:* "for here is a *Bold Attempt indeed, not only to dispoil the House of some particular Piece of Furniture, but to throw it quite out of Windows, not only to take away some of its Ornaments, but to blow up its*

Foundations." Gunpowder Treason all over again! This "Combination of Work-men Disaffected with the fashion of the Old Fabrick" is "something in the manner of Nehemiah's Men on the Wall, Neh. 4.17," seeming to mend with one hand, "[b]ut in Reality . . . all hands at work Banging the *Platform* in Pieces, upon which the old Fabrick is Built" (43). And Wise invites "the Church and all their Lovers" to "sigh and complain, as once Cicero did, *O Tempora! O Mores!* who would have expected such Times and such things from such men?"

Being Protestants, to say nothing of being Bay Colony men, those who favor the *Proposals* seem so particularly out of place because they do not adhere to the traditional Protestant source of wisdom, "Holy Scripture, . . . the Clergy-mans Pandects, whence he takes the Rules for the Management of his Trust": Wise professes to find "that it is very Amusing that the Bible should be forgotten in drawing up such Schemes as these; as tho' the usage of the Popes Conclave, which turns the Bible out of doors for a Wrangler, and gives the chief Seal to Tradition, &c. were here in fashion" (46). The proposals smack of Rome not only because they put human invention above the Bible's sacred word; in addition to raising "the *Spectre Ghost of Presbyterianism,* or the Government of the Church by Classes," the notion of an association has "something in it which *Smells very much of the Infallible Chair.* To Assume the Power of making Rules, to ingross all Principles of Process, The Right of Election, the last Appeal, the Negative Vote, and all Super-Intending Power in Matters Ecclesiastick . . . is but a few steps from that Chair of universal Pestilence. . . ." (50–51). Wise goes on to wonder "who can now withhold from them Infallibility . . . ?" Anticipating his subsequent evocation of Aaron's golden calf, Wise links his fears of Rome and of feudal despotism by foreseeing that "[t]heir Bulls can now, upon any affront, Bellow and Thunder out a Thousand terrible Curses, and the poor affrighted and Invassl'd Layity, both Princes and Subjects (being here as in the grave put under one and the same Topick) must forefeit their Salvation, if they don't tamely submit . . ." (51).

Fears of Rome and of loss of liberties: Wise extrapolates both sorts from the Presbyterian flavor of the *Proposals* as it contrasts with "the *Platform,* the Ecclesiastical Political Charter of these Churches" (29). The word "classes" (or "classis") comes up again and again (e.g., 64, 68, 76, 102, 103); one hierarchy becomes the equivalent of another, and before the "Honourable Brethren," the "Fraternity of the Churches," know it, they will find themselves "supported and Well Ordered by Suffragons, Metropolitans, and other great Pillars of those Churches" (70). The part of the *Proposals* that calls for a careful watch over each other by the Associated Pastors "might have been Ingrost with the first Canons of the Dominicans or St. Bennets Laws, when first entering upon their Monastick Life; but it in no ways agrees with this Constitution [the Cambridge Platform]" (70). The comparatively democratic liberties and powers written into the *Platform* ought to stand. The "Proposal" in question seems to be, must be, "a Plot to Introduce the Enemy [Rome] that is in the Reer," and Wise worries about "the great Damage we shall sustain by swopping Governments upon these Terms" (67).

2. THE TRIUMPH OF THE COUNTRY
EARTHY AND CONSERVATIVE VULGARITY

When he isn't being primarily a lawyer, with each "Proposal Arrested and brought to Tryal," and pleading "*Not Erring,* or *Not Guilty,* as is usual with all Criminals, when indicted" (112); or a Protestant, who finds that the proposers of the *Proposals* "have out-Pope'd the Pope himself" (123); or a freedom-loving Englishman committed to the rule of law, Wise adheres to the specifically New-England qualities of institutions, laws, and perspectives. He becomes a sharp-eyed and sharper-tongued countryman who enters into no disadvantageous "swopping." Nor does he brook officious meddling into private matters. Specifically, because the *Platform* clearly allots to the individual churches the power to elect their own ministers, the *Proposals* would be "ingrosing the Right of Jurisdiction, not only over the visible Freedom and Liberties, but Con-jugal and Secret Powers of Christs Virgin and Widdow Churches." The common sense of the "Satyre' "s author rises to the occasion, and

> it seems to [him] very Adviseable (if this Proposal may stand for a sound Precept) that forth-with another Office be erected, and put into the hands and under the Government of a few men, exactly skilled in Phisiognomy, and deeply studied in the Sympathies and Antipathies of Humane Nature, with an absolute superintending Power to Controul and direct all Wooers in the Choice for the Marriage Bed; for that there is many a fond Lover who has betrayed the glory of Wedlock, by making an unwise and unfortunate Choice; And why may not perticular Beds be over-Ruled, as well as perticular Churches? both being for the good and service of Mankind, and that for both parties, Husband and Wife, Pastor and Church, by our sort of Government, are bound for Term of Life. . . . (89–90)

After further play with his metaphor of an "Office . . . erected" at "the Nuptials" and the "Marriage Day of two Lovers," he ends the paragraph with a return to "the theam and subject of [his] pains" (10) by observing the threat to both "the Churches Liberties" and "the Government; for that our Platform in *Chap. 2.* treating of the Nature of the Churches, asserts, *Sect. 5. That the State of the Visible Church since the Coming of Christ, is only Congregational;* Therefore neither National, Provincial nor Classical; Then what does this Proposal do here?"

Like many another man from the country, Wise wants to "keep the good old Way of our Blessed Predecessors," in support of doing which he quotes three lines of Latin, ending the section with his translation:

> *Quicquid Praecipiti via.*
> *Certum Deserit Ordinem*
> *Loetos non habet exitus boetious.*
> Rashly to leave the plain and *good old way*
> Turns into Mournful *night a Joyful Day.* (93)

The legitimation of "These Proposals" will bring about "Chaos" and "Disorder" (52). A rural directness characterizes Wise's words, here:

> Indeed there is no Statute to be found that will justify the first Coitus of Parents, neither will any allow their Social Life; that the Birth must bear the Attender, of being both begotten and Born, out of Lawful Wedlock, and so in point of Honour fall under the Censure of the *Levitical Law,* and must be kept back from Promotion, for *Deut. 32. A Bastard shall not enter into the Congregation.* (52)

And the state of religion in New England suggests no need for any such additions. "Nay, consider well! are not the Flowers better wed, and the Weeds more kept down, than in most of the Inclosures in the World, belonging to the *Great Husband-man?*" (130) With regard to the flourishing of religion, "*non ex Codice, sed ex corde,* not out of Books, but out of Hearts," he

> may venture to affirm, there is no such Spot of Earth in the Earthly Globe . . . as is *New-England.* And if so, then what need have we of this late invention? Therefore to conclude, I shall, for my own part, with the Jealous Laocoon enter Caution against taking down the sides of the City, or opening the Walls of our ZION to let in this *Trojan Horse;* and let all *Israel* say, *Amen!* For, blessed be God, tho' we want to have our hearts Renewed dayly, but as for means, *tho' we have no glut,* we have Plenty enough, and want no new Institutions. (132)

Both plain-speaking countryman and classically educated lawyer turn to very plain speaking—often to vulgarity, as we have seen with the "Marriage Bed"—to find words strong enough to express their disgust: the *Proposals* "smell so strong of the POPES Cooks and Kitchen, where his Broaths and Restoratives are prepared, That they are enough to strangle a *Free-born English-man,* and much more these Churches, that have lived in such a clear Air, and under such enlargements so long a time" (141). "These Churches," once again, are the churches of New England, that for "four score years" have enjoyed the "high Immunities and Ancient Liberties" (141) spelled out with particular care in "the *15th* and *16th Chapters of our Platform*" (144). Given the greater congruence that exists between "our Church Government" and "the English Civil

Government" than between the latter and "the English Church" (54–55), how especially ironic that the proposers have not even followed "the Law and Custom of England," whereby "the *Convocation*, both the *Higher* and *Lower House* of that Learned and August Assembly," takes up only those matters specified by "our Soveraign" (146).

> What! for men to break from the Government they themselves have Established by Consent and Practice, and Arbitrarily to Rally together, And draw up a Direful Sentence . . . for the dissolution of a Country full of the best Churches of Christ in the World . . . ! What can this Import or Signify in the thoughts of Considerate Men, but a *Vertiginous Brain*? (145)

Wise contends that we would make ourselves a laughingstock: "The *Church of England* has been wont to look at us as men out of our Wits, therefore they Term us Phanaticks, or Mad-men, but much more now" (145), for we are acting as if we were "in *Esau*'s straits, who thought he might Sell his Birth-right for a mess of Pottage, if not to save his Life, yet to gratifie his Pievish and Distrustful Hunger" (144).

The "Birth-right" that most concerns Wise has, from the very beginning, been the liberty and rights of the ordinary church members, "the Fraternity of the Churches," whose "New-England Liberties have Cost your Progenitors" (17) so much. From beginning to end, the qualification of the general membership to serve as church elders, thereby obviating any need for an association, a presbytery, a classis, occupies Wise's attention almost as much as do the general principles of liberty and rule of law. "There are without doubt, in these Churches, many private Members, worthy Persons, suittably qualified for this Office, who (like some Edge-tools heedlessly left to Rust out in oblivion) lie hid, yet, when found, and put to use, will prove themselves truly Eminent" (20). With the Cambridge Platform as the orthodox and traditional guarantee of rational and democratic process, Wise declares "The Impartial Reason of the Churches" to be "the great Jury of Tryals," and proposes, in the light of all of his charges,

> that the Proposals be *Sentenc'd to Dye the Death of Hereticks*, and their Ashes Exposed to the four Winds; that the whole Scheme may, beyond all hope of Retrieve, be lost in Oblivion. And let the Churches, according to their *Platform*, Recover and Maintain their Authority, Liberties and Lustre so long as the Sun and Moon shall continue. (149)

Approaching his conclusion, Wise returns to "The Date,—*November the 5th, 1705*" (149). Addressing this "Blessed! Thrice Blessed Day!" (150), he asks it to "Uphold and Maintain thy *Matchless Fame* in the Kalendar of Time," and hopes that it will continue to reflect "a benigne Influence on the *English Monarchy*. And upon every Return in thy Anniversary Circuits, keep an Indulgent Eye open and wakeful upon all the Beauties (from the Throne to the Foot-stool) of that Mighty Empire!" (150). By calling the day "thrice blessed," Wise implies that it will signal to future generations the presence and the defeat, in 1705, as well as in 1605 and in 1688, of a threat to the Protestant order of the empire. With an eye to future threats, he prays—still to the date—that "when it is thy Misfortune to conceive a Monster, which may Threaten any part of the Nations Glory, let it come Crippled from the Womb, or else Travail in Birth again, with some Noble *Hero,* or Invincible *Hercules,* who may Conquer and Confound it."

Wise's last two pages (151–52) then simply bring his *Satyre* to a close. He promises that he will never reveal the names of the proposers, whom he refers to as "A council of War (by Adjournment met, without Commission) Consulting the most Plausible way to blow up the Walls of our Zion." He will allow them to "repose under a mantle of honourable Piety and forgetfulness," but hopes that next time they feel tempted to "Contrive how to subvert or alter the Government of the Churches, by such Dispotick Measures, especially in an Empire and Province so Charmed with such *Inchanting Liberties* as ours are," they will either

> write on the ground, or with the famous Domitian, spend the time in *Catching flies.* . . . For otherwise, they may chance to bring, if not the Old, a New House upon their heads, according to that saying,

> > *Debile fundamentum, fallit Opus.*
> > *A Work, if done, and no Foundation Laid,*
> > *Falls on the Work-Mens heads; Thus they are paid.*
> >   FINIS.

"Edge-tools heedlessly left to Rust" (20), "a sturdy Ox that will know no Whoa" (105), "Wooers in the Choice for the Marriage Bed" (89), and similar locutions characterize the straightforward countryman, just as legal terminology invokes the lawyer, and classical allusions the educated man. The antipapist, who is also anti-Presbyterian, likewise appears clearly enough. The only tangle of loyalties that seems to me serious, problematic, perhaps even disingenuous, emerges in the combination of claims concerning allegiance to the British Empire and loyalty to the Province (152). The point comes through clearly, even sharply, when we look at those last words about November 5 (150).

Whom has Wise in mind for the part of "Noble *Hero,* or Invincible *Hercules*" in 1605? in 1688? in his own day? According to tradition, James I received a direct inspiration from God that enabled him to decipher the real meaning of Lord Mounteagle's note: miraculous, certainly, but neither heroic nor Herculean. Were William and Mary heroic? Not particularly: again, the Lord provided a miracle on behalf of Britain so that the winds assisted rather than opposed the wonderful landing at

Torbay. As for the defeat of the *Proposals,* is Wise casting himself in the role of that mighty wrestler of antiquity? At one point he speaks with the kind of pugnacity one might expect from the wrestler of Chebacco Parish, sneering at the part of the *Proposals* that seems aimed at allowing particular pastors to hide behind the support of the Association "ere they proceed to any Action in their particular Churches, which may be likely to Produce Imbroylments" (67). So far as Wise is concerned, this proposal is merely

> a Covering of Figg-leaves, and may serve for a Harbour to Cowards and Fools but not for men of spirit and Conduct. The Dream [that is, the anticipation] of an Imbroylment, can never Counter-Poise Duty; If men are Trusted with Duty, they must consult that, and not Events. If men are plac'd at Helm, to steer in all weather which Blows, they must not be afraid of the Waves, or a wet Coat. (68–69)

Manly and direct this may be, but not heroic. It seems unlikely that Wise would cast himself in the role of hero or of Hercules; but what, then, does he mean?

When he asks the Day to "keep an Indulgent Eye open and wakeful upon all the Beauties (from the Throne to the Foot-stool) of that Mighty Empire!" (the one under the rule of "the *English Monarchy*"), he must be suggesting that New England does indeed occupy a subordinate place in the scheme of things political. But, on the other hand, he begins the apostrophe to the "Blessed Day" by calling it "Thrice Blessed Day!" Somehow, the defeat of the *Proposals* of November 5 signifies as great a blessing for the British Empire as the discovery of Gunpowder Treason and as the landing at Torbay upon the same date. Like the Mathers before him—like most, if not all, of his thoughtful New England predecessors— Wise wants the advantages of British tradition without its obligations. He evokes "the *Convocation,* both the *Higher* and *Lower House* of that Learned and August Assembly," but with no serious suggestion that New England church polity should be determined by those bodies of the Church of England: shades of William Binckes and Gilbert Burnet! Rather, just as convocation, "According to the Law and Custom of *England,*" take up only such matters as "our Sovereign by Commission Expressly alloweth of," so the proposers "should have done no less (in a matter of such weight and Moment) then have Petitioned the Publick Authority for Commission, before you had ventured this far" (146). But "the Publick Authority" in question cannot be the British sovereign, Anglican Queen Anne, "New-Englands Royal Nurse and great Benefactress" (32), but . . . who? Who indeed but the "Honourable Brethren," "the Fraternity of the Churches in the New-England Colonies"? The heroic suddenly becomes the commonplace, or, rather, the commonplace takes on the aura of

heroism. The "Foot-stool" of the Empire becomes as worthy of veneration as the throne.

Wise proposes as hero, as Hercules, not so much himself as those
church members, unused "Edge-tools" though they at present be, who
have the sharpness of wit to value their own capacities and to understand
the threat to their churches' integrity implicit in the latest November 5
plot. Wise also appeals to more than historical precedent. From high
principle to low interest, he covers all bets: one—to modern eyes, the
most innocuous—section of the *Proposals* suggests "That the several
Associations in the Country maintain a due Correspondence with one
another" (95). "If the Platonick Notion concerning the Universal Soul
of the World or Spirit of Nature (whereby one Body is affected by the
Operations of another at some considerable distance)" were enough to
enable "these Societies" to "circulate their Intelligence by the Power and
Echoes of this Mighty Essence," or were there "Doves trained up to
carry Males or Pacquets of Letters . . . , there might be some hopes for
Supporting this Mighty Correspondence, but to do it wholly by humane
Means, the Charge plainly threatens to eat out the Profit" (96). One might
well ask,

> what a Mighty business is a Six Penny or Four Penny Letter in such a good
> Cause? Nay, indeed there's no great matter in it self, yet these Six Pennys
> or Four Pennys are like the Sand on the sea shore, a great many of them
> put together grow very heavy, especially where Wife and Children are to
> be maintained upon 70£ or 80£ Income *per Annum.*
>
> Wise men may do as they please, yet for my part, I can see no good Policy
> in the Proposal, unless you can Court some Rich Potentate to espouse the
> Cause, and Sacrifice Annually some part of his Royal Revenue to Support
> the *Phantasie.* (96)

Wise, being himself a Wise man . . . but the punning allusion is pointed
enough, and Platonic "phantasie" is fantasy nonetheless: the "Notion"
is not "an Infallible *Theorem*"; it will transport no letters. The voice of
New England, one of the early voices of America, may seem like a
cheeseparing voice in some respects, but it has the ability to laugh at
itself as well as to hold to principles of liberty and privilege.

Still, it remains troublesome that these principles stem from England,
and from English civil practice, at that. The churches of New England
must somehow rise above, go beyond, the church polity of old while
holding to the examples of the British civil order. Wise, as will be the
case perhaps even more markedly in the more widely read *Vindication*
of 1717, recommends and defends democracy but never quite sees—or,
at any rate, never quite says—that monarchy, even of the best British
constitutional kind, by its very existence denies the equality between

men that he reiterates as an underlying pillar of the social compact that he borrowed from Baron von Pufendorf (see the *Vindication*, 32). His reference to Queen Anne as "New-Englands Royal Nurse . . ." (*Quarrel*, 32) may have more relevance than mere flattery. Rational, democratic, determined, brave, the wrestler from Chebacco still may be seeing the colonies as in need of the kind of care and nurture that a nurse who is also a "great Benefactress" supplies.

But these are murky waters. One thing remains indisputable: however much the churches of New England were at one time to serve as the model for the Church of England, the civil liberties of Englishmen provided the model upon which the government of the New England churches had to take its stand. The upshot of Wise's rational defense and satiric attacks was to insist upon a divided allegiance. The conditions of New England, its geography and climate that made travel and communication so expensive and so tedious, called with especial urgency for the liberties promised not only by the Cambridge Platform of 1648 but by the specific documents and hallowed traditions of British law. Insisting upon the democratic spirit latent in Congregational church polity, Wise defends it from attack by evoking the threat to the royal family and the Established Church of England commemorated—in Old England but not in New—every Fifth of November.

3. "THE SIMPLE COBLER" AND THE MASKS OF WISE, VERSUS POLLY BAKER
OR, HUMOR SLIPS IN WHEN THEOLOGY BLINKS

Exactly a century apart, Wise's Ipswich predecessor, who called himself a "Simple Cobler," and Wise's most clever Bostonian successor, whose pen names were legion but who was best known as Poor Richard Saunders, humble almanac maker of Philadelphia, both published in England exhortations written from behind masks of different sorts. Each document throws considerable light upon what the British heritage meant to colonials, as well as upon the uses of reason in argument and upon the strategies that allowed satire and the vernacular to come together in ways that strengthened the position of common folk, of perspectives represented by people of low degree. Nathaniel Ward's *The Simple Cobler of Aggawam in America* (1647) and Benjamin Franklin's "The Speech of Polly Baker" (1747) both appeared first in England, printed only later in the colonies—in Ward's case, many years later. Although the social status of Ward's cobbler may by definition be low, he cannot legitimately be perceived as ill-educated, unless his unconventional vocabulary be seen as mark of ignorance rather than expression of an exuberant feistiness. (The *OED* lists a number of words as appearing only in Ward's book.)

But Ward's use of vernacular—the speech of the supposedly uneducated local populace—is even sketchier than Wise's.

Ward-the-writer, the trained lawyer, shows considerable ability at preserving the distance between himself and his mask as "Simple Cobler," but he does not try to keep his own personality out of the fray as Wise tries to do—with uneven success—and as Benjamin Franklin will succeed so spectacularly in doing. Ward, for reasons worth considering, had no practical need to do so—and no aesthetic need, either. But I suggest that the two are absolutely inseparable, or at least that I am unable to separate them in estimating the effect of Ward's volume. Although Ward speaks as the "Simple Cobler," eager "to help mend" the "sole" of "his Native Country" (3), he speaks, finally, for himself, with his own passionate commitment to his causes. His first person trembles with the sort of rage and disappointment that are altogether in keeping with Ward himself. He speaks as the cobbler, to be sure, and scores many points with bad puns on the subject of his concern for the soles (souls) of his fellows. When, however, he launches into violent diatribes against the folly of tolerating religions other than one's own if one has the power to suppress them, the emotion is Ward's as well as his cobbler's. "If the whole conclave of Hell can compromise . . . such a multimonstrous maufrey of heteroclytes and quicquidlibets quietly; . . . they can do more than the Senate of Heaven" (23). Ward has no need to hide his own anger in this context, any more than in the matter of women's dress: he

> mislikes a bullymong drossock [a drab, untidy woman] . . . but when I
> heare a nugiperous Gentledame inquire what dresse the Queen is in this
> week: what the nudiustertian fashion of the Court; with egge to be in it
> in all haste, whatever it be; I look at her as the very gizzard of a trifle, the
> product of a quarter of a cypher, the epitome of Nothing, fitter to be kickt, if
> shee were of a kickable substance, than either honour'd or humour'd. (26)

His oft-quoted neologisms against the fashion-conscious ladies of the town have an inimitable ring to them, but the tune is not that of a maker of shoes. Just the reverse: to be true to the economic role of his persona, Ward would have been compelled to have his cobbler commend a wasteful extravagance.

In 1647, Ward could let his own feelings out because his message was the Lord's. What he felt, as well as what he thought, he could perceive as coming from righteous indignation, not smug self-importance. Even though many of the citizens of his "Native Country" disagreed with him—if they hadn't, he wouldn't have needed to write in the first place—Ward's stance takes on the vulgarity not of a cobbler but of a man absolutely sure of the eternal verity of his positions. Less than two years before his brethren in Old England beheaded their king, and looking that possibility squarely in the face, Ward urged Charles to mend his ways because "your good subjects are now rising into a resolution to pray you on to your throne, or into your Tombe." If Charles will not respond to God's directions—identical to the drift of those prayers—then he deserves to lose his kingdom, his crown, and his life itself. With the self-righteousness of total certainty, Ward reminds the king of the fundament upon which his majesty's humanity is based, predicting that "God will . . . convince you, that it had [been] and will be farre easier to sit downe meekely upon the *Rectum*, than to wander . . . into bottomlesse Seas of sorrowes" (57).

Until Anglicans began to turn against zeal in any cause at all as more likely to lead to works of devilish disorder than to constructive godliness, zeal for truth, zeal in a righteous cause, to both Anglican and Puritan preachers, was seen as providing the only psychological force powerful enough to override the natural propensities of fallen humanity. Ward's seventeenth-century New England intolerance reflects a frame of mind, not simply a doctrinal preference. Deviations from the true and the good deserve no toleration; those who deviate need—perhaps even deserve—correction. But, as John Cotton had so memorably spelled out to Roger Williams, anyone who does ignore the truth, "after the first and second admonition" (Titus 3:10), makes a choice to close his eyes to what the Lord has imprinted upon his very soul. Therefore, whatever persecution comes his way occurs not "for cause of conscience," but, rather, accrues to him because "he sins against his own conscience." That circumstances were forcing toleration upon Cromwell and the other Puritans back in Ward's "Native Country" needs no documentation at this date, nor does New England's principled objection. Innate depravity exists, a fact of life; human weakness needs correction, not cosseting.

Under the guise of bragging for his fellow colonials as he calls to account the manners of the court of King Charles, Ward—or his Simple Cobler (the distinction expresses no difference)—both warns his readers and allows them to share his righteous anger.

> I thank God I have lived in a Colony of many thousand English these twelve years, am held a very sociable man; yet I may considerately say, I never heard but one Oath sworne, nor never saw one man drunk, nor ever heard of three women Adulteresses, in all this time. . . . If these sinnes bee amongst us privily, the Lord heale us. I would not bee understood to boast of our innocency; there is no cause I should, our hearts may be bad enough, and our lives much better. (58–59)

Needless to say, the colony's reality differed considerably from this account;[7] Ward is having his cobbler speak for specific effects. On the one hand, no matter how admirable the appearance of our lives, the

---

7. See, inter alia, Janette Bohi, "Nathaniel Ward, a Sage of Old Ipswich," 5.

actuality of our external behavior, the condition of our hearts remains human, which is to say fallen. At the same time, blasphemous Prince Rupert, with "all his God-damne mee's" (58), and any "nugiperous Gentledame" as well, justly receives our condemnation. Ward does not so much persuade through argumentation as condemn through excoriation. The alleged facts elicit feelings in the cobbler that any right-minded, though inevitably somewhat sinful, human being ought to have. Ward's tone of vulgar irreverence will be echoed through the years by other Americans.

Wise, like Bishop Burnet, faces what he takes to be a different world. Burnet, despite his position, encountered the ire of the Houses of Convocation. Unlike Salisbury Cathedral in England, Chebacco Parish cannot be called a significant power base in early eighteenth-century Massachusetts. Wise, with relatively little position at all, either could not, or perhaps did not even try to, publish the first edition of *The Church's Quarrel Espoused* in the Bay Colony of the Mathers. In his "Satyre," he uses such a variety of masks as, at times, leads him into inconsistencies of tone and of pretended bias. A plausible intention behind such shifting as we have seen in the speaker's fictional identities might well have been to cast as broad a net as possible. Wise creates one kind of appeal with the voice of a simple countryman, concerned with his pennies and in touch with the homely realities of edged tools and of the marriage bed. A quite different voice, though related, is that of the sharp-tongued lawyer, distinguishing between the God-given "Miraculous Gifts and Indowments of Mind Impresst upon Christs Ambassadors, whereby Fisher-men Commence (*per Saltem*) Doctors of Divinity, and in an instant were stocked with such Principles of Religion, Reason and Philosophy, that they were capable to dispute with Athens it self" (78), and the more painfully acquired learning necessary for ministers in these later times. Because "it is very Reasonable that the Churches should be well assured of the Sufficiency of the Learning of those Persons, e're they presume on the Ministry," someone must certify to the learning of each candidate. But that certification, says Wise, not only need not, but ought not, be attended to by elder ministers, members of the proposed "Association," who are removed in time from the details and even the general rubrics of academic learning, whose Latin has grown rusty and who may more probably embarrass themselves than probe the supposed deficiencies of recent students. No, says Wise, coming in a bit from the country, but retaining a country metaphor nevertheless: "Our Accademy is the Store-house of Learning, and this all Mankind will Assent to" (78–79).

And then Wise tries—and succeeds in his attempt—to have the best of both learnèd and unlearnèd worlds. He insists, in one of his favorite country similes—the one that he earlier used in decrying the *Proposals'* apparent lack of faith in the existence of men competent to serve as elders by likening such men to "Edge-tools heedlessly left to Rust out in oblivion" (20)—that the standard of Harvard College more than suffices,

> That of all men living, the best and most Infallible Standard for the Philosophical Accomplishments of our Candidates, is the Judgment of the Honourable President and noble Fellows of our Famous Colledge; for this I am sure must needs stand for a verity, that the Judgment of a real Honest and skilfull Artificer (keeping close to his Shop) concerning the Nature and Qualities of an Edge-Tool which he hath wrought, and hammered on his own Anvil, out of its first Rude Matter, must certainly Excel him that hath been long from the Trade, that only takes it, turns the Edge slightly, or has but a Transient view of it! So that hence we may fairly infer, that (as to humane Learning) *Harvards Commendamus* is most valuable and sufficient, and justly Supplants these Testimonials. (79)

Wise speaks through one mask and then another, appealing to one and then another anticipated fraction of his readership. In all cases, however, he appeals not to truths established by divine fiat but to truths known through human experience and by human reason.

Wise's ironies on occasion have the effect of humor: they surprise us, while amusing us, into viewing the *Proposals* from a perspective totally different from that intended by their proposers. But Wise, reason and all, still writes from the vantage point (with the advantage) of one who knows the Truth. He may know it as much through human reason as through divine revelation, but the divine sources of knowledge still pertain. Also, although New England Puritanism was by his time dead, in the sense that no one hoped any longer to reform the Church of England, Wise was very much a Puritan in the high seriousness of his purpose. Some of his locutions, as we have seen, make (and must have made) readers smile; but, like Nathaniel Ward before him, he would have disdained to acknowledge humor as a useful weapon in the Lord's polemical battles.

William Prynne's *Histrio-Mastix*, at which we will glance much later, back in 1633 had presented the Puritans' definitive statement against the dangers of laughter. I do not mean that Ward and Wise deliberately stayed their hands, deliberately capped any continuous welling-up of risible material—although, of course, that may have been the case. My belief is that, like most writers, they went with what "felt right"; and deliberate humor would have felt wrong, especially in anticipation of its effects on one's readership. The time had not yet come for the kind of delight in playing a role for humorous as well as polemical—for humorous even more than for polemical—effects, of which Mark Twain will speak so knowingly in "How to Tell a Story." But that will be in 1895; and by then, a case for humor needed little, if any, arguing. In Ward's, and then in Wise's, New England, almost any display of humor would have been seen as self-indulgence and would have damaged the earnest writer's serious cause. Still, by adopting different masks, by playing different roles, such writers, even though their primary concern was with nonhumorous effects, could strengthen their impact by the sudden shifts of perspective engineered by the sudden changes of mask.

Yet even so, how much effect Wises's variety of personae, or Ward's combination of personal rage and clever mask, had on their various readerships we cannot say. The British did not abandon their tendency toward toleration any more than Charles I learned to sit meekly upon his throne; the *Proposals* against which Wise inveighed appear to have been a dead issue in eastern Massachusetts; but, farther west and south, the *Saybrook Platform* of 1708—very much in the spirit of the 1705 *Proposals*—became law before Wise had even written. Today, *Quarrel Espoused* and *Simple Cobler* seem extremely effective as polemic, and highly enjoyable as literature. They bristle with energy, with cleverness, and with authenticity of voices. Ward's work, however, had no discernible impact upon his purposes, and Wise's purposes remain to this day cloudy: if they included making the Mathers look inconsistent, and therefore foolish, Wise succeeded (from a modern reader's point of view), but how many of his contemporaries ever saw a copy of the book, and how did those who saw it react to it? Still, the interplay between concern for colony and regard for mother country, the shift from more to less direct expression of specifically personal attitudes, and the increasing experimentation with consistency of invented perspective all suggest that Wise was shaping language to his deliberate purpose.

Not so many years later, Benjamin Franklin, literary and political genius that he was, operated out of a firm grounding in an active tradition. Franklin did not need to look abroad at Jonathan Swift, whose blowing up of John Partridge anticipated, and contributed to, Franklin's destruction of Titan Leeds.[8] Instead, authors on his own side of the Atlantic provided Franklin with examples of how beguiling and how effective a mask might be. One of the elements that Franklin added, however, was the deliberate use of humor to disarm opposition. As everyone knows, he could use appeals to the divine, too; but he used them as one more weapon carefully chosen from his arsenal, not as a direct presentation of personal belief. When it comes to the question of belief, we may never know the "real" Mr. Franklin. Commentators ever

8. See quoted passages and discussion in Frank Donovan, ed., *The Benjamin Franklin Papers*, 51–52.

since D. H. Lawrence (in 1923) have testified that Ben Franklin was a master of the art of disguise. Where he failed in his intended effects—and he seems to have failed infrequently—at least one shrewd commentator has found him failing precisely on the grounds of misjudging his readership because of an inability to subordinate his feelings to his rhetorical purposes. Leo Lemay's discussion of the *Narrative of the Late Massacres in Lancaster County* (January 1764) makes especially persuasive reading in light of a letter that Franklin wrote to Lord Kames about a year-and-a-half after the event. What Franklin intended to do, what he thought he was doing, was "to strengthen the hands of our weak government by rendering the proceedings of the rioters unpopular and odious."[9] He appears not to have anticipated that the effect of his words might have been to lead middle-class and lower-middle-class men to take violent steps, independently of that same "weak government," to protect their property at less rather than more expense, rather than to refrain from massacre and revolt. Carla Mulford argues with considerable ingenuity that Franklin's efforts took a quite different direction.

Of particular interest is that the issue arises and has significance. Where Professor Mulford sees "a strategic manipulation of the communal values and capitalistic interests of mid-century Philadelphia rather than . . . an emotional response peculiarly attributable to Benjamin Franklin,"[10] Professor Lemay finds that "Franklin was so outraged by the massacres that he gave vent to his true feelings, ignoring the almost certain consequences . . . [of] his failure to appeal to his primary audience."[11] But whether or not he failed, and whatever his intention, one finds both of these scholars taking into account the impact on readers of Franklin's successes and failures in controlling his own emotions in favor of those appropriate to a coherent and consistent speaker. And, really, the absence of such a fictional (i.e., non-Franklinian) speaker cannot be determined on the basis of any given reader's failure to feel its presence. Projection and transference are mighty forces indeed. D. H. Lawrence's noisy rejection of Franklin includes a total misreading of Mark Twain's view of him.[12] When our great humorist and satirist lambasted Franklin's "early to bed and early to rise,"[13] siding instead with an invented quotation that he attributed to

9. *Benjamin Franklin's Autobiographical Writings*, 147.
10. Carla Mulford, 348.
11. J. A. Leo Lemay, "Rhetorical Strategies . . . ," 200.
12. In D. H. Lawrence's *Studies in Classic American Literature*.
13. "Rise early. It is the early bird who catches the worm. Don't be fooled by this absurd saw; I once knew a man who tried it. He got up at sunrise and a horse bit him" (*Mark Twain's Notebook*, ed. Paine, 12).

George Washington,[14] Twain was rejecting Poor Richard, not Lawrence's Benjamin.

The poker-faced Franklin, as students have come to recognize, anticipated Twain himself. This is the Franklin who created Polly Baker in 1747 and who, forty years later in the *Autobiography*, commented dryly on the fatalism expressed by the Indians of Carlisle in acquiescing in their own destruction by the white man's rum. Later, I shall return to Lawrence's reaction to this latter passage. Franklin, like Twain, used humor as part of the mask; he could launch his attacks from that protected position. Just as Twain will do in a number of his stories (e.g., "The Celebrated Jumping Frog" and "His Grandfather's Old Ram"), Franklin, in the two small examples that I shall be using, attacks the conventional acceptations of what he views as a smug and moralistic society. Just as Twain's silly narrators with genteel sensibilities lack the awareness that their narratives communicate to readers, so Franklin's purported speaker serves often to communicate an awareness of the similar gap between moral pretensions and lived values that, ironically, led Twain to reject Franklin's Poor Richard. Franklin's Richard, and many another, serves as a mask behind which readers are invited to look in order to laugh, and also to examine their own preconceptions. The invitation to readers to do such looking forms the means of the attack; its success must depend on a complicated array of factors, including the importance of the preconceptions under attack, the strength of the readers' defenses, and the skill of the writer in controlling the speaker's perspective.

14.   *Early to bed, and early to rise,*
                 Makes a man healthy, wealthy and wise.
                         —BENJAMIN FRANKLIN.

                 I don't see it.
                         —George Washington.

Now both of these are high authorities—very high and respectable authorities—but I am with George Washington first, last, and all the time on this proposition.
    Because I don't see it, either.
    I have tried getting up early, and I have tried getting up late—and the latter agrees with me best. As for a man's growing any wiser, or any richer, or any healthier, by getting up early, I know it is not so; . . . You observe that I have put a stronger test on the matter than even Benjamin Franklin contemplated, and yet it would not work. . . . I am not any healthier or any wealthier than I was before, and only wiser in that I know a good deal better than to go and do it again. And as for all those notable advantages [urged on Twain by others], . . . I don't see them, any more than myself and Washington see the soundness of Benjamin Franklin's attractive little poem. (Twain, "Early Rising . . . ," 44, 45, 50)

4. From Wise and Franklin, Mark Twain's Triumphant Vernacular

If readers can laugh at their own insufficiencies, for instance, while retaining the illusion that they are laughing simply at another's, the writer succeeds in charming an audience, and perhaps succeeds even in advancing a point of view. Old Ben understands perfectly well the regimen of exercise and diet that he should follow. His 1780 "Dialogue Between Franklin and the Gout"—reading in many ways like the dialogue between "Mark Twain" and his conscience in "The Facts Concerning the Recent Carnival of Crime in Connecticut" (1876)—charms primarily because it allows us to chuckle at our perception of a weak human: the speaker is caught, as we all so often are, between preachment about responsible behavior and distaste for direct experience of it. Furthermore, by using the name of the grand old man of American international diplomacy, Franklin adds particular reassurance to readers: how heartening to be able to feel so superior to, so much more aware than, the renowned Dr. Franklin. The next step feels less comfortable, alas, for we must either go on to demonstrate our own self-discipline or else give up our unearned sense of superiority.

In 1747, Polly Baker, whose activities have led to the birth of some five children, all healthy and well formed, but none having a legal father, argues that she deserves neither fines nor whippings for her part in supplying the new country with needed population, but a medal or a statue. So persuasive was she that, as the totally impersonal narrative voice reports before reporting the speech itself, one of her judges subsequently married her, and the happy union in time produced another fifteen citizens for the new world. Franklin places Polly "before a Court of Judicature, at Connecticut near Boston in New-England," and has her speak only with the authority of human, secular reasonableness to defend her sexual self. She plays the role of reasonable woman, wondering if it can really "be a crime (in the nature of things, I mean) to add to the king's subjects, in a new country, that really wants people?" Neatly emphasizing what to her is the irrationality of a supposedly rational society, she puns away the allegedly immoral nature of her acts: "Abstracted from the law, I cannot conceive (may it please your honors) what the nature of my offense is." As for "the precepts of religion . . . how can it be believed that heaven is angry at my having children, when to the little done by me towards it, God has been pleased to add his divine skill and admirable workmanship . . . ?" To abstain would be to violate "the duty of the first and great command of nature and nature's God, *encrease and multiply* . . . [but w]hat must poor young women do, whom custom and nature forbid to solicit the men" (into becoming husbands, that is)? Men unwilling to marry and reproduce commit a real crime, one "little better than murder," Polly insists. And so on.

Franklin's language is a remarkably effective combination of the formally legal and the delightfully conciliatory, and nowhere in the speech does Franklin allow Polly to make the mistake of implying that there might be anything pleasurable in the sexual act itself. The real audience for Polly's speech, the readers of *The Gentleman's Magazine* in April 1747, and of numerous other British publications (over three months elapsed before the piece was reprinted on this side of the Atlantic),[15] may have retained—almost undoubtedly did retain—their self-righteous, or legalistic, or simply habitual, attitudes; but Franklin managed, if only for the moment, to arouse their aesthetic and intellectual awareness of discrepancies between society's conventional acceptations and what was really and truly self-evident to an unbiased observer of nature and nature's laws. Max Hall argues persuasively for Franklin's exposure of the discrepancy between a conventional double standard for sexual behavior and the preoccupation of contemporary novelists with women's rights, or at least with the rights of women to be treated less exploitatively in matters of sexual behavior. This interpretation seems very likely. At the same time, Franklin sticks pins in a tradition of sexual hypocrisy that he had long loved to attack.

Polly speaks in a way that blots out all facets of the human personality not immediately useful to her creator's argument. On the one hand, this selectivity creates much of the power of her effort. At the same time, it presents for delighted ridicule a kind of emotional isolation well known to readers of, and about, New England. Polly's expressed concern for the public, barely disguising what readers easily perceive to be self-interest, echoes Cotton Mather's *Bonifacius, or Essays to do Good*, the inspiration for Franklin's own Silence Dogood letters twenty-five years before Polly's speech. When Mather urged his readers to admonish their neighbors, he displayed—apparently with no sense of self-irony—the same single-tracked moral vision, the same disregard for the feelings of people, on which Polly's speech depends for its humor and, in its fictional context, for its success. Said Mather, "lovingly and faithfully admonish them . . . prudently dispense your admonitions unto them till you have persuaded them to set up the worship of God. . . . Whatever snare you see anyone in, be so kind as to tell him of his danger to be ensnared, and save him from it."[16] Mather's humor, obviously, was totally unconscious.

15. See Max Hall, *Benjamin Franklin and Polly Baker . . .* , 70.
16. Cotton Mather, *Bonifacius. . . .* I quote from Perry Miller's *The American Puritans*, 218–19.

Another perspective on Polly's speech emerges if we go back still further, to Cotton Mather's grandfather, John Cotton, and the concept of Christian Calling.[17] The three necessary qualities by which one can identify one's calling as truly Christian Polly has no difficulty discovering in her own. She points out that God has given her the natural abilities to do well what she has been doing, the "gifts for it," in Cotton's words; and certainly the healthy and comely results of her labors are there for all to see. That her endeavors have been to the advancement of "the public good"—part of Cotton's second criterion—she has made clear from her mention of the need for population in a new country. Most striking of all, she can show that even the occasion that allowed her to initiate her calling has been divinely blessed, at least for her partner, although not for herself. Her own lack of reward she puts down to the laws, "but since laws are sometimes unreasonable in themselves, and therefore repealed," she argues for the repeal of the one that keeps on hauling her up for punishment. As for her initial partner, after having proposed marriage and then abandoned her after getting her with child, he has received more than ample encouragement from both God and man: "[Y]ou all know, he is now become a magistrate of this country; and I had hopes he would have appeared this day on the bench, and have endeavored to moderate the Court in my favor." She sees it "as unjust and unequal, that my betrayer and undoer, the first cause of all my faults and miscarriages (if they must be deemed such [Polly seems to have experienced no "miscarriages" of the obstetric variety.]), should be advanced to honor and power in this government that punishes my misfortune with stripes and infamy." Finally, Cotton said that the third distinguishing mark that "makes a calling warrantable" is that one "would not come unto it by deceit and undermining of others": Polly has "debauched no other woman's husband," nor has any virginal young man ("youth," as she says) known her bed.

Not only does Polly present a wonderfully parodic argument whereby her sexual activities appear in the light of having received divine sanction; she also presents her argument in a manner that owes much to that mysterious Puritan sense of "weaned affections," also articulated by John Cotton, among others, whereby the sojourner through life is to pursue with all his (or, in this case, her) might her God-given calling, but still focus her "affections," her emotions, her libido, we might say, on the Kingdom of God. So Polly's cool, totally passionless explication of her passionate past recreates, in an unconventional context, the Puritan mystery of emotions so dedicated to the holy will of the Lord as to

17. John Cotton, "Christian Calling." I quote from Miller's *The American Puritans*, 174–75.

be separated from the things of this world, even from the strenuous pursuit of one's calling, as well as from the material fruits of it. As in Swift's "Modest Proposal," offspring are economic counters and material objects, examples of God's "admirable workmanship." Although Polly acknowledges that God has "furnish[ed them] . . . with rational and immortal souls," she says nothing to suggest that they are beings with whom one experiences any emotional involvement.

Franklin's Polly succeeds so beautifully in part because she plays upon the outmoded, though still respected, pieties of her society. At the same time, she parodies them. John Wise could allow his country lawyer persona or his farmer's voice to invoke the past directly because Wise wants his readers to revere it and then to dismiss the new-fangled innovations of the present *Proposals* in part because they contradict the good old ways. Even though Wise's principles have a modern—that is, a rationalistic and prodemocratic—ring to them, Wise argues on the basis of revered precedent.

Our sly Ben is up to something a lot more subversive, however. In this sense, Lawrence's observation that Franklin was quite deliberately setting about "the breaking of the old world," even while "the American spiritually stayed at home in Europe," becomes an immensely complex, and extremely ambiguous, proposition.[18] Certainly Franklin engaged, as did Wise, in establishing the sufficiency, and perhaps even the autonomy, of human reason, but not against the paternal control of Europe so much as against the authoritarian theocracies of the past, on both sides of the Atlantic. Bishop Burnet had been engaged in doing the same thing. Lawrence's most crushing condemnation of Franklin had to do with the Lawrencian sense that excessive respect for conscious reason leads to the repression of feeling, a repression that Lawrence found in the Puritans on the one hand, and in modern Americans on the other. By turning us all into moral and laboring machines, that is, Franklin helped bring about the worst excesses of the modern world, whereby humans act out of their consciousness alone, with insufficient awareness of their deeper passional selves. Lawrence's indictments have received such widespread attention that I shall take them as read. Their bearing on twentieth-century America-in-general differs considerably from their bearing on Ben Franklin-in-particular.

Franklin's subversiveness in the speech of Polly Baker has a great deal in common with the subversion Franklin performs in a passage in the *Autobiography* that Lawrence sees as epitomizing the "barbed wire fence" within which the good doctor would confine us all. Lawrence

18. See the last eight paragraphs in chap. 2, "Benjamin Franklin," in D. H. Lawrence, *Studies in Classic American Literature.*

pounces upon the passage as an example of Franklin's smug superiority, the epitome of what he takes to be Franklin's true self. Instead, the passage turns out to be another example of Franklin's irony, of Franklin's created voice. Franklin, in the section of his autobiography written in 1788, describes the Indians during a meeting at Carlisle, in 1750, at which a "treaty was conducted very orderly, because they [that is, the Indians] could get no liquor." Afterwards, upon receiving their promised rum, the Indians proceeded to a drunken and shockingly disorderly orgy, "a scene the most resembling our ideas of hell that could be well imagined." Franklin concludes his two-paragraph account, first with the explanation of the Indian orator, who "acknowledged the fault, but laid it upon the rum; and then endeavored to excuse the rum," and then with his own brief comment.

Although the two paragraphs in question have been quoted often, I present the two "speeches" from the second:

> "The Great Spirit, who made all things, made everything for some use, and whatever use he designed any thing for, that use it should always be put to. Now, when he made rum, he said, 'Let this be for the Indians to get drunk with,' and it must be so." And, indeed, if it be the design of Providence to extirpate these savages in order to make room for cultivators of the earth, it seems not improbable that rum may be the appointed means. It has already annihilated all the tribes who formerly inhabited the sea-coast.

Franklin's disdain for, even fear of, the "hell" of Indian anarchy reveals—I believe authentically—Franklin's awareness of how thin was the ice of rational self-control over which civilization had to skate. But the passage's last two sentences do not represent anything like the complexity of Franklin's seriously held attitude toward Indians. Too many other documents exist to show that Franklin understood, as clearly as Roger Williams or William Penn did, precisely whose land was being expropriated and who was the more likely to break treaties.[19]

Franklin's commentary promises the "annihilation," the "extirpation," of "savages" in favor of "cultivators of the earth," all brought about through the impersonally predetermined means of the Calvinistic "Providence" and punctuated by repeated use of the unassailable, because so coldly impersonal, "it." Through his prose, Franklin sticks pins into the smugness of those who would smugly see themselves as leagued with God's supposedly most scrutable purposes. But he does more than that. His controlled, though bitter, and in this context not especially amusing, rage has for part of its target the inability of the Indians to pursue

19. See, inter alia, Franklin's *Narrative of the Late Massacres in Lancaster County* and *Remarks Concerning the Savages of North America*; also see Carl Van Doren, *Benjamin Franklin*, passim, especially 205–9, 307–10, 705–6.

their own best interests (at least as Franklin could understand them) by controlling their penchant for rum. The independence of the individual offers a glorious opportunity; it also carries tremendous risks. If the Indians—if any group—passively allow themselves to shuffle along as victims of the Almighty's purpose, their passive ignorance puts their independence into jeopardy.

Benjamin Franklin here both takes on and undercuts the tone of Cotton Mather's *Bonafacius*: as Bishop Burnet—and so many others—had been suggesting, even if the phrase "the design of Providence" denoted a sensible reality in a teleological universe, that design would undoubtedly frustrate the capacity of any mere human being to intuit, much less to formulate. In his autobiography, Franklin speaks from behind one (or more) of his masks. From behind the comic mask come incitements to understandings not just outward and societal but also inward and psychological. Those who equate the destroying of Indians with the Providence of God tended to be—at least in Lancaster County—the ill-educated, rough-and-tumble "Paxton boys" of Scotch-Irish descent, to whom Franklin seems to have felt considerably superior.

Indeed, Benjamin's self-effacement behind a variety of masks seems to me to belong to his awareness of himself as very superior indeed. How, then, to affect the views of others? Except when, as in his "Dialogue" with "the Gout," he wants to use the weaknesses of his biographical self, Franklin over and over again removes from his readers' view and consciousness the personality of the very superior Dr. Franklin. By allowing readers to persuade themselves that, instead of being guided by a superior writer, they were drawing their own conclusions, he moved them into position to see things as he did.

His purpose most often was the eminently practical one of swaying readers to do what he thought they ought to do but what they wouldn't or couldn't persuade themselves, or understand, that they ought to do. He writes as if he understood people so well that he had no need to maintain for long a sense of outrage even at their failure to appreciate Franklin himself. On the one hand, he manipulates them; they are means to his own beneficent—or, as the case may be, self-interested—ends. At the same time, they are free and equal individuals whom Benjamin Franklin wants to see act freely and independently, rather than give themselves passively up to the will of God or the designs of Providence.

Language serves as his engine, his lever. It is the medium in which he works, but it is not his subject. The masks themselves, made so skillfully from words, serve to make palatable the course of action that the writer hopes to bring about. But Franklin tends to avoid one linguistic tool that had already begun to be a source of humor, of pleasure, in American (as well as in British) writing, the use of vernacular speech in contrast to the more formal standard usage of the day. The novels of Henry Fielding, for instance, abound—as had the plays of William Shakespeare—in the use of vernacular to distinguish between social classes in a humor-producing way. Apparently even the groundlings at the Globe could be expected to identify themselves strongly enough with characters of noble birth, of significant social status, to enjoy the contrasts between the speech of high and of low. Similarly, in reading a Fielding novel, we find ourselves amused by the colorfully inappropriate—that is, non-standard—speech of yokels. The characters whom we are to take seriously, however, speak standard English. Even such unpromising heroes as Tom Jones and Joseph Andrews speak—and Joseph certainly writes—"well."

Franklin stays away from vernacular, perhaps in large part because he is aware of its potential for divisiveness. As a teen-aged printer's apprentice and thorn in the side of the Boston establishment, he had cleverly, and subversively, presented Silence Dogood's dream of Harvard College, with its slothful and dishonest scions of the upper classes.[20] Even then, with the example of Addison's *Spectator*-prose ever before him, he had maintained a gentlemanly elegance in his own excoriation of elegant young gentlemen. But Franklin knew well as an adult member of the governing elite that anything that would call attention to class differences, and thereby to a possible difference between the interests of classes, had best remain unnoticed. Franklin's straightforward, rational prose brings everyone into the theater of action under the premise that each person's choices and acts could have, if not equal, then significant consequences for the body politic.

One hundred years later, the gap between standard speech and vernacular had become so weighted with meanings of such variety that to ignore the commentary of levels of language upon character, as upon society, had become almost an impossibility. This gap embodied a number of social values, but the contrasts of immediate interest to us here are those between the hard-working and the lazy, the former considered as more "civilized," the latter as rudely unrefined. The contrast in language served to explicate a general contrast in aesthetic attitude toward life that in conventional terms at first may seem a contradiction: a sense of purpose and fulfillment in productive labor, or a sense of pleasure in contemplation of and participation in a process for its own sake. Readers of William Dean Howells's *The Rise of Silas Lapham* (1885), for example, will remember the persuasive but fictionally unusual case of Bromfield Corey, the Boston aesthete who contemplates everything and does nothing. In contrast to his civilized speech and unproductive ways

20. Number 4 of "The Dogood Papers," printed in his brother James's *New-England Courant*, reprinted in Franklin, *Autobiography*, ed. Ziff, 182–85.

stands coarse-grained Silas Lapham, with unacceptable grammar and a hard-working way of life. (Today we would call him a workaholic.)

The Silases make society possible; the Bromfields make it pleasant. Civilization demands both. Then Howells goes on to arrange for Silas's moral "rise" to bring an aesthetic pleasure to Bromfield Corey, just as he arranges for Corey's son Tom to combine both cultivation and hard work in expanding the paint business. The next generation will work hard and also appreciate the fruits of its labor in a more refined way than the crudities of the old Lapham house have suggested. But that will be then; this is now. Howells therefore also arranges for the speaker of vernacular, despite that moral rise, to return to the country, where he can give aesthetic pleasure to genteel society without offending its ears and eyes. Even so, readers could have had no trouble seeing that Silas, vernacular speech and all, cannot be said to represent a force in opposition to productive mainstream society.

Because Mark Twain remains the most interesting exploiter of the social implications of vernacular, let us return briefly to him. As auditor of Jim Blaine's memory-burdened non-story about "His Grandfather's Old Ram,"[21] Twain's narrator becomes the laughingstock of the initiated Westerners. "The tears were running down the boys' cheeks—they were suffocating with suppressed laughter—and had been from the start, though I had never known it. I perceived that I was 'sold.'" That is, as all but the narrator knew, Jim Blaine, when drunk enough to launch into the story in the first place, inevitably "maundered off" into irrelevancies. "What the thing was that happened to him and his grandfather's old ram is a dark mystery to this day, for nobody has ever yet found out." As with "The Celebrated . . ." (1865, 1867) or "The Notorious Jumping Frog of Calaveras County" (1875), Twain's speaker of standard English appears to want more than anything else to extract an articulable product from a vernacular informant. This naïve individual thinks that his purpose has social worth, genteel value. In the frog story, at "the request of a friend of mine, who wrote from the East," he is trying to find out about the Reverend Leonidas W. Smiley. The narrator's pedantically narrow intention, however, leads him to undervalue, indeed to miss totally, the delight in the sheer process of vernacular telling. "Good-natured, garrulous old Simon Wheeler," once reminded of "his infamous *Jim Smiley*," has nothing better in his infinite leisure to do than to "go to work and bore me nearly to death with some exasperating reminiscence of him as long and tedious as it should be useless to me."

That word "exasperating" is worth a moment's attention, for in the earlier (1865 and 1867) versions, when Twain perhaps had more difficulty

21. Mark Twain, *Roughing It* (1872), chap. 53.

noticing inadvertent descents to a way of speaking that had become part of his own western self, he had written "infernal," itself a euphemistic expression of participation in the western vernacular experience. Similarly, at the story's close, as Wheeler launches forth into yet one more "tedious" yarn, this one about Smiley's " 'yaller one-eyed cow that didn't have no tail, only jest a short stump like a bannanner,' " the 1867 narration concludes: " 'Oh! hang Smiley and his afflicted cow!' I muttered good-naturedly, and bidding the old gentleman good-day, I departed." But the ending of Twain's 1875 revision comes out much more in keeping with the mask of the irritated Easterner who has no empathy at all with Wheeler's unproductive way of telling: "However, lacking both time and inclination, I did not wait to hear about the afflicted cow, but took my leave." No longer "good-naturedly" tolerant of the "old gentleman," colloquially joining in the fun with the facetious wish to " 'hang' " both Smiley and the cow, Narrator has become a true stuffed shirt, too busy to waste any more "time," and too driven to allow himself any "inclination" toward sheer narrative pleasure. Something has happened. Nathaniel Ward's cobbler of Aggawam, Bishop Fleetwood's Curate of Salop, John Wise's farmer, and Benjamin Franklin's prostitute Polly may be vernacular characters, but they do not speak in the vernacular, or at least not very much. Wise, with his "swoppings" and direct reference to bastards, perhaps transgresses against the standards of the most polite eighteenth-century good taste, but not even he can be said to revel, much less to wallow, in the language of the uneducated. These voices from the people spoke their unvarnished good sense as a reminder to the more formally educated classes of what their own God-given reason was probably telling them already.

On the one hand, there remained something amusing simply in reading about a cobbler, a country curate, a farmer, or a prostitute: Thomas Hobbes, with his theory of laughter as a "sudden glory," a feeling of superiority over people or situations presented on the page or stage or street, would nod in agreement, as would partisans of various "incongruity" theories of humor. But on the other hand, these characters who have made their appearance so incongruously into socially sophisticated print culture have common sense on their side. They speak with a reasonableness that their society must condone. Although the cobbler blasts a king, and Polly questions her judges, and all of them find fault with specific actions and attitudes, they have not yet taken to criticizing their "betters" in any all-encompassing way. Just as Aristophanes put common sense into the mouths of "mere" women in his *Lysistrata* in order to emphasize the failure of male political leaders to recognize the necessity of waging peace, not war, so Ward, Wise, and Franklin use spokes-personae of a lesser respectability, a lesser social value, in order to sway the respect-worthy to adapt positions in keeping with what is truly respectable.

Almost at a stroke, with the invention of vernacular-speaking Simon Wheeler and the standard-speaking narrator of the "Jumping Frog" story, our man from Missouri has broken the pattern of underlying respect for respectability. Twain's pompous or obtuse narrators with genteel sensibilities and a total commitment to a materially constructive expenditure of time, and having little if any tolerance for or understanding of mere pleasure, communicate to readers the author's underlying criticism of the very society into which Sam Clemens (as well as many of his readers) was trying to fit. This kind of ambivalence twentieth-century readers take almost for granted. But if we look back to Polly Baker, or slightly ahead to Tom Sawyer in *Tom Sawyer Abroad* (1896), the waters deepen. Let us by all means dive in.

V

The Basis of Laughter
WHAT'S SO FUNNY?

1. HOW DO WE READ POLLY AND TOM?

Franklin aims Polly's speech at a number of targets with representatively eighteenth-century natures. Like so much American humor of the nineteenth century, particularly the humor of what has come to be called the Old Southwest, Franklin has a sharp eye for affectation, for the pretending to virtues, qualities, habits in order—as Henry Fielding put it in his "Author's Preface" to *Joseph Andrews* in 1742—either through vanity "to purchase applause" by "affecting false characters" or through hypocrisy to "endeavour to avoid censure, by concealing our vices under an appearance of their opposite virtues." The young man, now a judge, who seduced Polly under promise of marriage is Franklin's ethical villain, his infamy understated but apparent to all readers. Whether the readers will take his case to heart is another story, but the blow against affectation seems directly given, unambiguous, sharp, powerful, and memorable because the reader, not Polly, forms the judgment. Polly's rational evaluation of fornication, and the resultant bastardy, in the context of "a new country that really wants people," turns out to be more difficult to explicate with certainty.

Even though I shall be arguing that behind the eighteenth-century issue of affectation, actually embedded in it, lies the assumption of an unambiguously knowable moral reality, I shall also be insisting that the idealizing assumptions of what George Santayana was to call the genteel

137

tradition work to smooth over the ambiguities and uncertainties that give to the writings of a Ben Franklin, a Jonathan Swift, the richness that makes them continuously rewarding. The element of mystery, of human and social complexity, whether in the frontier writings of a Thomas Bangs Thorpe or in the twentieth-century version of a lost frontier by F. Scott Fitzgerald, aligns some seemingly ill-sorted mavericks. If one thinks about the issues carefully enough, one could make a strong case, e.g., for including nitty-gritty, apparently anti-idealist Ernest Hemingway among the purveyors of a new genteel tradition. The idea so often determines the event in his work that he might well be seen as a latter-day Josiah Holland. But that will be a safari for another day. I want now to get back to how humor works, to some of what it accomplishes, and to how it can be both comforting and subversive.

Most simply, does one read Franklin as proceeding in the tradition of Jonathan Swift and the last book of *Gulliver's Travels*, wherein the Houy-hnhnms, totally rational as they are, mean something quite different to Gulliver from what Swift makes them mean to an eighteenth-century (or to a very careful twentieth-century) reader? The Houyhnhnms, after all, in their utter incapacity to comprehend human emotion, and in their consequent inability to make any sense out of such elements of Christian belief as Lemuel Gulliver can inform them of, remain, despite Gulliver's delight in their attractive reasonableness, monsters totally lacking in both religious feeling and every other variety of human sensibility. That they still manage to do as comparatively well, morally, as they do without the leavening of Christianity simply casts even harsher opprobrium upon European humanity, who ought to be so much better than they (we) are because of the incentives offered by the Christian religion. Where Gulliver uncritically approves, we censure.

When Polly so colorlessly and coldly refers to the "natural and useful actions" that only the law's "prohibitions" have turned into "crimes," one can (as a follower of D. H. Lawrence might) sigh over the betrayal of passion by reason, and see Franklin's target as the emerging ratio-nalism of the era. Or one can, as Lawrence no doubt would have done, simply equate Ben with Polly and find him participating in, rather than attacking, such rationalism. Or one can equate the practical perspective of a Poor Richard with Franklin's own—and I find much evidence allowing one to do so—and enjoy Franklin's attack on the inequities and irrationalities of an archaic legalism that sanctions needless human suffering in the name of religion and in the cause of propriety. All of these readings have been made; each offers a specific interpretation of social reality. Whatever Franklin intended, each sanctions an attitude toward a clear interpretation of an equally clear account of—or assumption about—that reality. Several of them certainly contradict each other and complicate a modern reader's response. E.g., if the betrayal of passion by mere consciousness is the target, then passionate, even if judicial, commitment to religious truths may justify Polly's punishments. It does, however, seem unlikely that this would have been an eighteenth-century response.

Still, we have no reason to believe that Franklin's first readers were at all confused. Perhaps some put an emphasis on the appeal of Polly's reasonableness and its attack on archaic legalism, while others focused on the hypocrisy of her first lover or on the ludicrousness of pretending that children and sexuality could have no affect connected with them. Just as probably, the attack on the double sexual standard of the time—and of so much time before and after—caught the readers' eyes. I want to use the existence of these various readings, or emphases, to illuminate the contrast with a particular episode concerning the old Arabian Nights tale of a flying horse almost at the end of *Tom Sawyer Abroad*. Twain's early practice, as in the "Jumping Frog" story, will also be useful to keep in mind.

Although the essentially pot-boiling later work, which Twain seems simply to have stopped rather than concluded, might better have been titled "The Intellectuals Aloft," most of the time Tom simply dominates Huck and Jim. Because Huck tells the story, the quality of Tom's speech often remains somewhat in doubt. Tom speaks in the vernacular, but his voice also comes close to standard much of the time. Occasionally, Tom even speaks quite proper standard American English. Huck and Jim always speak vernacular. As befits traditional vernacular characters, they are ignorant. They have various other "traditionally" vernacular traits, too: they lack respect for law and order, as implied by their willingness to evade the protectionist duty on sand from the Sahara Desert; they respect large numbers, as in the area of the desert and the number of times a flea can jump its own length in a second—without considering the political or intellectual "importance" (Tom's word) of entities. Finally, they are extremely superstitious, not only in the matter of human ghosts but also about the ghost of what to them is a long-dead, and therefore supernatural, lake, but to Tom (and the reader) a perfectly natural, however immaterial, mirage.

At times, they show intellectual curiosity; but mostly they reveal a desire to win an argument, to get the better of Tom, rather than to get at "truth." Their response to the stories that Tom tells might seem at first simply to represent a reversal of the situation in the "Jumping Frog" and *Roughing It*, especially because the stories come after a number of episodes in which they have shown themselves to be inferior to Tom in appreciation as well as in understanding. Rather than the pleasures of aesthetic experience, for example, they cannot rise above a cash nexus when it comes to appreciating what it is that painters do. Although Jim does the talking in this particular encounter, Huck agrees with him, observing, when "Tom lost his temper[:] I notice a person 'most always does that's been laid out in an argument" (chapter 3). Jim's point has been that he knows, and Tom does not, " 'what chuckleheads dem painters is,' " with specific reference to one who has told Jim that a picture of Hank Wilson's cow will be worth one hundred dollars. " 'Mars Tom, he could a got de cow fer fifteen, en I *tole* him so. Well, sah, if you'll b'lieve me, he jes' shuck his head, dat painter did, en went on a-dobbin'. Bless you, Mars Tom, *dey* don't know nothin'.' "

Tom has invoked the ways of artists in a futile effort to explain to Huck and Jim why it is that maps do not lie when they show Illinois as green and Indiana as pink, even though from the balloon both look the same color. But Huck—with, in this early part of the "discussion," Jim's simple concurrence—insists that maps do indeed tell lies, for " 'if they don't, there ain't no two States the same color. You git around *that*, if you can, Tom Sawyer.' " There follows a page-and-a-half of Huck's glorying over his intellectual triumph—"I never felt so good in my life," and so on—while the reader, as happens so often in the course of the story, laughs at Huck (and at Jim), and shares Tom's, and undoubtedly Twain's, frustration over the ignorant self-satisfaction of what H. L. Mencken would soon be calling the *Boobus Americanus*. Twain, it would seem, has retreated into the eighteenth century.

Although Huck and Jim, at least in this case, reject the pleasures of art for the immediate practicalities of experienced reality, preferably with a price tag, we notice that Tom himself does not quite qualify as a champion of aesthetic enjoyment. Over and over, he uses the materials of art— analogy, metaphor—for the purposes of logical disputation. Here and in the subsequent "Tom Sawyer, Detective," Twain does a considerable amount of retracing his steps from *Adventures of Huckleberry Finn*: Tom, in the earlier book Twain's representative of a corrupt, sensation-seeking, hypocritical society, now becomes increasingly admirable as a clear-headed, competent, essentially honorable lad. Nevertheless, just beneath the presentation of Tom as the praiseworthy pragmatist who uses his information and his intelligence to solve problems, even to save lives, a great deal of the familiar Tom remains. Not only is he still the seeker after personal glory and "reputation," no matter who gets hurt in the process of acquiring them, Tom's concern for practical results, for product, puts him finally, surprisingly, in the same camp as Twain's naïve and genteel narrator of the "Jumping Frog." The difference would seem to be that Twain shows a good deal more sympathy with this side of Tom in 1896 than he did with the first-person relater of Simon Wheeler's yarns about Jim Smiley thirty-one, and especially twenty-one, years earlier, as my previous discussion of Twain's revisions of the story suggests.

Specifically, Twain had seemed to share Huck's mockery of Tom's Arabian Nights at the start of *Adventures of Huckleberry Finn*. Here, however, Twain-as-author seems to have switched sides. "Tom said we was right in the midst of the Arabian Nights now" (chapter 7), and proceeds to tell Jim and Huck a story about an encounter between a man walking over the desert and a camel-driver in search of his camel. On the basis of Sherlock Holmes-like observation, the man describes the camel in considerable detail, including its blind left eye, lame hind leg, missing tooth, and specific load—" 'the ants told me that' "—concluding, " 'I know all about your camel, but I hain't seen him.' "

Both Jim and Huck express their involvement, but not of the sort that Tom intended: " 'Go on, Mars Tom, hit's a mighty good tale, and powerful interestin',' " prompts Jim. And then he wants to know what became of the camel. When Tom confesses to ignorance on that score, Jim concludes that it's " 'de beatenes' tale' " he ever struck: it gets to the place " 'whah de intrust is gittin' red-hot, en down she breaks.' " When Tom turns to appeal to Huck, Huck agrees and has to say "that as long as the tale stopped square in the middle and never got no place, it really warn't worth the trouble to tell." Tom's reaction to their rejection of the story surprises Huck: " 'stead of being mad, . . . he seemed to be only sad; and he says: 'Some people can see, and some can't—just as that man said. Let alone a camel, if a cyclone had gone by, *you* duffers wouldn't 'a' noticed the track.' " Huck concludes that this response is "just one of his irrulevances, I reckon." They'd "spotted the soft place in that tale sharp enough, he couldn't git away from that little fact. It graveled him like the nation, too, I reckon, much as he tried not to let on."

Poor Tom has had to put up with a curious blend of intellectual competition and ignorance from his two companions. His occasional impatient rages seem very much like the sort of response frequently attributed to Mark Twain himself, as when Huck wonders how Tom can possibly " 'ask such a jackass question' " as " 'is the sun standing still?' " Huck knows, and confidently proclaims, that " 'Anybody that ain't blind can see it don't stand still.' " Tom has been trying to get across the point that just seeing something does not necessarily demonstrate the validity of one's interpretation of what one has seen. " 'There used to be forty thousand million people that seen the sun move from one side of the sky to the other every day. Did that prove that the sun *done* it?' " So far as Huck and Jim are concerned, the obvious answer is obviously correct. " 'Well,' [Tom] says, 'I'm lost in the sky with no company but a passel of low-down animals that don't know no more than the head boss of a university did three or four hundred years ago' " (chapter 8).

In his exasperation at the ignorance of his companions, Tom's language becomes almost vitriolic. Trying, and failing, to get across the idea of metaphor leads Tom to explode: " 'Do you want to drive me crazy? Keep still. . . . Oh, give us a rest! You can't get the simplest little thing through your thick skull. Now don't bother me any more' " (chapter 5). "Tom lost his temper. . . . He told us to shut up, and maybe we'd feel better" (chapter 3). From high up in the balloon, Tom spots a caravan of camels, but Huck, after looking through the spyglass, is disappointed: " 'Camels your granny; they're spiders.' " " 'Spiders in a desert, you shad? Spiders walking in a procession? You don't ever reflect, Huck Finn, and I reckon you really haven't got anything to reflect *with*' " (chapter 6).

The ignorance that Twain attributes to Huck and Jim at times approaches the unbelievable. Even so, its effect is to put most readers squarely on the side of Tom against the great unwashed, a feeling that Twain no doubt shared. But on the other hand, Twain's commitment to Tom often wavers. When Tom and Huck leave Jim on the Sphinx, "with an American flag to protect him," and "sail off to this and that and t'other distance, to git what Tom called effects and perspectives and proportions" (chapter 12), Tom identifies as "bugs" what turn out to be men and horses, guns and ladders. Back they speed to rescue Jim, but Twain has created for Tom the same sort of error for which Tom earlier condemned Huck. When Tom tells the story of the camel-driver's encounter with the observant man, his own interest in the story is at best one-dimensional. Its moral, its point, its product, blots out, for Tom, any possibility of narrative pleasure for its own sake. And the last three pages of chapter 12, once more pitting Tom against Huck and Jim in intellectual combat, either make clear that Tom knows neither himself nor what he's talking about, or—at the very least—reduce Tom to the level of Huck and Jim. Earlier, the two ignoramuses had valued cash and rejected art. Here, pragmatic Tom values the product of modern engineering and rejects the delights of a creative imagination.

The episode itself is far simpler than my explication may make it seem: Tom tells the Arabian Nights story of the flying horse whose movements the prince controls by manipulating a peg. Huck and Jim don't believe it. Tom waxes indignant when Huck suggests, " 'Tom Sawyer, *you* don't believe that, yourself.' " Tom, not for one minute acknowledging that the story is a story, a fiction, pleasurable for its own sake, insists that " 'there ain't an atom of difference' " between the buttons that control the balloon and the peg that controlled the horse because " 'the principle is the same in both.' " Were Twain here indulging in a bit of twentieth-century metafiction—and perhaps he is, although I doubt it—the "principle" would indeed be "the same in both": both Twain's balloon and Scheherazade's horse do fly on wings of human imagination. But this would seem not to be what Tom means; and, in any case, Huck doesn't buy it. He wants to ask Tom some questions, "and I see Jim chirk up to listen": the intellectuals aloft then engage in their final argument, with Jim the supportive audience for Huck's Socratic maneuvers. At the end of the argument, and of the chapter, "Jim was so full of laugh he got to strangling"; "Tom was that mad . . . that all he could manage to say was that whenever he heard me and Jim try to argue it made him ashamed of the human race"; and Huck, "feeling pretty well satisfied," says nothing more, "for I consider that if I was in his [Tom's] place I wouldn't wish him to crow over me. It's better to be generous, that's what I think."

Once again, Tom has taken the position of the smugly genteel narrator in Twain's early accounts of the West: no significant pleasure resides in a story told for its own sake; moral or intellectual or, at the very least, factual profit alone legitimates narration. Although the last chapter ends by reestablishing Tom as competent leader—he plots out the course for the balloon to take so that Jim and their hired guide can go back to St. Petersburg for Tom's spare pipe—the damage has been done. Even in the last chapter itself, before Tom's navigational expertise emerges, we have had both Tom's explanation that a Moslem "was a person that wasn't a Presbyterian," leading Huck to infer that "there's plenty of them in Missouri, though I didn't know it before," and Huck's eulogy to Tom's Falstaffian "instink" that gives Tom the ability unerringly to pick up the one remaining brick of a house celebrated in the Arabian Nights. "I know he done it," says Huck, "because I see him do it."

Huck's gullibility shares the stage with Tom's self-aggrandizement: what in truth does Twain want us to make of Tom? Of Huck? What is the basis for our laughter? Whatever it may be, we—along with Twain's first readers—find ourselves dealing with a reality far less neatly defined than that behind Polly Baker's "Speech." Twain has moved from an "objective" view of the external world and into the far less certifiable provinces of the interior. In doing this, he was departing from, not continuing, the traditions of his predecessors of the Old Southwest.

2. Affectation, Again — and Certainty

I do not intend to have yet another go at trying to explain why people laugh, why they find funny the odd or common things that provoke laughter. The impossibly long bibliography on this fascinating subject needs no addition. By way of summary—very incomplete summary— books by John Morreall and Norman N. Holland deserve special attention: the first efficiently digests the principal theories traditionally expounded, especially those having to do with the laugher's senses of superiority (Hobbes's "sudden glory"), of incongruity, and of relief, whether conscious or unconscious; the second develops a way of thinking about those individually subjective responses that lie behind what Professor Holland thinks of as the laugher's sudden recognition, or discovery, of self in the external cause of the laughter. Each proposed theory has its merits. Almost any laughable tale can be shown to fit each of these paradigms that accounts for a reader's amusement. The feelings and recognitions set loose within the individual reader's psyche do seem potentially useful toward that individual's self-knowledge, and a perceptive psychiatrist could undoubtedly draw interesting conclusions about the underlying state of a population's communal mind from a study of what that mind finds amusing.

My present interest is simpler, more obvious, and literary. I want to look at what it is that readers were smiling over in some of the works to which I've already referred, and at some of the social norms implied by—that is, in a way causing—the smiling. Rather than concerning myself with the interior perceptions or sensations of incongruity, superiority, relief, and self-recognition, I am trying to infer some of the assumptions that gave what seemed at the time to be coherence or meaning to the materials in the external world. As I mentioned at the very start of this chapter, and have shown at some length elsewhere,[1] affectation, in Henry Fielding's eighteenth-century sense of the term, underlies a great deal of the humor coming out of the Old Southwest. This region, geographically fluid over time, offered immense literary opportunities to the educated editors, lawyers, doctors, bankers, and other literate newcomers from the East as they reported on the odd behavior, and ways of life, suddenly before their eyes, under their feet, and in their ears. Although these authors were nineteenth-century Americans, they seem to have seen through eyes attuned to an eighteenth-century British way of looking.

At least three impulses run through the works often collected under the rubric of the region: the reportorial, the political or social, and the envious.[2] The reportorial seems self-evident: all this strange behavior is "news" simply because it's strange; it's "strange" because it differs from what the writer has been accustomed to. The impulse to share the newly encountered with the people back home—an impulse older than Xenophon and *The March of the Ten Thousand*—informs the pieces written from the new lands for publication in journals and collections in the East, most notably in William Trotter Porter's *The Spirit of the Times* in New York City, 1831–1861. With this urge to share often came the urge

    1. Covici, chap. 1 of *Mark Twain's Humor: The Image of a World*, reprinted in Inge, *The Frontier Humorists: Critical Views*, 233–58, and in Sloane, *Mark Twain's Humor: Critical Essays*, 51–83.
    2. See, inter alia, Hennig Cohen and William B. Dillingham, eds., *The Humor of the Old Southwest*.

to evaluate: the behaviors they witnessed often struck the observers as not only new but also boorish. Sometimes with explicit political—that is to say, Whig—leanings, sometimes with broader social concerns, the writers seem to have wanted their readers to understand just how much of an affront to the feelings and expectations of decent human beings life in the backwoods could be. But one finds shocking only what matches something buried deep within one's self, so it should not surprise us that a tone of wistful longing often creeps into the accounts of, and responses to, Simon Suggs's successful swindles, Sut Lovingood's offenses against decency, and Huck Finn's idle and ungrammatical rafting-rapture.

With the exception of Thoreau's insight into the shocked response of many readers to the poetry of Walt Whitman,[3] this last element appears to have escaped comment until well into the twentieth century. What seems likely to have been the reaction of early readers? What did authors do to encourage the responses they wanted? However we may read the tales of a century-and-a-half ago, Henry Fielding's eighteenth-century formulation describes pretty well the efforts of early nineteenth-century Americans, with values and attitudes rooted in the East, to present their experience of the Old Southwest. When Johnson J. Hooper's Simon Suggs pretends to a religious conversion in order to pick the collective pocket of a camp meeting, he succeeds in large part because those who contribute to his appeal for money with which " 'to start a little 'sociation close to' " where he lives pretend to a pious generosity that they do not have. On the point of leaving, they respond to the "insinuation" behind Simon's bland plea that " 'ef you ain't able to afford any thing, jist give us your blessin' and it'll be all the same!' " Hooper tells us that because Simon has stirred up "the pride of purse of the congregation," appealing to their competitive, though not to their Christian, impulses, he succeeds in collecting "a very handsome sum . . . in a very short time."

Earlier, Simon has prepared the way for ministerial backing of his enterprise by singling out as the agent of his conversion

> the reverend gentleman . . . who Simon was convinced was the "big dog of the tanyard". . . . "*I-I-I* can bring 'em!" cried the preacher alluded to, in a tone of exultation—"Lord thou knows ef thy servant can't stir 'em up, nobody else needn't try—but the glory aint mine! I'm a poor worrum of the dust," he added, with ill-managed affectation.

Whether in "lavishing caresses" upon only the attractive young women or in claiming credit for what he ought to perceive as God's

---

3. "A writer can communicate to us no experience [that we have not imagined for ourselves], and if we are shocked, whose experience is it that we are reminded of?" (Thoreau, "Letter to Harrison Blake.")

grace, each minister affects a piety that he does not possess. Members of the congregation, described at some length by Hooper, pretend not only to pious generosity but even to piety itself, an affectation that Hooper seems to delight in exposing. Pretending to virtues that they either lack or else have to a much smaller degree than they try to suggest, they lose their money because they want to be thought well of by their neighbors. As Henry Fielding would put it, they affect false characters in order to purchase applause. Simon, on the other hand, pretends in order to gain cash. He shapes his appearance to the measure of his audience because he values their money for his pocket's sake, not their good opinion for the sake of his ego. Also, there is no question of his lying to himself about his attitudes, however much he lies to others. As witness to the selective attentions of amorous ministers, Simon understands perfectly: " 'Well! who blames 'em? Nater will be nater, all the world over; and I judge ef I was a preacher, I should save the purtiest souls fust, myself!' " Human nature is to be accepted, not railed at; at the same time, it is to be exploited: this is the working attitude of Simon Suggs.

Johnson J. Hooper, however, has a different agenda, at least so far as his stories communicate his conscious intentions. Hooper addresses his readers confidently, as if secure in the knowledge that they share his view of what constitutes acceptable behavior and what does not. The "huge, greasy negro woman" who, "in a fit of the jerks," squashes flat "a diminutive old man" and the "delicate woman in that hysterical condition . . . termed 'the holy laugh,' . . . with a maniac's chuckle," represent perversions of the religious impulse and also of what has social acceptability. Delicacy befits respectable womanhood; hysteria does not. "Huge, greasy" women, especially if black, by their very adjectives exclude themselves from respectable nineteenth-century society. Hooper presents their vulgarity—"the holy laugh" appears within quotation-marks—to call into question their piety. Lest some readers miss the point, Hooper even adds a footnote to the effect that he intends "no disrespect . . . to any denomination of Christians." Asserting "that camp-meetings are not peculiar to any church, though most usual in the Methodist," he goes on to call the latter "a denomination whose respectability in Alabama is attested by the fact, that *very many* of its worthy clergymen and lay members, hold honourable and profitable offices in the gift of the state legislature; of which, indeed, almost a controlling portion are themselves Methodists." Hooper can assert whatever he pleases, knowing that his irony will communicate what he means and not what it only seems to say. Real respectability, he expects all of his readers to agree, cannot have anything to do with the Methodists of an earlier Alabama, whether in their secular or in their religious exercises.

Similarly, George Washington Harris expects his readers to enjoy the outrageous behavior of Sut Lovingood, but he also assumes that their sympathies will be with the affronted "George" when Sut asks, " 'How would you feel if I went to your church pew dressed like that?' " and George answers, " 'I'd shoot you dead.' " As I have already suggested in Chapter I, the pleasure we are to take from Sut's vernacular telling of his stories is the pleasure of *carnival*, of vacation, of play; it has nothing to do with any suggestion that respectable society fails in a serious way to nurture adequately the totality of the human spirit. Even twentieth-century readers, with assumptions far less genteel than those of the readers who first met Sut, cannot mistake Harris's assumption of superiority to his "natural born durned fool." About to relate one of his more outrageous escapades, Sut asks: " 'Say, George, much talk 'bout this fuss up whar yo're been?' For the sake of a joke I said yes, a great deal."[4] Condescendingly, "George" humors Sut in his delusions of importance, and we readers snuggle down for a titillating glimpse of raw impulses turned loose, impulses to which we ourselves, of course, share Harris's superiority. Although our own twentieth-century sympathies may well be more involved with Harris's vernacular creation than Harris himself could have anticipated, we cannot mistake Harris's own horrified fascination with, and ultimate (conscious) condemnation of, Sut's perverse sadism. Author and reader share a sense of what is right and proper.

This shared sense characterizes the fictive world of Henry Fielding and the satirical worlds of Nathaniel Ward and of John Wise. These are worlds in which objective truth exists for all to see. However great the recalcitrance of individual human beings, the world itself, the reality in which people operate and that they must interpret, turns out to be something about the rights and wrongs of which people of good sense can pretty much agree. Each of us can have direct apprehension of the moral truth. In his dictation for Tuesday, January 23, 1906, Mark Twain inserted into his *Autobiography* a piece written twenty-two years earlier (when he was finishing *Adventures of Huckleberry Finn*) in which he discusses "certain sweet-smelling sugar-coated lies current in the world." Among them, and of considerable interest to Twain (and to us in the present context), is the lie "that conscience, man's moral medicine chest, is not only created by the Creator, but is put into man ready charged with the right and only true and authentic correctives of conduct—and the duplicate chest, with the self-same correctives, unchanged, unmodified, distributed to all nations and all epochs."[5]

---

4. Harris, "Parson John Bullen's Lizards," in *Sut Lovingood*.
5. *Mark Twain's Autobiography*, 2: 8–9.

With his usual perspicuity, Twain was noting the assumptions of the people with whom he had grown up, even of the people among whom he lived, and certainly of the majority of human beings who enjoyed the works of Henry Fielding and of Fielding's early nineteenth-century heirs. When we laugh at affectation, "the only source of the true ridiculous" to Fielding, we laugh not only because we know exactly what constitutes appropriate, socially approved behavior, but also because we read as insiders who share an unquestioned standard. When people behave in an affected manner, when they are guilty of affectation and therefore have become legitimate targets for our laughter, they acknowledge that the standards against which we measure them are appropriate standards, correct standards, legitimate standards, the only standards that count. Otherwise, they would not bother to try to appear to be measuring up. Affectation, by its very nature, affirms what it seeks to emulate.

Without repeating a great deal that has already been said elsewhere, I take as established the assertion that much of the humor of the Old Southwest depended for its effect upon the reader's amusement at affected behavior. At the same time, important distinctions need to be drawn when we look closely at the humor of particular writers; Sut Lovingood's adventures elicit deeper and more complex responses than those of Simon Suggs. Both adventurers, however, show up the foibles of the affected; Harris's Parson Bullen and Hooper's Bugg (and anonymous others) pretend an adherence to approved patterns of behavior from which they are shown to deviate. Readers chuckle over their undoing and withhold sympathy.

Simon and Sut, however, cannot legitimately be seen as equivalent forces. Although Hooper gave Simon the unforgettable aphorism, "It's good to be shifty in a new country," Simon remains primarily (not exclusively) a mechanical creation, usually triggered into action by greed, on occasion by the desire to dominate. He suppresses, perhaps represses, his bodily desires in the interests of money or power, although even these words suggest a more deeply imagined character than Hooper usually manages to create. The reader's enjoyment of the stories lies not in reveling in Simon's successes or sympathizing with him in his occasional failure. Rather, because his victims seem even less attractive than he himself does, one somewhat smugly approves their downfall without exactly approving of Simon's triumph.

In this connection, commentators note that Hooper objected to being referred to as "Simon Suggs."[6] Taking the form of a campaign

6. W. Stanley Hoole, *Alias Simon Suggs: The Life and Times of Johnson Jones Hooper*, 102–3. Also see M. Thomas Inge, *High Times and Hard Times*.

biography—for the worthy captain will most probably soon be a candidate for office, and Hooper feels "bound in *honor* to furnish the Suggs party with such information respecting himself, as will enable them to vindicate his character whenever and wherever it may be attacked by the ruthless and polluted tongues of Captain Simon Suggs' enemies"[7]— his book opens with unflattering reference to the "'counterfeit presentiment'" of two recent Democratic Party presidential candidates, Martin Van Buren of the "foxy smile" and "'Major General Andrew Jackson,'" whose lithograph will be used to frighten "future generations of naughty children" into their beds, "their mammas" presenting it to them as "a faithful representation of the Evil One—an atrocious slander, by the bye, on the potent, and comparatively well-favoured, prince of the infernal world." Hooper's social sympathies seem in harmony with his politics: the roughnecks of the frontier, whether Simon's victims or Simon himself, represent behavior worth laughing at, worth keeping at an emotional distance, and worth condemning. No subversion that I can see lurks below the surface of the text.

Yet, by the mere act of writing vernacular humor, Hooper, as his biographer of 1872 made clear,[8] forfeited "the respect of men," or, anyway, of some men whose respect he coveted. We may take this with a reasonable amount of salted reservation, considering that, at the time of his death in 1862, Hooper was secretary to the Provisional Confederate Congress. Still, the general attitude of the leaders and representatives of mainstream American nineteenth-century culture, as demonstrated by its brutal effect on Mark Twain following his vernacular extravagance at the *Atlantic* dinner of 1877, saw in the vernacular nothing with which respectable people might care to identify themselves. Hooper's vernacular persistently provides a contrast between the qualities of the characters who use it and those of the educated, standard-writing narrator who reports, with repeatedly noted disapproval, the escapades in which those low characters find themselves.

George Washington Harris, on the other hand, seems to have had no objection to being called "Sut Lovingood." Professor Inge notes that by 1858, Harris "had become identified with him to such an extent that he used the name as a pen name and was called 'Sut' by his friends."[9] Not that Harris was any less the representative of propriety in his own life than was Hooper: a recent biographer suggests that "a sense of social separation from the 'lower orders,' reinforced by strict Presbyterian upbringing, had already [by the age of 19, in 1833] produced a reserved,

7. Hooper, *Some Adventures of Captain Simon Suggs*, chap. 1.
8. Blair, *Native American Humor, 1800–1900*, introduction, 108–9.
9. Inge, *High Times and Hard Times*, 41.

sedate, rather formal character," perfectly in keeping with Harris's self of three years later, who already "was making long-range plans for genteel living."[10] "George's" reaction to the hypothetical appearance in his sedate Presbyterian pew of a scandalously attired Sut seems close enough to what one might expect of the real George W. Harris for it to stand as autobiography. Unlike Hooper, however, Harris had the need, and developed the ability, to bring to life the gusto and vitality, the cynicism and shame, of the infantile facets of Sut. Because these lurk within all human beings, even readers who found Sut's yarns disgusting also found them fascinating.

3. DISGUST AND GENTILITY

Although readers of Harris have fairly to wallow in the underworld that Sut inhabits; and even though in at least one story—"Eaves-Dropping a Lodge of Masons," referred to in my Chapter I—Harris sets up the language of super-refined gentility to receive not only Sut's but the reader's scorn; and although in several places Harris presents with extremely plausible sympathy Sut's condemnation of the sentimental excesses of Longfellow's "Excelsior"; and despite the fact that a list of examples of an anti-genteel perspective in Harris's work could be stretched to considerable length: still, even modern readers of Sut's adventures find his world repulsive. Certainly the delight that we today take in Sut's doings, and certainly the similar delight taken by Harris's contemporaries, suggests no seriously held wish to relinquish civilization, however constricting and demanding, for the libidinal jungle that is Sut's experience. But Harris did make vivid the fascination of that jungle. Harris further differs from Hooper in that he finally eliminated the voice of the educated speaker from his character's tales. By doing so, he gave weight to the vernacular, and to the vernacular world, to a far greater extent than had been done previously. But, as if to counter this emphasis, his presentation of that world, especially in combination with his vernacular character's difficulties in coping with any world at all, can make the modern reader, however fascinated, extremely queasy. Edmund Wilson, the most prestigious critic to comment on poor old Sut and poor dead Harris, put the matter this way:

> One of the most striking things about *Sut Lovingood* is that it is all as offensive as possible. It takes a pretty strong stomach nowadays—when so much of the disgusting in our fiction is not rural but urban or suburban— to get through it. . . . I should say that, as far as my experience goes, it

10. Rickels, *George Washington Harris,* 21, 22.

is by far the most repellent book of any real literary merit in American literature.[11]

Wilson's overreaction does not change the fact, perhaps even makes it more apparent, that the effect of Harris's work was to strengthen the grip upon readers' minds and hearts of the relatively safe, relatively known world that propriety offered. And the world of propriety was indeed a knowable world. Although some of the inhabitants of the Tennessee backwoods whom Sut most discomforts are those who in one way or another would interfere with his taste for barbaric freedom, many turn out to be hypocrites, guilty of precisely the sorts of affectation that Henry Fielding found so damning and so amusingly ridiculous. Although "reverence"—in Josiah Holland's sense of the term—seems an odd word to use in connection with the writings of any of the humorists of the Old Southwest, and perhaps especially so in thinking about Harris and his Sut, this humor often, even mostly, reinforces the claims of the conventionally suppressive and repressive society whose ways Sut and the others so pointedly flout. A quick look at one more of the "Yarns Spun by a 'Nat'ral Born Durn'd Fool' " will show just how radically respectable Harris's fiction can be, despite its violence and apparent disrespect for law and order.

"Trapping a Sheriff" concerns a gruesome revenge taken against the adulterous Sheriff Doltin by the cuckolded Wat Mastin, along with Wirt Staples (Wat's rip-roaring cousin), Wirt's wife, and Sut. The planning and execution of the terrible things that happen to Doltin form the framework of the story, and the descriptions of Doltin's sufferings comprise about half of its actual content. A surprisingly large portion of its language, however, celebrates three sorts of preoccupations close to the hearts of readers of the genteelly idealizing fiction of the day. First, Doltin's wife, dying of tuberculosis, elicits from Sut a most poetic description, including the angelic nature of her smile, which, Sut expects, "will go back up wif her when she starts home, whar hit mus' a-cum from." Contemplating Mr. and Mrs. Doltin, Sut finds himself absolutely committed to the existence of a hereafter. "Yes, *two* herearters, by golly. . . ." Sut's description of the hell that he wishes for Doltin has a vividness that most ministers could not have equaled, but the idea itself is precisely in keeping with George Washington Harris's reputation as "an old Blue," a kind of Presbyterian, Milton Rickels informs us, "notable for the strictness of his life at a time when the ordinary Presbyterian Sabbath meant morning

11. Edmund Wilson, *Patriotic Gore: Studies in the Literature of the American Civil War*, 509.

and afternoon church services—the prayers long; the sermons, dry and logical."[12]

In addition to the sentimental portrayal of Mrs. Doltin as an angelic forerunner of Emmeline Grangerford, so congruent with Sut's confirmation of traditional notions of heaven and hell, Harris presents both a rapturous celebration of true marriage and a traditional warning to sinners to mend their ways. The experience Doltin has suffered drives him into joining the church; parts of Sut's share in the revenge include pretending to be the voice of the Devil for the terrification and edification of both Doltin and Mary Mastin. That they respond as they do testifies, to be sure, to their superstitious dread; in context, however, one sees Sut as using the rhetoric of belief not simply to add to his own fun but also to try to engineer the reformation of people whose behavior has violated the sanctity of marriage. (The references to "sly courtin'" and "rar ripe garden-seed" have to do with Doltin's adultery with Mary Mastin.)

> "I put my han[s] roun my mouf, an' bellered thru 'em in the mos' doleful way yu ever hearn, frum the thicket—
> " 'Margarit Mastin, the lawful wife ove Watson Mastin, the blacksmith, prepar tu go down whar thar's no sly courtin', nur rar ripe garden-seed. Margarit, thar's rath tu cum, yer crap's laid by, prepar,' an I groaned.
> "She arched her naik, an' tuck a wild blazin look over at the thicket, like she wer studyin 'bout sumthin, an' sez she, short an' vigrus—
> " 'Durn my soul ef I go a step,' an' jis busted thru the standin corn like a runaway hoss. Thinks I, that ar blade will never git religun frum a skeer."

Sheriff Doltin, after his own, more extensive, "skeer" and considerable physical pain, may have learned something. Sut's suggestion that this is the case ends, as does the story, with Sut's retreat from any shadow of propriety:

> "George, them ar tom-cats mus' a-scratched into his conshuns afore they died, fur he jined church jis' es soon he got abil tu walk thar. Hits strange, haint hit? In ole times I hearn tell they hed cities what fellers run tu, an wer safe arter they'd dun sum pow'ful devilmint."
> "Yes, Sut; cities of refuge."
> "Well, durn my rags ef gittin ove religun ain't the city ove rayfuge now-a-days; yu jis' let a raskil git hissef cotch, an' maul'd, fur his dam meanness, an' he jines church jis' es soon es he kin straitch his face long enuf tu fill the pius standurd, an' that's eighteen inches fur lean peopil, an' fourteen fur fat ones. I hes a city ove rayfuge myself, what I allers keeps along wif me," and Sut looked down proudly and fondly at his legs.

But before helping Doltin to a place in the church that he himself will never know, Sut basks in the genteel bliss of dinner with the Stapleses. His

---

12. Rickels, *George Washington Harris*, 27.

appreciative description of the material and spiritual blessings evident in the home of Wirt and Sally Staples leads him to conclude that an accurate picture of Sally's devoted expression and the accompanying dinner table could "make more men hongry, an' hot to marry, a-lookin' at hit in one week, nor ever ole Whitfield convarted in his hole life; back-sliders, hip-percrits, an' all, I don't keer a durn." Harris here, and over and over again, presents the odd-seeming circumstances of Sut's simultaneous rejection of civilized norms of behavior and support for some of the central ideals of genteel culture. Harris has Sut almost literally gild the lily:

> Es we sot down, the las' glimmers ove the sun crep thru the histed winder, an' flutter'd on the white tabil-cloth an' play'd a silver shine on her smoof black har, es she sot at the head ove the tabil, a-pourin out the coffee, wif her sleeves push'd tight back on her white roun' arm; her full throbbin neck wer bar to the swell ove her shoulders, an' the steam ove the coffee made a movin vail afore her face, es she slowy brush'd hit away wif hur lef' han', a-smilin an' a-flashin hur talkin eyes lovinly at her hansum husbun.

Here Harris employs the vernacular for an effect very like that of James Russell Lowell's in "The Courtin'," making us smile condescendingly, as well as appreciatively, at the simple bliss of simple people. Notice that although Sut's appreciation of the coffee, as of other drinkables and edibles, rings true, the Sut who appreciates that "white tabil-cloth" is a Sut whom we have not seen or heard before. This self-indulgent sentimentality—gentility, really—reassures us that we, too, participate in the common humanity shared by members of all social classes.

Although nothing suggests that the thinker who coined the phrase, *the genteel tradition,* did much reading around in the works of Harris, Hooper, and others of their relative obscurity, one of George Santayana's casual observations in his 1911 talk at Berkeley remains especially suggestive.[13] Wondering about "any successful efforts to escape from the Genteel Tradition, and to express something worth expressing behind its back," he considers "the humorists, of whom you here in California have had your share." He concludes that they "only half escape": "They point to what contradicts it in the facts; but not in order to abandon the genteel tradition, for they have nothing solid to put in its place." Then he goes on to draw an analogy between the situation in late nineteenth-century (and early twentieth-century) America and the case of Italy during the Renaissance, considering the attitude of Italian humorists toward the Catholic tradition. He saw them as

> not intending to deny the theory of the church, but caring for it so lit-
> tle at heart, that they could find it infinitely amusing that it should be

---

13. Santayana, "The Genteel Tradition," 38–64.

contradicted in men's lives, and that no harm should come of it. So when Mark Twain says, "I was born of poor but dishonest parents," the humor depends on the parody of the genteel Anglo-Saxon convention that it is disreputable to be poor; but to hint at the hollowness of it would not be amusing if it did not remain at bottom one's habitual conviction.[14]

So Harris's Sut voices the cynical truths that "The Tradition" kept trying to hide, as in his observation that religion is becoming merely a "city of refuge," or that it's simply "univarsal onregenerit human nater" to feel "a streak ove satisfackshun" at the misfortunes of another, "I don't keer ef he's yure bes' frien, an' I don't keer how sorry yu is fur him."[15] This attitude does have a lot more of Harris-the-Presbyterian in it than do most of Sut's aperçus.

A more obvious example of the appropriateness of Santayana's remark might well be in Sut's statement of his " 'sentimints ontu folks: Men wer made a-purpus jis' tu eat, drink, an' fur stayin awake in the yearly part ove the nites: an' wimen wer made tu cook the vittils, mix the sperits, an' help the men du the stayin awake.' "[16] This phrasing, appealing to male sexist fantasies but shamefully vulgar in its earthy materiality and physicality and its denial of both ideality and reverence, is one of the many passages in which Harris does absolutely provide evidence for Santayana's sense that "the humorists" fail to escape from the Genteel Tradition because "they have nothing solid to put in its place." The case of Harris may be more satisfyingly ambivalent than most—satisfying from the point of view of twentieth-century students of American culture, I mean—but not, surely, by very much: in case after case, readers of the actual humorists (as opposed to readers of commentators on their work) can see easily enough that the authors cling to the polite standards that some of their characters ignore, and that, in many cases, the bedrock of gentility has no disguise at all.

4. GENTILITY, IDEALITY, AND RESPONSES TO MYSTERY
NICK CARRAWAY AND JIM DOGGETT

Now what I mean by the bedrock of gentility, the foundation upon which its sometimes very elaborate structures are based, comes down to the matter of certainty, the very perception that characterizes Nathaniel Ward's performance as Simple Cobler, John Wise's as country lawyer, farmer, et al., and also the atmospheric comfort, even smugness, that pervades the reader's response to the created worlds of humorists intent on exposing the affectation of their characters. This certainty provides

14. Ibid., 51–52.
15. Harris, "Contempt of Court—Almost," in *Sut Lovingood*.
16. Harris, "Sicily Burns's Wedding," in *Sut Lovingood*.

the heuristic force and the psychic energy necessary to keep in place the repressive and suppressive structures of "excessive" propriety that one usually thinks of when encountering the notion of gentility, the energy that also enables its possessors to keep clearly in their minds' eye not material reality but "the poet's ideal" as "the embodiment of God's will."[17] When Santayana speaks of Emerson's supremely important intuition about "his notions"—"he felt in his bones that they were myths"[18]—he applauds Emerson as one who refrained from making "a system out of" them because "he coveted truth." "A system" is precisely what Josiah Holland coveted, under the mistaken impression that he was interested in the truth. Said Santayana:

> No system would ever have been framed if people had been simply interested in knowing what is true, whatever it may be. What produces systems is the interest in maintaining against all comers that some favorite or inherited idea of ours is sufficient and right. A system may contain an account of many things which, in detail, are true enough; but as a system, covering infinite possibilities that neither our experience nor our logic can prejudge, it must be a work of imagination, and a piece of human soliloquy. It may be expressive of human experience [as Santayana says of myths], it may be poetical; but how should any one who really coveted truth suppose it to be true?[19]

Although Santayana's essay and the famous phrase in its title suggest a variety of interesting directions in which to explore American literature, this impatience with ideal constructions, with intellectual systems that more or less ignore material reality, seems to me to be at the agnostic heart of Santayana's objections to the American writers whom he labeled "genteel." Certainly it enabled him to appreciate Emerson, despite the latter's great propriety.

When Emerson, in his 1838 talk to the graduates of the Harvard Divinity School, spoke of the orthodox Christianity of his day as having mistaken the figurative language of the New Testament for literal fact, he was in effect asserting that Christianity was a myth, rather than a system of truth. He saw the myth of Christianity as truly expressive of the divinity in all persons, but a myth nevertheless, one that had, during the centuries, been turned into a cult by the institution of the church. No wonder that Professor Andrews Norton of the Divinity School condemned Emerson's address as "the latest form of infidelity in Cambridge," and that Emerson had to wait for almost thirty years, and appointment to the Board of Overseers, before speaking at Harvard

17. Holland, *Lessons in Life*, 286.
18. Santayana, "The Genteel Tradition," 48.
19. Ibid., 49.

again.[20] Propriety may have been, may be, the most obvious component of the genteel tradition in American life, but it was—is—also the most superficial.

Although the power of the ideal realm might seem an odd recognition for the archetypal writer of the iconoclastic 1920s to have so many of his narrators insist upon, the flappers, golf-caddies, and assorted other golden girls and boys who saunter and speed through his pages embrace ideality wherever they think they find it. When F. Scott Fitzgerald's genteel narrator, Nick Carraway, recognizes that "Jay Gatsby of West Egg, Long Island, sprang from his Platonic conception of himself" and had "invented just the sort of Jay Gatsby that a seventeen-year-old boy would be likely to invent" (chapter 6), Nick provides at least one answer to the question raised at the very start of the book.

Sophisticated, proud of his tolerance, Nick now wants, as a result of his Gatsby experience, "the world to be at a sort of moral attention for ever." Why, then, a reader wonders, does he say that Gatsby "was exempt from my reaction—Gatsby, who represented everything for which I have an unaffected scorn"? We can surmise by chapter 6 that, in part, the answer must be that Nick is mistaken about himself when he says, after admitting that his tolerance has its limits: "Conduct may be founded on the hard rock or the wet marshes, but after a certain point I don't care what it's founded on." Nick's error lies in his ignorance of the power that the ideal—any apparent manifestation at all of the ideal—holds over him. Although Fitzgerald's novel of 1925 may seem unrelated to Emerson's essays of almost a century earlier, the novel brings the essays "up to date." Emerson's open-minded search for truth has become a closed system, a formula that, like any other embodiment of collectively held dogma, saves one "the vexation of thinking" (*Journal*, June 20, 1831).

Gatsby's closed system, the ideal construction of himself to which, asserts Nick, Gatsby "was faithful to the end" (chapter 6) and that leads him to his death, turns out to be based on vulgarizations of Benjamin Franklin and of the Myth of the West. The list of James Gatz's schoolboy resolutions that Mr. Gatz shows Nick just before the funeral (chapter 9) is inscribed on the flyleaf of "a ragged old copy of a book called *Hopalong Cassidy*," emblem of a world that, like Gatsby's dream, like the unravaged "green breast" of Long Island that was at one time "commensurate to [humanity's] capacity for wonder," Gatsby "did not know . . . was already behind him." Still, Nick's perception of Gatsby as powered by an ideal construction of any sort at all partially accounts for Nick's enduring sympathy for, even empathy with, Gatsby.

20. Ralph R. Rusk, *The Life of Ralph Waldo Emerson*, 435.

Equally important is Nick's temporary fascination with the corrupt world represented by Gatsby and by the East, the world that Nick conjures up in two unforgettable images just after Gatsby's funeral. The "West" (the "Middle West" Nick calls it first, with geographical rather than figurative accuracy) comes down to a realm where the imposition of human ideas on material reality can be taken for granted, a place "where dwellings are still called through decades by a family's name." It's a world made for human beings, a world of Christmas parties, "and sleigh bells in the frosty dark and the shadows of holly wreaths thrown by lighted windows in the snow," and of human voices and human names. In contrast, the East, even when it "excited [Nick] most," haunts his imagination like "a night scene by El Greco: a hundred houses, at once conventional and grotesque, crouching under a sullen, overhanging sky. . . ." The "four solemn men in dress suits," carrying the "stretcher on which lies a drunken woman in a white evening dress . . . turn in at a house—the wrong house. But no one knows the woman's name, and no one cares." This city of dreadful night, where houses crouch like malevolent beasts untamed by the associations that go with family names, denies meaning, even reality, to the merely human.

Finally, Nick retreats into the familiar, the known, the safe world. But that other world of impossibly opulent, as well as vulgar, parties, of incredible, but true, accidents and horrors, retains a hold over him. What Fitzgerald has made clear about Nick Carraway's fascination with what repels him we have already seen to be the case with George Washington Harris, to say nothing of the other creators of the humor of the Old Southwest. For the latter, the repulsion more than the fascination tends to receive written emphasis; but the generalization holds. And another parallel emerges between what Fitzgerald shows us about Nick and what we can see for ourselves about the early humorists of the Old Southwest. This concerns the element of mystery in contrast to that of certainty. Nick recognizes the existence of an indefinable mystery about the East. "Perhaps," he speculates at the end of the book, "we [the principal characters in the story, "all Westerners"] possessed some deficiency in common which made us subtly unadaptable to Eastern life." Nick further confesses that "after Gatsby's death the East was haunted for me . . . , distorted beyond my eyes' power of correction. So . . . I decided to come back home."

Just before retreating into the fastnesses of his safe home, Nick pays a last visit to what had been Gatsby's house. There it is that, "as the moon rose higher[,] the inessential houses began to melt away until" Nick has his epiphany, experiencing if not quite articulating the sheer hold of the land itself, and of the American past, upon the mind and psyche of even modern Americans. That "vast obscurity beyond the

city, where the dark fields of the republic rolled on under the night,"
is itself mysterious, beyond all human attempts to encompass in words
(unlike Nick's sense of his particularized, known "Mid-West"), not only
because one can never reach it and, in vain attempts to do so, finds oneself
"borne back ceaselessly into the past": it is mysterious because its very
existence is, as Edgar Allan Poe said in another context, "out of Space—
out of Time."[21] It has to do with the time and space of psychology rather
than of this material world. It is, in a word, ideal.

Fitzgerald allows—that is to say, forces—Nick to encounter this realm
in order to retreat from a permanent immersion in it. Mark Twain's
predecessors tended to look away from it as much as they could, but in at
least one striking case, that sense of mystery overwhelmed both author
and character, although each attempted to shake off the experience.
Before going back to wonder once more about what it is that readers find
amusing in Twain's *Tom Sawyer Abroad,* and about why anyone should
care, let us think about Thomas Bangs Thorpe and his most celebrated
story, "The Big Bear of Arkansas." The title of one of his collections of
some of the tales that he published in William Trotter Porter's *Spirit of
the Times* is worth noting: *The Mysteries of the Backwoods; or Sketches of the
Southwest.* Although "the big bear school" of fiction, named for Thorpe's
most famous and popular story, came to stand for productions that we
now call "tall" tales having to do with the exaggerated feats of hunters
fictional or real, the story itself Thorpe anchors in mystery. Its humor is
mild, though real, and it offers the beginnings of my counterstatement
to Santayana's easy assurance that American humorists offer no real
escape from "the genteel tradition, for they have nothing solid to put
in its place." (What they will turn out to have we have already seen
adumbrated in John Wise's vernacular equation of ordinary church
members with "edge-tools," more than sharp enough for the task at
hand but unappreciated by a genteel theocracy.)

First, an overview of Thorpe's story. The "Big Bear" yarn has three sec-
tions: the first sixth of the story presents a steamboat scene, with Thorpe
as the outsider, hiding behind his newspaper, but then interrupted by "a
loud Indian whoop" and the entrance into the main cabin by the noisy
stranger, who gives a loud " 'Hurra for the Big Bear of Arkansaw!' "
and proceeds to make himself most familiarly at home. The next third
consists of a series of brief accounts by Jim Doggett ("the Big Bear") of life
in Arkansas, " 'the creation State, the finishing-up country,' " accounts
of a sort that leads one of the auditors to observe "that our Arkansaw
friend's stories 'smelt rather tall.' " The second half, and third part, of

---

21. Poe, "Dream-Land," in *The Viking Portable Edgar Allan Poe.*

the tale consists of the Big Bear's account of his hunting and killing of the biggest bear (four-legged) he ever encountered. "His manner was so singular, that half of his story consisted in his excellent way of telling it." Jim tells his tale, uninterrupted, and then three brief paragraphs in Thorpe's standard English conclude the whole.

Only in this second half of the story do I find the emphasis on mystery, but the emphasis there seems unmistakable, and unmistakenly deliberate. Jim sets up the contrast between this bear hunt and all of his other ones with the observation that hunting a bear has become for him as routine a matter

> "as drinking. It is told in two sentences—A bear is started, and he is killed. The thing is somewhat monotonous now—I . . . could give you the history of the chase with all the particulars at the commencement, I know the signs so well—*Stranger, I'm certain*. Once I met with a match, though, and I will tell you about it; for a common hunt would not be worth relating."

This hunt is indeed "worth relating," but not because the bear was so big: its other attributes have made the hunt memorable, as Jim's language suggests. He, the man who has always been so "certain" in the matter of bears and the hunting of them, is led to use the following locutions: " 'I never could understand' "; " 'puzzling' "; " 'past my understanding' "; " 'I wasted away' "; " 'in this shaky fit' "; " 'I was mistaken' "; " 'onaccountably curious' " [that is, " 'strange' "—one might say, "mysterious"]; " 'convinced that I was hunting the devil himself' "; " 'the thing was killing me' "; " 'he loomed up like a *black mist*' "; " 'Twould astonish you to know' "; " 'something curious about it, that I never could understand' "; and finally, most perplexing, and perplexed, of all is Jim Doggett's very last sentence, after he has shot, killed, and skinned the bear: " 'My private opinion is, that that bar was an *unhuntable bar, and died when his time come*.' " Then Thorpe, as narrator, sees that "there was a mystery to him connected with the bear whose death he had just related," for the Big Bear "sat some minutes with his auditors in a grave silence." As one of those silent auditors, narrator Thorpe himself has been affected: as he leaves the boat, he "can only follow with the reader, in imagination, our Arkansas friend. . . ." His imagination, no less than that of his vernacular creation, has become possessed by reverberations too deep for words.

"The Big Bear of Arkansas" is, therefore, more than just a "tall tale." It also goes far beyond its primary importance to William Faulkner as a nostalgia-laden reminiscence about the gradual clearing away of "the big woods" and therefore as a forerunner of Faulkner's own *The Bear*. It takes its place, along with Samuel Sewell's prose encounter with Plum Island and Melville's *Moby-Dick* and parts of Cooper's Leatherstocking saga, et al., among the important American "aesthetic contemplation[s]." "Neither understood nor desired," as Nick Carraway puts it, these sudden encounters with the transcendent bring those who experience them "face to face . . . with something commensurate to [their human] capacity for wonder."

I find it more than merely fanciful to see in Jim Doggett, whose underlying senses of foreboding and of mystery he covers over with noise and drink, a somewhat less rapacious, but ultimately no more content, James Gatz/Jay Gatsby. That Jim calls himself "the Big Bear of Arkansaw" and loved "like a brother" the big bear he hunts and unaccountably kills suggests an early intuition that, in the American vastness, success and death come together in unexpected ways, from unexpected sources. The real-life Thomas Bangs Thorpe even shares with Nick Carraway a kind of failure in the region to which he has come, in which his story is set, and performs a retreat to a less mystifying, a more secure, realm. That he retreats to the Northeast rather than to the Middle West is a matter of chronology alone: in the early nineteenth century, there was little in the midcontinent to which to retreat. Whatever the underlying source, a perceived threat to equanimity, and perhaps even to sanity, looms in the recalcitrant and raw vastnesses before the human mind has shaped them to accord with human imagination. Wallace Stevens's jar on that Tennessee hill might well have spoken to Thorpe and others of like sensibility.

All this has nothing to do with overt influence, but a great deal to do with ways of looking at experience, as well as with ways of experiencing in the first place. From 1869 until his death in 1878 (except for a period of about six months), Thorpe held a political appointment in the New York Custom House. Did he know Herman Melville, four years Thorpe's junior? Did they talk of bears and whales? Both men published in *Harper's Monthly Magazine*. Did they ever meet in the offices? Did they discuss their craft, or anything else? Just as the tattooing on Queequeg's body is a "devilish tantalization of the gods" to Ahab (*Moby-Dick*, end of chapter 110), so might readers and critics and biographers find themselves tantalized by such idle speculation. What a subject for a new "Imaginary Conversation" by a modern Walter Savage Landor.

But this possibility of probably non-existent fellowship between two writers, who endow the common man, whaler or woodsman, with a rare perceiving power, has merely the realm of the ideal in which to wander. Thorpe's "Big Bear" is quite real enough to serve as a landmark on the way to solid opposition to the genteel tradition. By itself, it is merely suggestive in that it raises tremors of feeling that pass quickly away, although not as quickly for the reader as for Jim Doggett, whose own story has affected him at least as strongly as it has his auditors. "He was the first one, however, to break the silence, and jumping up, he asked all present to 'liquor' before going to bed,—a thing which he did, with a number of companions, evidently to his heart's content." In the words of a perceptive Japanese scholar, "Jim Doggett . . . exaggerates everything to subdue his pain. He must speak loud so that he may not hear his mind."[22] That is, he must laugh so that he will not think.

Apart from profundities of mood, the humor of this tale exhibits a quality that sets it apart from the pattern of the stories that it superficially resembles. Thorpe writes of life on the frontier, but his humor, we notice, has nothing to do with a showing up of affectation. As in the matter of mystery, this appears to be a matter of Thorpe's deliberate decision rather than of mere lucky chance. When Jim Doggett first begins to talk, Thorpe tells us that "his perfect confidence in himself was irresistibly droll." This observation would seem to be an invitation to Thorpe's readers to rub their metaphorical hands together in anticipation of seeing Doggett shown up in some way. When he goes on immediately to set himself up as a brash hick from the sticks, what would be more likely to follow than an account of his self-confident errors in New Orleans, the city from which the steamboat has just sailed? But see for yourself; here is Doggett's opening gambit, after his general greeting: " 'Prehaps,' " he self-confidently twice mispronounces, " 'prehaps you have been to New Orleans often; I never made *the first visit before*, and I don't intend to make another in a crow's life. I am thrown away in that ar place. . . .' " One expects him to follow this introduction with a defensive account of the ridiculous scrapes into which his affectation of knowledge or experience surely must have led him. But then he openly admits to having been " *'green'* "; never for a second does he pretend to a sophistication, or to any other conventionally desirable trait, that he does not possess. Whatever satisfactions the story provides, an exposure of affectation is not among them.

One of the repeated motifs in the story, on the other hand, is the uncertainty provided by the Big Bear's oscillation between tall tale and large fact. Are we to believe the size of the beets and mosquitoes in Arkansas? No. Are we to believe the size of the bear? Yes. Are we to believe the manner of the bear's escape from Jim on an island? I don't know. And so it goes. What defines the in-group, the intimate circle of informed listeners sitting around the campfire and drawing comfort from their ability to preserve a straight face while the uninformed greenhorn gets taken in by the skillful teller of fantasy? Does the circle of initiates around the metaphorical campfire consist of knowledgeable city sophisticates

22. Norio Hirose, "Humor in *The Big Bear of Arkansas*," 20.

(us readers) or of ignorant country naïfs, Jim's fellows? Who is at home? And where? Thorpe may not have an explicit program, but he sets up reverberations the effects of which clash with those of the traditional humor of the Old Southwest. When one reads Thorpe's "Big Bear," one has to move beyond the values and mindset of the traditional educated narrator. The real sources of interest and power lie in the perceptions and responses of vulgar Jim Doggett. Something democratic (with a small "d") this way comes.

5. MYSTERY WITHIN

Now "The Big Bear" is a minor masterpiece of American art, representing its author at his best; in contrast, *Tom Sawyer Abroad* is a minor work by a harassed major writer trying to pick up a few dollars by reviving the characters of an earlier triumph. Its author's indecisions about those characters, however, make the book especially useful for my purposes. Both Huck's celebration of Tom's "instinck" and Tom's definition of *Moslem* as any non-Presbyterian allow a reader the luxury of a superior smile. Huck's repeated inability to cope with metaphor; his ignorance about maps, galaxies, and the motion of the earth around the sun; his obtuseness over the story of the observant desert denizen and the man hunting for his camel: all of these create sympathy for Tom and generate one's laughter at Huck. It seems almost as if Twain has thrown in his psychological towel and, as writer, has joined the ranks of genteel propriety as represented by that lovable philistine, Tom Sawyer.

Tom tells stories to an audience that fails to understand what the stories are about. So Twain: we remember his expression of pleasure over the ability of the *Atlantic*'s readership to allow him to appear before them without requiring that he "paint himself stripèd & stand on his head every fifteen minutes."[23] Tom feels himself surrounded by the ignorant. Twain saw himself living among a vast majority who believed the "lies" that their culture taught them. In *Adventures of Huckleberry Finn*, Twain had put into the mouth of the despicable king the perception that having " 'all the fools in town on our side' " would constitute " 'a big enough majority in any town' " (Chapter 26). Despite its suspect source, that turns out to be a pretty valid observation. By *Pudd'nhead Wilson* (1894: the last two pages of the first chapter), Twain goes to some lengths to dramatize the stupid literal-mindedness of Dawson's Landing's "majority." When readers see Tom, then, as the impatient and aggrieved victim of a similar obtuseness, they see what Twain has put there for them to see.

23. Twain and Howells, *Letters*, 1: 49.

On the other hand, Tom himself becomes a target for our laughter. Despite all his courage and quickness, which allow him to save the day for himself and his companions when the mad professor decides to kill them; despite all of Tom's intellectual abilities-in-general that allow the three to survive not only the professor but the balloon-voyage itself, Twain has great fun with Tom's clay feet. The Tom who insisted on freeing Jim according to the "books" now finds himself in the very land so celebrated in one of his favorites, *The Arabian Nights*. A book is all the authority that Tom needed in the past, whether for silencing the other boys' questions about "orgies" in the robbers' cave or for insisting on the particular nonsenses of Jim's "evasion." After he tells the story of the flying bronze horse, he insists that there is absolutely nothing to "hender" his believing in its factuality. Huck's observation, that " 'it couldn't happen, that's all,' " leads into a long argument-by-analogy, a ludicrous one indeed, that Tom loses when Huck turns his own analogical weapon against him. By the end of Chapter 12—the penultimate chapter of the book—Tom looks as credulously naïve as ever Huck or Jim have looked.

So what is the basis for our laughter? First of all, let us be clear about what it is not. None of the three characters is guilty of affectation. The superiority we feel toward them, the incongruity we perceive in their remarks, the relief of psychological tension we may experience as complex scientific or social structures suddenly lose, however temporarily, their power over us: all these pleasures we owe to the text, but not because a character is pretending to be what he is not, whether "to purchase applause" by "affecting false characters" or through hypocrisy to "endeavour to avoid censure, by concealing [his] vices under an appearance of their opposite virtues." When Huck insists that the map tells lies because Indiana and Illinois as seen from the balloon have about the same color, even though the map shows one as green and the other as red, and because he can see no meridians of longitude or parallels of latitude on the flat, clear desert sand, Huck's certainty, however ignorant, is not a matter of pretense. When Tom insists that the principle of flight is just as likely to inhabit the shape of a bronze horse as of an aeronautically designed balloon, Tom, too, demonstrates ignorance without affectation. Tom's ignorance, however, carries us a bit further than Huck's does into whatever slight significance Twain's text might have.

Even in so trivial a piece as this one, Twain appears not to be able, or not to want, to abandon the central preoccupation of his mature work. People, he shows us over and over again, do not understand their real selves, their real interests, their real obsessions. The contrast between an elite Eastern establishment, secure in its educated commitment to standard English and correct perception, and a boorish population of

Southwestern clowns and knaves no longer has either force or relevance. Instead of affectation and social standing, the real question turns out, practically, to be classless: what is it that human beings, educated or not, ought to (but do not) know about themselves? The interior world is every bit as mysterious as the external, if not more so. Tom has no notion that his belief in the possibility—in the probability—in the reality—of a flying bronze horse derives from his enslavement to the authority of the written word. But Twain sets up this dependence on such authority in Tom's explanation of a crusade to Huck and Jim in chapter 1. When they object to the apparent immorality of Tom's plan " 'to march against them ["the paynim"] and take it ["the Holy Land"] away from them,' " Tom insists that, unlike " 'common low-down business . . . this is higher, this is religious, and totally different.' " Huck and Jim have trouble with this arbitrary distinction: " 'Religious to go and take the land away from people that owns it?' " asks Huck. Jim says:

> "I's religious myself, en I knows plenty religious people, but I hain't run across none dat acts like dat."
> It made Tom hot, and he says:
> "Well, it's enough to make a body sick, such mullet-headed ignorance! If either of you'd read anything about history, you'd know that . . . the most noble-hearted and pious people in the world hacked and hammered at the paynim . . . —and yet here's a couple of sap-headed country yahoos out in the backwoods of Missouri setting themselves up to know more about the right and wrongs of it than they did! Talk about cheek!"

By the end of his harangue, Tom thinks that he's talking with the literal backing of those "noble-hearted and pious people"—" 'Richard Cur de Loon, and the Pope, and Godfrey de Bulleyn, and lots more' "— even though, as so often will be the case with Tom throughout the book, the written word alone serves as his authority. Huck's inspired misspellings, whereby Richard the Lion-Hearted becomes Richard the Loony Dog, underlines the doubleness of Twain's aim.[24] At the very end of the chapter, however, Twain returns to one of the problems with Tom's reliance on his beloved authorities: the text yields what the reader brings to it. Says Huck:

> Now Tom he got all that notion out of Sir Walter Scott's book, which he was always reading. And it *was* a wild notion. . . . I took the book and read all about it, and as near as I could make it out, most of the folks that shook farming to go crusading had a mighty rocky time of it.

24. Without rehashing the tangled tale of the story's text, I note only that "Cur de Loon" appears in the editions published in Twain's lifetime. The University of California Press edition of 1980 reads "Cur de Lyon."

It's easy enough to enjoy Tom's foolishness, but our amusement at it does not stem from any affectation on Tom's part. Tom does not know himself well enough; therefore, even though he knows a great deal more than Huck and Jim do about the external world, he often shows himself in as ridiculous a light as that in which they so often appear. But affectation is not, in these cases, the source of the ridiculous.

Twain shows us a world that lacks the clarity of moral and psychological outline on which the conventions of his craft have insisted, thereby muddying waters kept transparent by his predecessors. Laughter having affectation as its basis rests on the secure sense of readers that they themselves know the truth, not only about the characters on the printed page but about the world, about their society and its standards, and even about themselves. This clear-eyed, eighteenth-century sort of amusement brings together civilized people for whom the writer, at least temporarily, has managed to push away any nagging intuitions of mystery, of the unknown or unknowable. Let us think for a moment about what Mark Twain, in Chapter 20 of *Adventures of Huckleberry Finn*, does with Johnson J. Hooper's camp meeting episode. The cause-and-effect sequences of the two stories sound identical: a man without money (Simon Suggs; the king) attends a camp meeting, pretends to a conversion experience, takes up a collection in order to do religious works elsewhere, and leaves with the blessings of the rejoicing congregation as well as with their money. As Hooper tells the story, we scorn Simon's victims because their affectations—to appear pious, to appear rich—make them ridiculous, just as Henry Fielding said should be the case. As Huck tells Twain's version, nobody reveals any affectation at all. The people seem to be pious and generous, and so they are.

Most readers, even so, derive great amusement from the scene. As in *Tom Sawyer Abroad*, the basis for laughter turns out to be one's perception of at least two sorts of ignorance. First—and, though necessary, really trivial—the people whom the king fools show a laughable ignorance of geography: as everyone undoubtedly remembers, the king asserts that he owes his presence in Arkansas to the unquestioned "fact" that his Indian Ocean pirate "crew was thinned out considerable last spring in a fight" and needed "some fresh men." But, says he, his recruiting mission ended when "he'd been robbed last night and put ashore off of a steamboat without a cent," a misfortune that, he now sees, "was the blessedest thing that ever happened to him" because it led to his conversion "in Pokeville camp meeting." So we begin with the people's nonskeptical acceptance of the notion that an Indian Ocean pirate would travel all the way to Arkansas (and even farther upstream) to find replacements for a depleted crew.

More important, however, is the avidity with which they welcome the king because he is not merely a converted sinner, but a converted pirate. Lest we miss the point, Twain spells it out for us through the king's reaction once he's back on the raft with "eighty-seven dollars and seventy-five cents," as well as "a three-gallon jug of whiskey": not only had it been the most profitable "day he'd ever put in in the missionarying line. He said it warn't no use talking, heathens don't amount to shucks alongside of pirates to work a camp-meeting with." As Twain makes clear through Tom Sawyer's fantasies at the start of the book, and in *The Adventures of Tom Sawyer* as well as in *Life on the Mississippi*, the pirate icon carries with it a heavy charge of sensationalistic association.

These village people, bored in the drabness of their small lives, welcome the excitement of a camp meeting, and welcome even more fervently the fantasy that an Indian Ocean pirate can brush against the monotony of their days. They do not know themselves well enough to understand their own susceptibilities, so they part with their cash to enjoy an illusion. For the same reason, *The Royal Nonesuch*, later on, after the duke has changed his advertising poster from an announcement of Shakespeare to a promise of the kind of show to which women and children will not be admitted, "fetches" a sell-out crowd because the duke is quite right in assuming that the men of a dismal Arkansas village will pay a good deal more for something improper and entertaining than for something that they associate with the polite culture in which they feel that they themselves have no part. The Phelpses' gullible belief in Tom's incredible rescue of Jim costs them no cash, but almost costs Tom his life. As the archetypal representative of his society, Tom, as has been noticed often enough, uses the literature and even the music cherished by his society in order, supposedly, to subvert it by freeing a slave.

But the slave has already been set free, and Tom's strategies include imitations not only of sensational literature but also of the ways of one of Mark Twain's "real-life" crooks: the alleged member of "a desperate gang of cutthroats from over in the Indian Territory" who has "got religgion" and therefore "will betray the helish design . . . to steal your [the Phelpses'] runaway nigger" announces a conversion as unsubstantial as the king's at Pokeville camp meeting. Tom is as much a con artist and a thief as is the king. Even though he is after a different sort of plunder— glory, not cash—Tom plays upon the same sort of love for the theatrical, for the sensational, for the "romantic," as does the king in his inspired pretension to piracy. Also, both sets of victims do not know themselves.

In his last years, Mark Twain explored the ways in which this lack of self-knowledge enslaves the human race despite our illusions of freedom and independence. Most of the writings in which he did so have received either posthumous publication or none at all, and therefore were not accessible to George Santayana (who, however, could have seen "The $30,000 Bequest," available in book form in 1906, before Santayana's 1911 pronouncement). "The Great Dark," "The Mysterious Stranger" manuscripts, and a number of other works, both completed and unfinished, a few published in Twain's lifetime, most only recently (or still not publicly) available, make clear how intent Twain was on exploring ways in which one's various levels of consciousness conflict with each other and constitute unknown, perhaps unknowable, traps and delusions. As he says in "The $30,000 Bequest," he marvels at "how soon and how easily our dream life and our material life become so intermingled and so fused together that we can't quite tell which is which, any more."

In the ordinary way of speaking, this insight is hardly something "solid" to put in the place of the genteel tradition, however porous. But in Santayana's sense of the word, it is very solid indeed. The genteel tradition, emphasizing propriety and a Victorian denial of the body, had at its base the same sense of certainty that underlay the often vulgar, and even physically repulsive, humor of the Old Southwest. Edmund Wilson's reaction to Eugene Field's "compulsive fondness for puerile and disgusting jokes," to Sut Lovingood as "always malevolent and always excessively sordid, . . . a peasant squatting in his own filth," to the "crude and brutal humor" in general "that was something of an American institution all through the nineteenth century,"[25] indirectly reveals how firmly those writers drew their boundaries. Yes, life among the boors is like that, but we educated gentlemen know better how to behave. Although their humor did indeed point out the discrepancies between their experience and the assumptions of the genteel tradition, their dismissal of their characters as merely quaint or vulgar or igno-rant or stupid (or any combination thereof) puts them solidly within Santayana's categorization.

6. Dr. Holland Once More, and the Plight of the Humorless

The most important way in which this is true seems to me to be the certainty with which most of them, most of the time, implicitly lay down the law of the knowable. It is as if they were promulgating the material complement to Josiah Holland's favorite doctrine concerning the ideal, as if they were demonstrating that the objective truth of the visible world is perfectly knowable, has nothing to do with the viewer's perspective, and is simply a matter of (unfortunate) fact. For Holland, who seems

25. Wilson, *Patriotic Gore*, 509, 510, 512.

to have spoken for, as well as to, vast numbers of his unsophisticated contemporaries,[26] truth is equally knowable, but by a different route. Holland's "argument"—really a series of assertions built on unexamined assumptions, rather like the way most of us "argue" most of the time— emerges most clearly in Lesson 22 of *Lessons in Life*, "The Poetic Test" (284–97 of the 1893 edition), from which I have already quoted an account of the "proper" way of perceiving an idyllic-seeming village whose inhabitants are miserable, even to the children suffering with measles. For fear of being thought to distort—Holland's essay is precisely what an unscrupulous twentieth-century scoffer at the genteel tradition would want to invent—I shall quote extensively, but I believe its entertainment value will compensate for any strain that its substance may put upon a reader's attention.

Dr. Holland did indeed study to be, and did briefly practice as, a doctor, a materially oriented healer. As we have seen, he was quite sure that "no unwarped and unpolluted mind can fail to see that the poet's ideal is the embodiment of God's will" (286). At the same time, he knew very well, saw very clearly, that God's will had yet to be realized on earth. He knew a hawk from a hand-saw; he saw, for example, that, despite the fine lines that patriotic poets had written, the ballot box too often turns out to be a miserable object that

> stands in a corner grocery [by which he means what we would call a liquor store], and that the poor voter is led up to deposit his priceless ballot so drunk that he cannot walk without help. Mr. Whittier would have us believe that the poor voter sings:
>
>> "Today shall simple manhood try
>> The strength of gold and land;
>> The wide world has not wealth to buy
>> The power in my right hand."
>
> The truth is that gold and land try the very "simple manhood" as a rule, and very much less than the wide world is sufficient to buy the power in a great multitude of voters' hands. (293–94)

Holland has no intention of saying that Whittier's poem describes material reality in its usual configurations. "The poet sees what the ballot-box may be, ought to be, and, in some rare instances, really is." Except for those "rare instances"—and Holland is perfectly willing to give them up, as he does on the next page—the poet does not tell the truth of things-as-they-are. The "truth" that most concerns him is a far more Platonic

---

26. Harry Houston Peckham, *Josiah Gilbert Holland in Relation to His Times*, refers to Holland as "the major prophet of the unsophisticated, the supreme apostle to the naïve" (2) and as "the chosen and anointed Apostle to the Naïve!" (67).

truth than that: "The great truth of human equality inspires him, and he uses the ideal and possible ballot-box to illustrate it, and thus furnishes the standard by which the real ballot-box is to be judged."

Holland, we can safely interject, would not have been sympathetic with Herman Melville's perspective, had he chanced to encounter it. For a quick reminder of what I essentially am referring to, consider the passage, in the first chapter of *Moby-Dick*, where Ishmael announces that the story of Narcissus "is the key to it all." The "it" refers to the fascination that water, especially the ocean, holds for contemplative individuals: Narcissus, in Melville's artfully revised summary of Ovid's story, sees in a particular bit of water the object of all desire. Not knowing that what he sees is his own reflection, he tries to reach it, and drowns. "But that same image, we ourselves see in all rivers and oceans. It is the image of the ungraspable phantom of life; and this is the key to it all." What we find is what we project. Chapter 99, "The Doubloon," is probably Melville's most detailed working out of this proposition. So Ishmael finally (Chapter 94) comes to accept "that in all cases" a person's "conceit of attainable felicity" must lie not in an ideal realm (not "in the intellect or the fancy") but in material reality ("in the wife, the heart, the bed, the table, the fire-side, the country").

Not that Holland simply ignores what is "out there" in the material world. He even goes on to take a quite Mark Twainian view of some American institutions. He doesn't quite say that Congress is America's only native criminal class,[27] but he does say:

> No greater fiction was ever conceived than the pleasant one that the people of America govern themselves. The people of America, except in certain political revolutions, have always been governed by a company of self-appointed and irresponsible men, whose principal work was to grind axes for themselves. The poetry of American politics is then the severest standard by which to judge the reality of American politics.
>
> Religious freedom is another poetical idea in which America glories. It is essentially a poetical thought that every man is free to worship God according to the dictates of his own conscience—that there is no Church to domineer over the State, and no State to domineer over the Church, that the Bible is free, and that each individual soul is responsible only to its Maker. This great and beautiful liberty stirs us when we think of it as music would stir us, breathed from heaven itself. It is grand, God-begotten, belonging in the eternal system of things, full of inspiration. This religious freedom we claim as Americans. Some of us enjoy it; but the number is not large.

27. "It could probably be shown by facts and figures that there is no distinctly native American criminal class except Congress.—*Pudd'nhead Wilson's New Calendar.*" *Following the Equator*, chap. 8.

Even Holland's use of anticlimax—as with his reference earlier in the essay to "the measles" afflicting the children in his poetically seen village—has the ring of the American humor of which Santayana will speak half a century later. And Holland goes on to rip explicitly into shreds any notion that the poetic truth matches the lived experience.

> I would as soon be the slave of the Pope or the Archbishop as the slave of a sect. . . . Take any town in America that contains half a dozen churches, representing the same number of religious denominations, and it will be found that, with one, and that probably the dominant sect, it will be all a man's reputation and religion are worth to belong to another sect. Perfect religious freedom in America there undoubtedly is; but it is the possession of only here and there an individual. Prevalent uncharitableness and bigotry are incompatible with the existence of religious liberty anywhere. (295–96)

But Holland's purpose is not to debunk America or Americans. He is, instead, boosting "the poetic instinct" because

> Litmus-paper does not more faithfully detect the presence of an acid than the poetic instinct detects the false and foul in all that makes up human life. All that is grand and good, all that is heroic and unselfish, all that is pure and true, all that is firm and strong, all that is beautiful and harmonious, is essentially poetical, and the opposite is at once rejected by the unsophisticated poetic instinct.
>   Verily the poets of the world are the prophets of humanity! They forever reach after and foresee the ultimate good. They are evermore building the paradise that is to be, painting the millennium that is to come, restoring the lost image of God in the human soul. When the world shall reach the poet's ideal, it will arrive at perfection; and much good will it do the world to measure itself by this ideal, and struggle to lift the real to its lofty level. (297)

So Holland concludes. We can easily imagine how someone of Mark Twain's persuasion would read aloud to a Lyceum audience that "much good will it do the world" clause. After being inundated by Holland's optimistic dismissal of the merely material, however, can there be any reader who needs assurance that Holland means no irony in his last sentence? "The poet's ideal," that toward which "the unsophisticated poetic instinct" unerringly points, constitutes "the transcendent truth," synonymous with

> the highest poetry, . . . and there is no true poetry this side of the highest truth. Poetry follows the universal law, and is dependent for its quality upon its materials. In the degree to which its materials are fictitious and artificial, is it poor and false. The Pilgrim's Progress is essentially better poetry than the Paradise Lost, because it contains more truth as it is in the divine life of man. (287)

And Holland goes every bit as far as this last judgment might suggest. After arguing that criminals must be punished, not simply wept over until they repent, he goes on to draw what to him constitutes a crucial contrast between "sentimental sympathizers with criminals" and those with a true "poetic sense":

> "Poetic Justice" maintains its purity. The reader of a novel, no matter how good or how bad he may be, demands that the villain of the book shall be punished, as a matter of justice alike to him and to those who have been his victims. Nothing but justice—nothing but a fitting retribution— will satisfy. The poetic instinct demands a perfect system of rewards and punishments, and is as little satisfied when a hero succeeds indifferently, as when a scoundrel fails to be punished according to his desserts. There is no poetic fitness without justice—retribution pound for pound, and measure for measure. Set any audience that can be gathered to watching a play in which criminal and crafty art is made to meet and master a guileless spirit and pollute a spotless womanhood, and the sympathies of the vilest will follow the victim, and, in the end, demand the punishment of the victor. . . . Now I would trust this poetic instinct of fitness further than I would all the sympathies of the humanitarians, all the sophistries of the philosophers, all the subtleties of the theologians, and all the milder virtues of Christianity itself. To me, it is as authoritative as a direct revelation from God, and is equivalent to it. (289–90)

A lifelong Congregationalist—only the exigencies of geography led him to join the Presbyterians toward the end of 1872—Holland in principle was non-sectarian.[28] As he wrote in the *Springfield Weekly Republican* (February 16, 1861), "Every denomination or form of religion has its excellencies, . . . but none of them hold [sic] exclusively the keys of happiness."[29] For all his elitist gentility, his denial of importance to vulgar materiality, he expresses an audacious trust in the "poetic instinct" of the mob at least as arresting as that of John Wise (also, though earlier, a Congregationalist) in his "edge-tools." Clearly, Holland embodies that decadence of Calvinism from which Santayana traced the Genteel Tradition; and, just as clearly, he embodies the decadence of Transcendentalism, "the other chief element in that complex system" that Santayana also calls "current idealism."[30] Direct revelation from God, as an earlier generation well knew, was simply, in Andrews Norton's previously quoted words, "The latest form of infidelity in Cambridge," by which Norton had meant precisely Emerson's insistence that the individual soul could have direct access to what Holland came to call "transcendent truth" and to equate with "the highest poetry."

28. See Peckham, *Josiah Gilbert Holland*, 193–95.
29. Ibid., 194.
30. Santayana, "The Genteel Tradition," 44.

Looked at from an angle the legitimacy of which Holland would surely have repudiated, his rejection of the "sentimental" in favor of a poetic justice that has the moral authority of divine revelation turns out to be a distinction without a difference. If sentimentality is emotion cut loose from behavior, then Holland's prizing of an audience's reaction to nineteenth-century melodrama does seem to be a prizing of the sentimental. Twelve years after Holland's death, Scribner's judged it profitable to issue a second edition of Holland's 1881 revision of his 1861 *Lessons in Life.* That was the same year—1893—in which Stephen Crane's *Maggie: A Girl of the Streets* appeared and received almost no notice at all. In part of Chapter 8, Crane summarizes Maggie's experience, and that of "the rest of the audience," with what to them is the "transcendental realism" of "these melodramas":

> Shady persons in the audience revolted from the pictured villainy of the drama. With untiring zeal they hissed vice and applauded virtue. Unmistakably bad men evinced an apparently sincere admiration for virtue. . . . Those actors who were cursed with the parts of villains were confronted at every turn by the gallery. If one of them rendered lines containing subtle distinctions between right and wrong, the gallery was immediately aware that the actor meant wickedness, and denounced him accordingly. . . . Maggie always . . . rejoiced at the way in which the poor and virtuous eventually overcame the wealthy and wicked.

What amounts to Holland's belief in Mark Twain's great lie about the "moral medicine chest" Crane presents as the projections and transferences of an ignorant and exploited underclass, although without my distancing and arrogantly certain vocabulary. Both Crane and Holland agree upon the facts: viewers of such plays react in favor of virtue and in opposition to vice. What Crane presents as extreme sentimentality, however, Holland dignifies as "the embodiment of God's will."

Laughter in response to humor that refuses the assumption of metaphysical certainty manifested both by Holland and his idealizing ilk on the one hand and by the continuers of the eighteenth-century tradition articulated by Fielding on the other has the capacity to push its readers into at least a fleeting comprehension of their need to know themselves better. Professor Carolyn Heilbrun, writing as "Amanda Cross" in one of her Kate Fansler detective stories, has an elderly gentleman suggest, in 1986, that his own generation " 'knew the world we were living in wasn't much good, but that didn't stop us trying to change it. These young [assorted "yuppies"] think that "making it" is all there is. Perhaps because their doubts, if they had any, would be too profound to bear.' "[31]

31. Amanda Cross, *No Word from Winifred,* 14–15.

The humor that has concerned itself with confounding easy assumptions about the transparency of God's will, of the real world, of the human psyche, does indeed offer something "solid" to put in the place of the genteel tradition. Such humor may not—of course it cannot—remove those doubts "too profound to bear." It did, it does, function to help readers to cope with mystery as well as with pain. Both abound when we cut the ties to what we have known, culturally or psychologically. We have to cope with loneliness and with the psychologically still-uncharted immensity of America. The laughter that takes us outside ourselves, however briefly, has always helped. Nick Carraway, that very serious young man defeated by the East, had no sense of humor. Neither did Huckleberry Finn, whose life Twain foresaw as ending in madness.[32] The solidity offered by the humor of a Twain, the irony of a Crane, the humor and irony, both, of a Melville and a Hawthorne, rests on the affirmation that ordinary human beings can confront the mystery and the pain not so much triumphantly as with open eyes, and without the palliative of genteel ideality. And if we cannot, readers may infer, we had better learn how.

32. "Twain envisioned Huck as a broken, helplessly insane old man" (Lynn, *Mark Twain and Southwestern Humor*, 245).

VI

The Puritan Roots of American Humor

1. RECOGNITIONS OF THE SELF

From Josiah Holland to Norman Holland, the previous chapter has surveyed some of the territories that various people have claimed for, and denied to, American humor. George Santayana saw that "the modern American" of 1911 was "usually joking" rather than making serious statements about his condition.[1] Although he did not discuss why that might be so, he might have agreed that mystery, pain, and guilt have long formed the underpinnings of American humor. He seems to have made no mention of Herman Melville, but he does refer to the work of Hawthorne, Poe, Emerson, and Thoreau. We have looked at Hawthorne and Melville already, but we need to do so again, as well as to glance briefly at Edgar Allan Poe, Ralph Waldo Emerson, and Henry David Thoreau. These few will take us to the heart both of the matter of revelation, American style, and of the humor-filled mind-set through which the revelation comes. Let us begin with Ishmael in chapter 49 of *Moby-Dick*, "The Hyena," after he has experienced loneliness and immensity.

Adrift in a swamped whale-boat in the midst of an ocean storm after his first encounter with a whale, "in the heart of that almighty forlornness" (end of chapter 48), Ishmael and his fellows finally are rescued by the *Pequod*. Soaked through after his night on the deep in an

---

1. Santayana, "The Genteel Tradition," 43.

open boat, but back on the ship's deck at last, Ishmael—in an oft-quoted rumination—notes that "[t]here are certain queer times and occasions in this strange mixed affair we call life when a man takes this whole universe for a vast practical joke, though the wit thereof he but dimly discerns, and more than suspects that the joke is at nobody's expense but his own." After developing this idea at some length, he observes: "That odd sort of wayward mood I am speaking of, comes over a man only in some time of extreme tribulation; it comes in the very midst of his earnestness, so that what just before might have seemed to him a thing most momentous, now seems but a part of the general joke" (first paragraph, chapter 49). There follows an amusing series of exchanges between Ishmael, on his first whaling-voyage, and three veteran whalers. After his friend, Queequeg, assures him that there was nothing unusual in their misadventure, he questions first one mate and then another:

> "Mr. Stubb," said I, turning to that worthy, who, buttoned up in his oil-jacket, was now calmly smoking his pipe in the rain; "Mr. Stubb, I think I have heard you say that of all whalemen you ever met, our chief mate, Mr. Starbuck [in whose boat Ishmael has just spent the night], is by far the most careful and prudent. I suppose, then, that going plump on a flying whale with your sail set in a foggy squall is the height of a whaleman's discretion?"
>
> "Certain. I've lowered for whales from a leaking ship in a gale off Cape Horn."
>
> "Mr. Flask," said I, turning to little King-Post, who was standing close by; "you are experienced in these things, and I am not. Will you tell me whether it is an unalterable law in this fishery, Mr. Flask, for an oarsman to break his own back pulling himself back-foremost into death's jaws?"
>
> "Can't you twist that smaller?" said Flask. "Yes, that's the law. I should like to see a boat's crew backing water up to a whale face foremost. Ha, ha! the whale would give them squint for squint, mind that!"

"Here, then," concludes Ishmael, "from three impartial witnesses, I had a deliberate statement of the entire case." After further rumination, "I thought I might as well go below and make a rough draft of my will. 'Queequeg,' said I, 'come along, you shall be my lawyer, executor, and legatee.'" Ishmael shows that he can enjoy his own "part of the general joke," even though he "more than suspects" that it's at his own expense.

Melville's sense of the absurd might almost be a commentary on some of the work of his friend Hawthorne. Ishmael's laughter as he accepts the reality of risk, the high odds against a safe return from the briny, has a certain kinship with the laughter of Hawthorne's Robin as his fantasy of dependence encounters the stormy reality of Major Molineux's disgrace. As a strategy for coping with "extreme tribulation," however, Robin's laughter has to do with unconscious, rather than conscious, perspective and will. Still, Robin and Ishmael are making progress toward an understanding and acceptance of the world as they encounter it rather than as they have wished it to be. One of Hawthorne's other laughers, Young Goodman Brown, both encounters and produces laughter, but Hawthorne distinguishes it from the laughter that signals the possibility of growth for Robin, Brown's young predecessor. Rather than seeing himself from the outside, and understanding that what most threatens him comes from within himself, Brown, "maddened with despair, so that he laughed loud and long," feels "as if all Nature were laughing him to scorn."

> "Ha! ha! ha!" roared Goodman Brown when the wind laughed at him. "Let us hear which will laugh loudest. Think not to frighten me with your deviltry. Come witch, come wizard, come Indian powwow, come devil himself, and here comes Goodman Brown. You may as well fear him as he fear you."

And "shouting forth such laughter as set all the echoes of the forest laughing like demons around him," Brown rushes through the woods, a "demoniac on his course." Condemned to repeat what he has come to accept as the sinful ways of his father and grandfather, and "more conscious of the secret guilt of others, both in deed and thought, than . . . of [his] own . . . [a] stern, a sad, a darkly meditative, a distrustful, if not a desperate man did he become from the night of" his ambiguous encounter in the forest that seems so like his own psyche. Because he rejects recognition of the legitimate sources of fear within himself, Young Goodman Brown laughs a laugh that rings most hollow. His laughter lacks any suggestion of either the self-discovery in Robin's laughter or the release from self-importance in Ishmael's. As we have seen, Ishmael, by the time he tells his story, has learned to renounce all hopes of metaphysical certainty, having come to the conclusion "that in all cases man must eventually lower, or at least shift, his conceit of attainable felicity; not placing it anywhere in the intellect or the fancy; but in the wife, the heart, the bed, the table, the saddle, the fire-side, the country . . ." (chapter 94, "A Squeeze of the Hand").

This voice reflects the elderly Ishmael, the narrator who has had time to savor and to develop the mind-set that led Stubb to insist, as if telling a tall tale around a campfire, that he has " 'lowered for whales from a leaking ship in a gale off Cape Horn.' " The shared humor of the initiated, into which group Ishmael has now earned membership, provides a kind of comfort. Quite different is the solitary laughter of little Pip—" 'Ha, ha! old Ahab! the White Whale; he'll nail ye!' "—in chapter 99, after Pip has been driven mad by "the awful lonesomeness" of "the open ocean" on which he has barely been buoyed up in chapter 93, "The Castaway." Similarly, Young Goodman Brown laughs in solitary despair, not in the context of a community like Robin's. Shared laughter serves characters like Robin and Ishmael—characters who stand for most of us—both as a catalyst for growth and as a barrier, or at least as a defense, against unmediated reality. Students of twentieth-century thought will remember the horror that fills Jean Paul Sartre's protagonist when he encounters directly the material realness and the ideological emptiness of those tree roots in *La Nausée*. Even Jim Doggett's "unhuntable" bear stretches to the breaking point the human capacity to cope. Jim, we remember, finally laughs so that he will not have to think.

Paradoxically, Howells's interest (*Criticism and Fiction*, 1891) in doing away with the unrealistic "good old romantic grasshopper"—in order to develop the revolutionary close focus on carefully chosen things-as-they-were—could offer comforting reassurance to the genteel reader in a way that ambitious quests for meaning could not. Readers should remember that five chapters after Melville leads Ishmael to his conclusion about the futility of trying to attain metaphysical truth, this same Ishmael comments upon the significance of the doubloon nailed to the *Pequod*'s mast: "And some certain significance lurks in all things, else all things are little worth, and the round world itself but an empty cipher, except to sell by the cartload, as they do hills about Boston, to fill up some morass in the Milky Way." Chapter 99, "The Doubloon," suggests that the "certain significance" in this particular object, and therefore in any object, is a function of the viewers' assumptions and projections. Insofar as natural facts serve as symbols for spiritual facts (because "nature is a symbol of spirit," in Emerson's formulation), Melville's resolution presents the natural fact as symbol of the spiritual, all right, but in the sense that no determinate final meaning exists. Ahab cannot begin to accept such a vision—he can barely tolerate his occasional thought that there may possibly be " 'nought beyond' " the mask that material objects present (chapter 36)—and, accordingly, he dies a defiant madman. Ishmael, however driven initially, however adrift finally, can laugh: Ishmael survives.

In America, where the human mind has had so much less time and opportunity than in Europe to create an intellectual envelope for a geography; in this country that, even now, still has not been whittled down to human proportions, taking things "seriously" has been perceived as very risky business. If the Puritans, who took things—including themselves—very seriously indeed, had landed on a coast like that of California, with its giant cliffs and redwoods, with a scale of things so out of proportion to the human, our early history might have been strikingly different. Santayana, as a matter of fact, suggests something very close to this at the end of his 1911 talk in Berkeley. He refers to the "crude naturalism" and "impassioned empiricism" that are turning the "flanks" of the genteel tradition. Then, addressing his audience directly, he says:

This revolution, I should think, might well find an echo among you, who live in a thriving society, and in the presence of a virgin and prodigious world. When you escape, as you love to do, to your forests and your Sierras, I am sure that you do not feel that you made them, or that they were made for you. . . . A Californian whom I had recently the pleasure of meeting observed that, if the philosophers had lived among your mountains their systems would have been different from what they are. Certainly, I should say, very different from what those systems are from which the European genteel tradition has [been] handed down since Socrates; for these systems are egotistical; directly or indirectly they are anthropocentric, and inspired by the conceited notion that man, or human reason, or the human distinction between good and evil, is the center and pivot of the universe. That is what the mountains and the woods should make you at last ashamed to assert. . . . They suspend your forced sense of your own importance not merely as individuals, but even as men. They allow you . . . to salute the wild, indifferent, noncensorious infinity of nature.[2]

Anyone who has encountered the hostile shores around Big Sur knows exactly what Santayana means. In contrast to New England's stern and rockbound coast, California's evokes not a human but a giant scale of beings. Whatever created the meeting of ocean with parts of Northern California clearly did not have in mind any accommodation to the human. As in Stephen Crane's "The Open Boat" explicitly (and implicitly throughout Crane's work), nature's indifference to the human condition presents the threat hardest for the human psyche to contain.

In contrast, Samuel Sewell's catalogue of nature's processes in the famous evocation of Plum Island in the midst of *Phaenomena Quaedam Apocalyptica ad Aspectem Novi Obis configurata. Or, some few Lines towards a description of the New Heaven As It makes to those who stand upon the New Earth* presents a nature very much in league with God's plans, plans that do indeed recognize "man" as "the center and pivot of the universe."

As long as Plum Island shall faithfully keep the commanded Post; Notwith-standing all the hectoring Words, and hard Blows of the proud and boistrous Ocean; As long as any Salmon, or Sturgeon shall swim in the streams of Merrimack; or any Perch, or Pickeril, in Crane-Pond; As long as the Sea-Fowl shall know the Time of their coming, and not neglect seasonably to visit the places of their Acquaintance: As long as . . . Nature shall not grow old and dote; but shall constantly remember to give the rows of Indian Corn their education, by Pairs: So long shall Christians be born there; and being first made meet, shall from thence be Translated, to be made partakers of the Inheritance of the Saints in Light.[3]

His recollection of the natural world as filtered through millennial hopes and salvationary expectations provided Sewell with infinite reassurance.

2. Ibid., 62–64.
3. Samuel Sewell, *Phaenomena*, Boston, 1797. This famous passage is quoted fre-quently, here as in *The American Puritans*, ed. Perry Miller.

Deprived of that assurance by his own direct experience of unmediated nature, Ishmael retires behind a curtain of humor; without the insulation of humor, Pip and sixty-year-old Huck go mad. Any declaration, or silent recognition, of metaphysical independence turns out to be no joke, although it may be something that one must joke about in order to survive.

2. THE LONELINESS OF THE SOLIPSIST
NO LAUGHING MATTER

Equally to the point, Ishmael's awareness stimulates, and at the same time validates, Melville's attribution of humor to Ishmael. To declare independence in this world, seeing that, willy-nilly, one has only one's own vision to rely on, suggests at least the beginnings of awareness. For all of Ishmael's embrace of democratic relatedness, the examples he gives of mutual dependence in "The Monkey-Rope" (chapter 72) point to the frailty of, not to any strength in, our umbilical connections with each other. Part of the capacity to laugh depends on the shift of perspective, of awareness, that accompanies such insight. Perhaps this is in large part why the "humorous" tales of Edgar Allan Poe strike few, if any, readers as terribly funny. The usual Poe protagonist finds himself cut off from all mediating agencies, not as a suddenly apparent condition, but as perhaps the one stable fact in a mad world. Church and state exercise no force over this world as he knows it; family does not exist as a nurturing force, with real parents or a healthy wife or sister (to say nothing of Poe's either non-existent, or implicitly antagonistic, fictional brothers).

Poe's most nearly successful funny stories—the two of them in tandem really constitute a unit—poke fun at what Poe knew best, the devices used by popular magazine writers to evoke horror, stimulate readers' sensibilities, and present the writer as erudite to an unusual degree, whether or not the image represented real attainments. The humor comes from the sudden change of perspective, a change for the reader, and perhaps for Poe, too. Instead of sources of prestige and chills, Poe presents many of his stock fictional elements as pitiful bids for attention on the part of an asinine would-be writer. "How to Write a Blackwood Article" and "A Predicament" concern the Signora Psyche Zenobia (known as "Sukey Snobs" to her detractors) and her efforts first to extract from Mr. Blackwood the correct recipe for writing a successful piece for his journal and then actually to write such a piece.

The popular *Blackwood's,* the one journal sure to be found in the parlors of middle-class America in the first half of the nineteenth century, along with the tales of E. T. A. Hoffmann and similar sensationalistic fiction successfully exploited the cult of sensibility. As the ability to experience strong emotion (the possession of "sensibility") became increasingly a prerequisite to being perceived as having a good heart, a virtuous mind, and a moral disposition, readers valued the opportunity that fiction could provide to prove to themselves and to others how virtuously good-hearted they were.

Early on, writers used shows of emotion to demonstrate something about the fictional characters themselves. In eighteenth-century Britain, Tristram Shandy's Uncle Toby weeps at the death of a fly, thereby demonstrating his good heart, and so on, as thoroughly as if Tobias Smollett had involved him in episodes of complex moral dilemma and resolution. James Cooper, three years before he added the "Fenimore" to his name, in *The Spy* (1821) has his heroine, Frances Wharton, gamble the life of her brother on her correct reading of a stranger's emotional reaction to a sunset. "There can be no danger apprehended from such a man, thought Frances; such feelings belong only to the virtuous" (chapter 4). And of course she turns out to be correct, for the emotional "Mr. Harper" himself turns out to be none other than George Washington in disguise, the epitome of honesty and magnanimity. Before long, readers are putting themselves in the places of the characters, assuring themselves of their probity, kindness, and similar qualities, on the basis of their own ability to respond to the melodrama ridiculed by Poe and Stephen Crane but prized by Josiah Holland.

The tale of terror appears to have met the same need. The frissons of a Hoffmann, a Tieck, et al., both agitated and soothed; indeed, they soothed because they agitated safely, fictionally. And this is roughly the instruction that Poe's Signora Psyche Zenobia receives from Mr. Blackwood. After summarizing a number of his more successful publications, Mr. Blackwood generalizes from his examples to the effect that " 'Sensations are the great things after all. Should you ever be drowned or hung, be sure and make a note of your sensations—they will be worth to you ten guineas a sheet.' " Miss Zenobia vows to remember his advice, and remember it she does when she describes the "important event" that occurred after she had left Mr. Blackwood, "of which the following *Blackwood* article . . . is the substance and result." Entitled "A Predicament," her article details her stroll through Edinburgh upon quitting Mr. Blackwood's office.

Having ascended the circular staircase in the steeple of a Gothic cathedral to admire the view, she finds that the long hand of the cathedral clock has pinned her neck to the wall of an aperture through which she has been gazing at "the heavenly scenery beneath" her. "It had buried its sharp edge a full inch in my flesh," she tells us, and "my sensations now bordered upon perfect happiness." The pressure increases, and first one eye, then the other, is forced from its socket "and, rolling down the steep side of the steeple, lodged in the rain gutter"; both then "rolled out of the gutter together." Still in note-taking mode, she observes meticulously: "The bar was now four inches and a half deep in my neck, and there was only a little bit of skin to cut through. My sensations were those of entire happiness, for I felt that in a few minutes, at farthest, I should be relieved from my disagreeable situation." She is correct. Her head joins her eyes, rolling to the gutter and then into the middle of the street. Ms. Zenobia then "candidly" confesses "that my feelings were now of the most singular—nay, of the most mysterious, the most perplexing and incomprehensible character. My senses were here and there at one and the same moment." Finally, at the very end of the story, she asks and answers the question that for Poe himself persisted: "What *now* remains for the unhappy Signora Psyche Zenobia? Alas—*nothing!* I have done."

In the course of this extremely odd parody/satire, Poe has ridiculed most of the clichés, including the use of dubious quotations, he and others exploited. One hopes that he had a fine time doing it, and that he enjoyed himself with the thrusts at Emersonian and Bostonian transcendentalism, his equation of "Kant" with "cant," and various other common targets of his pen. What makes this pair of related tales significant here, however, has to do neither with their targets nor with their strange humor. Rather, it is the basis for whatever amusement they may create that calls for comment. Poe is not simply poking fun at the psychologically sensitive evocations that characterize so many of his tales. His target is the mechanical use of "devices," of materials, that have the effect of cheapening the effects that Poe at his best achieves. When he observed that his terrors "were not of Germany, but of the soul,"[4] he acknowledged his awareness not only of those corridors of the brain that Emily Dickinson knew surpassed "material place" ("One Need not be a Chamber to be Haunted," Johnson #670) but also of the source of many of the images and props that he was borrowing to evoke those inaccessible passageways.

Daniel Hoffman in 1972 summed up Poe's gift as well as it has ever been articulated: "Few writers have lived with their unconscious pulsations so close to the surface of their skins. Few have been as able to summon these images, or been as unable to escape them, as was Edgar Poe."[5] Even in a jeu d'esprit so clearly intended as such, Poe cannot "escape" those "images" that play such significant roles in his less playful works. He cannot totally suppress the vibrations of those "unconscious pulsations" that manifest themselves despite the attempted escape of the conscious mind. Even after her eyes and head have already rolled so far

4. Frequently reprinted. Here, as quoted by Daniel Hoffman in *Poe Poe Poe Poe Poe Poe Poe*, 324.
5. Ibid., 316.

away, after her slave has departed in terror at her altered appearance, and after her dog has been picked to the bones by a resident rat, there still remains more than "nothing." But the "*nothing!* I have done" with which the Signora ends her narrative portends the dissolution of her entire identity into the oceanic soup of eternity toward which Poe's less facetious characters are also bound.

What Poe finally presents as cosmology in *Eureka: A Prose Poem* (1848) he has over and over been presenting in his fictions of individuals who both fear and welcome death. The loss of identity, of an independent and separate soul that faces uniquely perceived horrors, appalls the Poe characters who are about to taste either madness or death. Madness and death both imply a merging into or an absorption by the universal soul, the mind of God. The aristocratic, the independent, the separate, identity that Poe's people have known and valued and cherished must be sloughed off and lost forever. But Poe's people also welcome that merge because it signals also the furthest possible extension of both democratic and aristocratic pretensions: the "heart Divine," as Poe exclaims at the end of *Eureka*, "*is our own.*" That is, everybody, finally, becomes part of the Universal Aristocrat, Who thereby becomes the universal democrat. More powerfully, less intellectually, in many of the tales, this final merge—death, that is—means, or at some unconscious level feels like, the return to the primal unity from which all separate entities with great pain emerged.

Anyone conversant with this view of Poe's work, even if not persuaded of its validity, can at least understand the approach by thinking of the narrator-protagonist of "Ligeia." "Sufficiently aware of" the mysterious Ligeia's "infinite supremacy to resign [him]self, with a child-like confidence, to her guidance through the chaotic world," after her death he sees himself "but as a child groping benighted." What stays with him the most vividly, however, is "the expression of the eyes of Ligeia!" He likens his efforts to account for that "expression" to "our endeavors to recall to memory something long forgotten. . . . And thus how frequently, in my intense scrutiny of Ligeia's eyes, have I felt approaching the full knowledge of their expression—felt it approaching—yet not quite be mine—and so at length entirely depart!" And then he tells us that after he has been possessed by the spirit of Ligeia—or, as he puts it, "subsequently to the period when Ligeia's beauty passed into my spirit"—he discovered, "in the commonest objects of the universe, a circle of analogies to that expression." At the tale's conclusion, with the dead Lady Rowena apparently revivified as the previously dead Lady Ligeia, the narrator, in his final outburst, begins to recognize who and what it is that stands before him as the "ghastly cerements" fall away from . . . whatever it is:

> And now slowly opened *the eyes* of the figure which stood before me. "Here, then, at least," I shrieked aloud, "can I never—can I never be mistaken—these are the full, and the black, and the wild eyes—of my lost love—of the Lady—of the LADY LIGEIA."

The story ends with Narrator's whole attention focused on those eyes that somehow put him at one with the whole universe. But they are also the eyes of a figure that has meant to him what the body of the mother at one time has meant to every human being. Because the two meanings are the same—for to the unborn infant, what can the whole universe be but the mother's body itself?—the story that in various forms Poe keeps on repeating resonates, at some deeply buried level of unconsciousness, with generally human desires for and fear of the total submersion of individual identity that signifies death. No wonder Poe's efforts at humor simply aren't very funny.

Those efforts do, however, reveal a substitute for the finally unsupportable view of Poe's work that sees in his detective stories, those tales of ratiocination, a projection of the human wish for order and for reasonableness in the universe. True, in the Dupin stories, however suggestive of the uncharted depths within the human psyche they may be, chaos finally does remain at bay; the human mind can win through to at least a kind of rational order. The universe does not simply overwhelm Poe's persona. But one cannot go very far into the tales involving Poe's private eye, C. Auguste Dupin, without encountering the nonrational, the intuitive, side of experience. Rational powers alone do not suffice. If one tries to read, for example, "The Purloined Letter" as a projection of desired order, one misses the heart of the story, as we will see later on. No, the real projections of reason upon the universe occur in the humor, or attempted humor, of some of the tales. There, the Poe people who think that they are encountering those liminal experiences that reduce so many Poe protagonists to quivering jellies or raving lunatics discover, instead, that they have mistaken firmly circumscribed order for the vast, unchartered wastes of their worst fears.

The Poe narrator at the end of "The Premature Burial" resolves henceforth to "read no 'Night Thoughts'—no fustian about church-yards—no bugaboo tales—*such as this.*" Dismissing "forever my charnel apprehensions"—he had long feared, and in the course of the story had thought that he had been experiencing, "living inhumation"—he discovers that he has thereby lost "the cataleptic disorder, of which, perhaps, they [those "apprehensions"] had been less the consequence than the cause." A good laugh at his own expense has cured him of his psychosomatic illness. But the reader's response to the humor is not that of hilarity, in part because those old "unconscious pulsations" manifest themselves in images that affect the reader as powerfully in Poe's humor as they do anywhere else in his work. The very unfunny "The Oblong Box," for example, tells of a real corpse and ends with the reminder of "an hysterical laugh which will forever ring within my [the narrator's] ear." Everyone remembers the similarly haunting walling-up of Fortunato in "The Cask of Amontillado." Although the reality of the threat in "The Premature Burial" turns out to be based on the narrator's serious misperception, the language that brings to life his fears has the same gripping intensity as in any of the tales of unrelieved terror. The reader's nervous giggle—it cannot be called laughter—tintinnabulates most hollowly.

Poe's attempts at humor, then—at least so far as my reading of individual stories goes—repeatedly find themselves betrayed by the underlying reality that manifests itself in most of what Poe wrote. Still, the humor itself presents an interesting variation on the workings of the Southwestern humor of the day, with which Poe was familiar. We know that he reviewed Longstreet's *Georgia Scenes* in the *Southern Literary Messenger* for March 1836. The brutalities of "Dr. Tarr and Prof. Fether" simply transport the violence in the stories of Longstreet, Harris, et al., to a lunatic asylum in the south of France. Physical deformity and violence filled the pages of *The Spirit of the Times* just as they do the pages of Edgar Allan Poe. An important difference (for my purposes, at least) lies in the nub of the "joke": for Poe, it turns out to have nothing to do with affectation, that staple of the humor of the Old Southwest. At the same time, it has everything to do with a character's failure to perceive accurately the very knowable and determinate reality that exists outside of the self.

When Poe turns to humor, he turns to a world, a universe, that signifies mere play, mere pretense, because it is so thoroughly knowable, and even known. It is a universe from which all suggestion of irrationality, of realities too overwhelming to be dealt with rationally, have been banished. So the Signora Psyche Zenobia, instead of experiencing terror and madness, prosaically recounts her "sensations" amidst the stages of her progressive dissolution. The narrator of "The Sphinx"—a story that begins as if it were going to end with the narrator's death or madness—works slightly differently because the source of the soul-saving truth, of rationality, comes from outside the narrator himself. If left to his own devices, he most certainly would have become another one of Poe's ecstatic lunatics:

> While I regarded this terrific animal [it seems to him a couple of hundred yards long], and more especially the appearance on its breast ["the representation of a *Death's Head*"] with a feeling of horror and awe, with a sentiment of forthcoming evil, which I found it impossible to quell by any effort of reason, I perceived the huge jaws at the extremity of the proboscis suddenly expand themselves, and from them proceeded a sound so loud

and so expressive of woe, that it struck upon my nerves like a knell, and as the monster disappeared at the foot of the hill, I fell at once, fainting, to the floor.

Unlike so many of Poe's similarly quivering jellies, however, this one has a friend—"a relative" in the first line of the story; "my friend" by the end of the fourth paragraph, and "my friend" or "my host" thereafter—whose language amuses the reader and reassures the narrator. Maintaining "that he saw nothing," this friend at first drives Narrator even further into his fears of "the vision either as an omen of my death, or worse, as the forerunner of an attack of mania." After questioning Narrator "very rigorously," he "went on to talk, with what I thought a cruel calmness, of . . . the liability of the understanding to underrate or to overvalue the importance of an object, through mere misadmeasurement of its propinquity." Somehow this magnificent locution fails to comfort the narrator adequately, perhaps because Poe uses the friend's words as stepping-stones to a brief warning about the false hopes raised by the possibility of " 'the thorough diffusion of Democracy,' " delusional hopes that are false because they leave out of account " 'the distance of the epoch at which such diffusion may possibly be accomplished.' " But after a brief ride on Poe's antidemocratic hobbyhorse, the friend returns to the matter at hand, reading to Narrator from " 'a school-boy account of the genus *Sphinx*, of the family *Crepuscularia*, of the order *Lepidoptera*, of the class of *Insecta*,' " an account that makes mention of both the death's-head " ' "insignia" ' " and the beast's " ' "melancholy kind of cry." ' " Then, seating himself where Narrator had been sitting when "beholding 'the monster,' " Friend delivers the last words of the story.

> "Ah, here it is," he presently exclaimed— . . . "and a very remarkable creature I admit it to be. Still, it is by no means so large or so distant as you imagined it; for the fact is that, as it wriggles its way up this thread, which some spider has wrought along the window-sash, I find it to be about the sixteenth of an inch in its extreme length, and also about the sixteenth of an inch distant from the pupil of my eye."

The terror was all a joke, a joke played on the reader by Narrator, and originally played on Narrator by himself, or by his "misadmeasurement" of the "propinquity" of the object of alarm.

I have referred both to the initial designation of the story's second character as "a relative" of the narrator and also to this character's expression of a Poe-like pessimistic view of democracy. The antidemocratic thrust of the story turns out to be a great deal more central to its point than my summary has suggested. Johnson Jones Hooper, let us remember, began his Simon Suggs stories with the explicit intention of satirizing Democratic political biographies and politicians. Fascination with the results of his own imaginative activity led him to do more than that, but Hooper's anti-Democratic sentiments control his presentation of the uneducated frontier democracy as well as of Democratic voters and legislators. So also here, with Poe, but only after a somewhat misleading, and probably unrevised, false start. Undoubtedly writing at speed, as was so often his necessity, Poe begins his story with Narrator and "a relative" on an equal footing. In aristocratic phrasing, the narrator speaks of his relative's *"cottage ornée* on the banks of the Hudson." They both suffer over the bad news from the cholera-infested city: "At length we [not just the narrator] trembled at the approach of every messenger." But by the end of the first paragraph, Poe has changed his mind. No longer "a relative" but now "my host," this other turns out to be "of a less excitable temperament" than Narrator, with a "richly philosophical intellect . . . not at any time affected by unrealities."

The narrator, on the other hand, cannot be said to be "philosophical" at all. That is, he has ideas, but not what one could call any rigorous basis on which to evaluate them. In a brief but crucial third paragraph, he places himself squarely among the ranks of the credulous mob and in direct contrast to his "host," the "relative" who becomes in the fourth paragraph simply a "friend":

> A favorite topic with me was the popular belief in omens—a belief which, at this one epoch in my life, I was almost seriously disposed to defend. On this subject we had long and animated discussions; he maintaining the utter groundlessness of faith in such matters, I contending that a popular sentiment arising with absolute spontaneity—that is to say, without apparent traces of suggestion—had in itself the unmistakable elements of truth, and was entitled to much respect.

This contrast between the democratic suggestibility of Narrator and the cool, aristocratic reason of Friend provides the story's underlying conflict. Although neither character says anything about the bearing of the events of the story on those "long and animated discussions," the superiority of Friend's perspective over Narrator's is clear. Poe expects readers to accept without question the effect upon the narrator of that insect on a thread so close to one of his eyes that it remains invisible to the other; but despite these weird optics, rational thought triumphs over uninformed unreason. The world is a stable, calculable place, however wildly the cholera may be raging in the distant city. To trust in the mental habit of the multitudes is to risk madness and despair; such trust amounts to perverse, to willful, self-destructiveness. Only aristocratic separation can provide proper stability, both psychological and social.

The reader of "The Sphinx" can have no doubt that this is indeed the case. A similar contrast between the one and the many also shapes much of the humor of the Old Southwest. Consider Augustus Baldwin

Longstreet's "The Horse Swap," wherein the narrator—indistinguishable from the educated and refined Judge Longstreet himself—witnesses a contest in sharp trading practices between two experts in the art of making a worthless horse appear valuable.

> The removal of the blanket, disclosed a sore on Bullet's back-bone, that seemed to have defied all medical skill. It measured six full inches in length, and four in breadth; and had as many features as Bullet had motions. My heart sickened at the sight; and I felt that the brute who had been riding him in that situation, deserved the halter.
> The prevailing feeling, however, was that of mirth.

The truth emerges with total clarity; the reaction of the mob—"the prevailing feeling"—stands in sharp contrast to the reaction of the aristocrat. The reader may share some of the low feelings of the mob, but the effect of the story is to insist upon their "lowness." In neither Poe's nor Longstreet's tale does the issue of affectation arise,[6] but in each, the correct judgment to be made raises the reader's appreciation of the aristocratic position and evokes scorn for the democratic one. As is emphatically not the case in Poe's less playful stories, that "correct judgment" stands forth in absolute terms: no mystery, no doubt, but a clear light of totally sufficient reason surrounds it. Inferior intelligences will misinterpret nature—the world out there—but the superior will avoid "misadmeasurement." I suggest that a careful testing of Poe's tales, one by one, would lead to the following generalizations: the more playful the story, the more rational independence does one or another of the characters successfully exhibit; the more seriously Poe seems to be taking his own work, the greater the failure of attempts at such independence.

Still more interesting is Poe's in-between world, a world of both ratiocination and infantilism. Among its inhabitants are Auguste Dupin and a certain Prefect of Police. Dupin, readers will remember, draws an analogy between his own method in locating the purloined letter and the method of an eight-year-old schoolboy " 'whose success at guessing in the game of "even and odd" attracted universal admiration.' " The narrator, Dupin's "Watson," quickly responds to Dupin's rhetorical question about the nature of such ability:

> "It is merely," I said, "an identification of the reasoner's intellect with that of his opponent."

So far, so good. But then the narrator oversimplifies in asserting that this " 'identification . . . depends, if I understand you aright, upon the

---

6. That is, in these stories, neither superior aristocrats nor lowly democrats are, generally speaking, guilty of affectation, although Longstreet's "The Horse-Swap" might be said to show up the affectation of one of the horse-swappers.

accuracy with which the opponent's intellect is admeasured.'" Because
he is not yet writing *Eureka*, nor rewriting "Ligeia," Poe keeps Dupin's
correction to a minimum, so much so that if one were not aware of Poe's
probable meaning (rather than simply of what seems to be on the page),
Dupin's response to the narrator's linking of intuitive "identification"
with self-conscious "admeasurement" would appear to be no correction
at all.

"'For its practical value it depends upon this,'" replies Dupin, and
then goes on to the practical particulars of the case at hand. But "practical
value" subsumes only a fraction of the interest that Poe builds into
Dupin's processes. The unexpressed remainder accounts for some of the
emotional reverberations of the story for which no explanation involving
simply rational processes can account. The prefect—whose reliance on
common-sense method has failed so completely—acts like an immature
and impatient child. After making out his check for fifty thousand francs
and receiving from Dupin the letter for which he has searched in vain,

> This functionary grasped it [the letter] in a perfect agony of joy, opened
> it with a trembling hand, cast a rapid glance at its contents, and then,
> scrambling and struggling to the door, rushed at length unceremoniously
> from the room and from the house, without having uttered a syllable since
> Dupin had requested him to fill up the check.

When we remember that the minister, (known only as "D——"), "'both
. . . poet *and* mathematician,'" and the first purloiner of the letter, has
a literary brother; that Dupin—the letter's second purloiner—admits
to having "'been guilty of certain doggerel myself'"; and that Dupin's
revenge upon D—— evokes that extreme case of sibling rivalry represented by Atreus and Thyestes, we readers may not know exactly where
we are, but we can sense that more is at issue, here, than a put-down
of the prefect's simple-minded dependence upon procedural routine. Is
the Minister D—— in fact Dupin's brother? Had the minister interfered
in a love-relationship between Auguste and a woman? If so, what sort
of a woman? A lover? A mother?

One facet among many twinkles behind Dupin's delight in that mysterious "identification" of self with other that springs not from any merely
rational admeasurement of an opponent's intellect, but from something
far deeper, far less comprehensible. Dupin reports the schoolboy's account of how he manages "the *thorough* identification" on which depends
his success:

> "'When I wish to find out how wise, or how stupid, or how good, or how
> wicked is any one, or what are his thoughts at the moment, I fashion the
> expression of my face, as accurately as possible, in accordance with the
> expression of his, and then wait to see what thoughts or sentiments arise
> in my mind or heart, as if to match or correspond with the expression.'"

The mind of the schoolboy, like the eyes of Ligeia, suggests the possibility of material as well as mystical union among all the fragments of this chaotic universe.

Desire for that oceanic feeling of which Freud spoke, that unconscious wish to experience total reunification with the mother, shows itself in the assumptions of Poe's most apparently successful rationalist. But this comes as no surprise to readers who have deliciously shivered over the terrors of Poe's tales because those shivers habitually evoke, and thereby force one to re-experience, the vague or forgotten emotions of an earlier period. Besides, even though Rufus Griswold's malicious and unfounded destruction of the dead Poe's personal reputation has become increasingly well known, that old notion that Poe was some sort of crazed drug-addict—one of his own characters, that is—dies hard. It may be that Poe's work presents an underlying ambivalence toward independence; but that, one might object, has more to do with the wounded psyche of Poe than with that perceptive writer's sensitivity toward the spirit of his times.

On the other hand, Poe's popularity says something about the emotional resonance of readers. One's response to literature, as we all know, does have an unconscious component. Readers need not be aware in order to be gripped; probably a writer's success with an audience, a readership, depends upon qualities about which the writer may well be unaware, whether in the work or in the self. Poe, over the years, has spoken to countless readers, although most of them may have little conscious, articulable sense of why. I am suggesting that Poe's popularity stems in part from the power of the writings themselves to cut through a reader's defenses, arousing emotion by an appeal to one's sense of the uncanny. By "the uncanny," I mean that with which one acknowledges no kinship because one has repressed all awareness of connections. Poe does not show us our suppressed feelings but, rather, makes us re-experience repressed feelings the objective correlatives of which we have also repressed. Because awareness is not his goal, humor tends not to be his effect.

Poe's universe comes increasingly to be that of a solipsist. *Eureka*, that long poem in prose that Poe published at the end of his life, is clear enough on this score. In seeming to look outside the self, Poe increasingly sees only within. After taking his readers on a tour of the universe, with its continuous process of disintegration followed by reintegration followed by more of the same, Poe insists that this "heart divine," the pulsations of which correspond to expansions and contractions of the universe, is that both of the Lord of All and of each one of us individually. We cannot believe in our own deaths because we are, in fact, immortally part and parcel of the divine.

This view seems remarkably similar to much that Ralph Waldo Emerson had to say. Yet Emerson, habitually seen as central to any understanding of nineteenth- and twentieth-century American thought and feeling, ought to offer as different a perspective from Poe's as one could find. After all, Mr. Blackwood's advice to Miss Psyche Zenobia fairly drips with Poe-ish irony as he urges her to " 'look over Channing's poems,' " suggests that " 'a little reading of the *Dial* will carry you a great way,' " and tells her, " 'Put in something about the Supernal Oneness. Don't say a syllable about the Infernal Twoness.' " These evocations, within one paragraph, of Emerson's protégé (whom Emerson puffed in *The Dial* for October, 1840—"The New Poetry"—as a "young Genius"),[7] of what was in effect Emerson's quarterly, and of Emerson's notion of transcendent unity suggest an awareness of Emerson that itself may well transcend mere animosity. For Emerson, like Poe, had his esoteric as well as exoteric audience. The example of Emerson, in all its multivalent interest, beckons.

3. EMERSON'S SAVING REJECTION OF THE "NOBLE DOUBT"

That Emerson evoked a variety of responses needs no explication at this late date. No one, however, would want to suggest that one of these responses would have been likely to be the laughter that indicates appreciation of an author's sense of humor. I wrack my brain in an effort to recall Emerson's humorous passages; I do not succeed. But, like so much American writing generally, Emerson provides sharp shifts of perspective that work the way humor works in the sense that they jolt readers into a new perspective from which to achieve a new awareness. And Emerson was nothing if not a jolter. Mild-seeming, kindly old Ralph Waldo Emerson certainly stirred people up in his day.

Many Americans beyond a certain age share my own recollection of the photograph adorning the back wall of countless high-school classrooms: it showed (in some schools, still shows) the other-worldly, very elderly, white-haired Emerson, his mind obviously on high and noble things, gazing abstractedly over the heads of generations of grubby adolescents, our own minds very much on concerns having, so we thought at the time, nothing whatever to do with whatever occupied the attention of the saintly transcendentalist. Perry Miller (1905–1963), in his lectures at Harvard, used to evoke this familiar image in order to contrast it with one provided to him, some time around 1940, by a woman, then most elderly herself, who had heard it often from her own mother, the original source. Of necessity, I paraphrase and condense:

7. Emerson, in *The American Transcendentalists: Their Prose and Poetry*, ed. Perry Miller, 247.

> Having set out in the morning, for the first time alone, to shop in Boston, the teen-aged young woman returned in the evening, flustered, nervous, clearly upset. "What's wrong, dear?" asked her perceptive mother. "What happened to you? Did someone try to steal your purse? Did anyone . . . ?" "Oh, no, Mother," she stammered. "No. N-n-nothing like *that*. But—oh, oh, Mother—at the North Station, while I was standing on the platform, waiting to board my train, I saw—oh, Mother, I saw—he was standing there, just about a car away from me—oh, Mother: it was Mr. Emerson!"

And Professor Miller used to conclude with the remark that it was as if his informant's mother, back in the 1840s, had expected to see horns and cloven hoofs and a tail.

Viewing Emerson as the devil incarnate does seem a bit extreme to us today, yet we must remember that contemporary reaction to Emerson did indeed reach extremes. It might fairly be said that Emerson reached them himself. As promulgator, in 1838, of "the latest form of infidelity in Cambridge," Emerson later laughed at "the shudder" that "ran around the sky" as "The stern old war-gods shook their heads" and "The seraphs frowned from myrtle-beds"; at "Uriel's voice of cherub scorn, . . . the gods shook, they knew not why" (426–28).[8] The pained but gentle Professor Henry Ware (one of the "seraphs") and the militantly angry Andrews Norton (a war-god if Harvard Divinity School ever had one) heard no cherub's voice behind the scorn. Heresy, not sanctity, seemed to many to be the tenor of Emerson's 1838 address. And, on the other hand, after Charles Eliot appointed him as a "saint" to the Harvard Board of Overseers, Emerson in 1874 was reported in Boston's *Commonwealth* as favoring the continuation of compulsory attendance at chapel for all Harvard students.[9] And also, if one tries to make a case that Emerson in 1838 and Emerson thirty-six years later cannot be expected to hold to a foolish consistency, one must first register an awareness that the earlier Emerson indulged in a similar varying of perspective, sometimes literally from page to page. How independent, how dependent, does Emerson present his "man in nature," his "man thinking," as in fact being?

Most obviously the 1838 "Divinity School Address," with its mildly stated but violently perceived shifts from Christian peace to all-out war against the taking literally of Christian doctrine, provokes considerable jolting from comfortable, because familiar, complacency and into the terra incognita of independent thought. But so does the 1836 *Nature* essay, which suggests that from the beginnings of his intellectual maturity, Emerson articulated an important ambivalence about the proper

---

8. "Uriel," published in 1846. Quotations from Emerson, unless otherwise noted, are from *Selections from Ralph Waldo Emerson: An Organic Anthology.*

9. Rusk, *The Life of Ralph Waldo Emerson,* 484.

stance of the individual soul toward the universe. On the one hand, the independent individual soul is all-in-all. On the other, the dependent individual soul requires metaphysical as well as physical sustenance from what is outside itself. More simply put, the issue comes clear if one asks oneself what it is that Emerson means by the word "Nature." In the "Introduction," he distinguishes between the term's "common" and "its philosophical import" (22). The common usage signifies "essences unchanged by man," that which is not "art"; and if the word "essences" raises questions, Emerson's brief paraphrase shows that he means birds and bees, forests and plains, water and air, and so on. The philosophical sense points to all that is "the not me," therefore to all that is not my own soul. This "all" includes not only the common sense of "nature" but also all that is "art," and even "my own body." He will use the term in both its senses, he says, but expects that "no confusion of thought will occur." That is, human "operations taken together are so insignificant, a little chipping, baking, patching, and washing, that in an impression so grand as that of the world on the human mind, they do not vary the result." Modern readers living in a post-industrial, post-atomic age may not be so comfortable with this estimate of those "operations," but Emerson's meaning is, so far, clear. The problem arises on the next page, two paragraphs later.

It turns out that what counts will be that very "impression . . . of the world on the human mind." By "nature," says Emerson, "We mean the integrity of impression made by manifold natural objects." Where does "integrity of impression," where does any impression at all, exist? But Emerson by no means is ready to slide into the mush of total subjectivity. If, as he will insist, "Particular natural facts are symbols of particular spiritual facts" because "Nature is the symbol of spirit" (31), then nature, although it may still function as an "integrity of impression," had better be a great deal more than that, or else each person's "impression" has as much validity as anyone else's.

Without the underpinning, or overarching protection, of the divine, Emerson can sound very like most modern Americans who have great difficulty understanding that each person's opinion is not as good as anyone's. Emerson, we need to remember, goes on to say: "This relation between the mind and matter is not fancied by some poet, but stands in the mind of God, and so is free to be known by all men. It appears to men, or it does not appear" (35). When, in the conclusion to section 6 ("Idealism") and in section 7 ("Spirit"), Emerson draws back from too exclusive a grasping of Nature as merely "Ideal"—in the mind—he does more than reject the "noble doubt" that "perpetually suggests itself" (42). It is not enough to say that Nature "is ideal to me so long as I cannot try the accuracy of my senses," for then there could be no "natural fact" to symbolize authoritatively any "spiritual fact."

The world proceeds from the same spirit as the body of man. It is a remoter and inferior incarnation of God, a projection of God in the unconscious. But it differs from the body in one important respect. It is not, like that, now subjected to the human will. Its serene order is inviolable by us. It is, therefore, to us, the present expositor of the divine mind. (50)

And just before this, Emerson has had the audacity to claim "that man has access to the entire mind of the Creator, . . ." Is Marshall Nathan alive and well and living in Concord? Or Josiah Holland?

But before wondering again about Anglican Arminianism and one of its early-eighteenth-century avatars, Marshall Nathan, let me quickly point to a few more facets of Emersonian illumination. In the course of his 1837 address to the Phi Beta Kappa Society at Harvard, "The American Scholar," he sketched out Man Thinking's proper stance toward the past. Practically speaking, he meant the past as embodied in books, in libraries. "We have listened too long to the courtly muses of Europe" (79). "Meek young men grow up in libraries, believing it their duty to accept the views which Cicero, which Locke, which Bacon, have given; forgetful that Cicero, Locke, and Bacon were only young men in libraries when they wrote these books" (67). "Give me insight into today, and you may have the antique and future worlds" (78).

Note the rapidity of, the shock in, Emerson's sudden juxtapositions. Both parts of them turn out to have equivalent value: "we" and those "courtly muses of Europe"; "meek young men" and the intellectual giants of the past; "today" and "the antique and future worlds." This was indeed an exhilarating declaration of intellectual independence, but it rang with an almost solipsistic self-sufficiency, too. "[I]f the single man plant himself indomitably on his instincts, and there abide, the huge world will come round to him" (79). "Books are for the scholars' idle times" (68). "I had better never see a book than to be warped by its attraction clean out of my own orbit, and made a satellite instead of a system" (67–68). As Santayana complained, Emerson "read transcendentally, not historically, to learn what he himself felt, not what others might have felt before him."[10]

But a page after insisting that being turned into "a satellite instead of a system" constituted a threat to be avoided even at the cost of ignorance, he "would not be hurried by any love of system, by any exaggeration of instincts, to underrate the Book" (69). Emerson's definition of "creative reading," to be sure, avoids all contradiction of the recommendation that one read only during those "idle times" when the scholar's soul is temporarily closed to the inspiration of the Over-Soul. It is the sort of reading of which only the truly inspired are capable, absorbing "only the

10. Santayana, "The Genteel Tradition," 43.

authentic utterances of the oracle" (69)—"Plato or Shakespeare"—and rejecting all that does not reflect "the seer's hour of [authentic] vision . . . were it never so many times Plato's and Shakespeare's."

Generations of pedagogues have found considerable comfort in the next paragraph that begins, "Of course there is a portion of reading quite indispensable to a wise man. History and exact science he must learn by laborious reading." Again as Santayana saw, Emerson "had no system"; "he never insisted on his notions so as to turn them into settled dogmas"; "he coveted truth" rather than the triumph of "some favorite . . . idea" of his own."[11] So when he voiced that determination to remain "a system" rather than "a satellite," his metaphor was astronomical rather than philosophical. But his perfectly conventional, and certainly important, reminder that to value the pontifications of ignoramuses is to be guilty of an "exaggeration of instincts" raises—as always in any careful look at Emerson's words—more questions than it resolves. And this seems to have been true for Emerson himself:

> Because our education is defective, because we are superficial and ill-read, we were forced to make the most of that position, of ignorance; to idealize ignorance. Hence America is a vast know-nothing party, and we disparage books, and cry up intuition. With a few clever men we have made a reputable thing of that, and denouncing libraries and severe culture, and magnifying the mother-wit swagger of bright boys from country colleges, we have even come so far as to deceive everybody, except ourselves, into an admiration of un-learning and inspiration, forsooth. (374)

Now who is this "we," this recipient of Emerson's scorn and impatience in a *Journal* entry for spring of 1857? At a certain level of consciousness, and probably a pretty well-buried one, "we," at first reading so safely distant from the writer, and then from the properly informed and aware reader, becomes not merely an "all of us-in-general" but an "even *you*," the *"hypocrit lecteur,"* Emerson's *"semblable"* and *"frère,"* even "I," even Emerson himself. "Especially Emerson himself," we might better say. The old tension between the antinomian and the Arminian kept playing itself out, and Emerson's explicit statements repeatedly insist upon the need to maintain a vital balance between the two energies. But with the anxieties that fed Calvinism fast being repressed by what seemed to be an appropriately cheerful, even an at least superficially guilt-free, response to the obvious facts of life in a booming America, ideas of Arminian effort and antinomian inspiration took on for most of Emerson's audience a magnificently optimistic application that Emerson, child of the Puritans, seems not to have intended, however latent it

11. Ibid., 48–49.

may be in the words of the "American Scholar" and then, a year later, of "The Divinity School Address."

When he asserted "[t]hat man has access to the entire mind of the Creator" (50), that the "relation between the mind and matter is not fancied by some poet, but stands in the mind of God, and so is free to be known by all men" (35), he made clear enough his belief that, although any particular person might have the spiritual capacity to perceive the divine truth that was there to be perceived, such truth was not at the beck and call of just anybody at any time: "It appears to men, or it does not appear" (35). But "the genuine impulses of virtue," "the truer inspirations of all,—nay," he goes so far as to say, "the sincere moments of every man" (111) do suggest that the appearance might almost run on schedule. That suggestion, built into Emerson's early work, he could not bring himself totally to undercut even in the 1844 "Experience." True, "this new yet unapproachable America I have found in the West" (267) may at first seem to be a land that offers possibilities unrealizable "[i]n this our talking America" where "we are ruined by our good nature and listening on all sides" (272). But although most of what Emerson called "the lords of life" (by which he meant the limitations of "Illusion, Temperament," and the other obstacles to clear vision) contribute to that unapproachability, "there is that in us which changes not" (267), that which, as almost always in Emerson's work, can "make inspiration by the Divine Soul [still not] impossible" (253).

This unceasing antinomianism carries with it as counterweight that part of the heritage from the Puritan past that insisted that every person struggle, exercising every spiritual and intellectual sinew in efforts to approach the unapproachable, to receive the divine breath even though success or failure was solely at the predetermined whim of the Divine. For the Puritans, most of the population in all probability would not be of the elect; their efforts to live good lives might well fail. All must try, however, for only God could know whom He would allow to succeed, and only God could know whose success was a sign of grace and whose simply a part of the communal rather than the individual covenant. So far as natural abilities are concerned, all men are created equal in their insufficiency to measure up to the requirements for sanctification and jus-tification. That, clearly, explained why a savior had to be sent. Emerson's perspective differed in this respect from that of his ancestors, distant and immediate; still, he knew, and showed, himself to be psychologically one of them. But not quite so much publicly as privately.

In his journal for December 9, 1834—less than three years before "The American Scholar," less than two before *Nature*—we can see how the dialectic of his thought reflects both the past's grim heritage and the optimism of the present.

Democracy, Freedom, has its root in the sacred truth that every man hath
in him the divine Reason, or that, though few men since the creation of
the world live according to the dictates of Reason, yet all men are capable
of so doing. That is the equality and the only equality of all men. To this
truth we look when we say Reverence thyself; Be true to thyself.

But capacity as a potential differs in important ways from actual realiza-
tions of it by individuals. Not to recognize the difference leads to what
for Emerson is "this stale sophism" that "a plain, practical man is better
to the state than a scholar, etc." He concludes this part of the entry: "And
because God has made you capable of Reason, therefore must I hear and
accept your selfish railing, your proven falsehoods, your unconsidered
guesses as truth? ["inspiration, forsooth"(!) (374)] No; I appeal from you
to your Reason, which, with me, condemns you" (18–19). John Cotton,
on remarkably similar assumptions, insisted to Roger Williams that
anyone who persisted in error "after once or twice *Admonition*, wisely
and faithfully dispensed," did so "not out of *Conscience*, but against *his
Conscience*, as the Apostle saith, *vers.* 11 [of Titus 3]. He is subverted and
sinneth, being condemned of Himselfe, that is, of his owne *Conscience*.
So that . . . such a Man . . . is . . . sinning *against* his Owne *Conscience*."[12]

Cotton's argument against toleration rests on the certainty that truth
is both unitary and accessible. Emerson, for all his principled abhorrence
of any infringement on freedom of inquiry and of speech, has only his
sense of the progressive nature of human insight to save himself from
however much intolerance he manages to avoid. The individual soul
can trust itself, finally, because the voice from within—despite what we
might call "projection," "introjection," "transference," and the like, and
that Emerson called "Illusion, Temperament, Succession, Surface, Surprise, ... Subjectiveness" (272)—turns out to be the voice of the divine,
not just audible, but intelligible and trustworthy as well. It goes not quite
without saying that some individuals are lower down on the spiral than
others. Although Emerson can make, and take, seriously the claim that
"God is here within," he is equally serious when he insists that God is
not to be found within "the intruding rabble of men" (159): "When he
wills, he enters: when he does not will, he enters not" (209). You may
read as much "history" and "exact science" as you like, Emerson does
not quite say, but grace, true to its name, remains gratuitous.

Emerson, that is, however obliquely, however urbanely, delivers jolt
after jolt. He may not be funny; but, like great writers of humor, he forces
his readers from one perspective to another—and then, often, back again,
too. His sense of the scholar's "idle times," those periods of intellectual

12. Quoted by Roger Williams in *The Bloody Tenent*, as printed in Miller and
Johnson's *The Puritans*, 218.

and spiritual deadness that come to all, confirms Emerson's link to his Puritan past. The mystery that so much of his writing, like Cotton's words on conscience, would seem to brush aside, remains nevertheless a mystery because the Divine is not to be commanded, bullied, or bribed by words or behavior, only experienced. But this side of Emerson's thought tends to make less of an impression than all the calls for a self-reliance that is founded upon the God within. Most modern readers—in large part, perhaps, because for those moderns who read Emerson seriously his articulation of the "Divine" has metaphorical rather than substantive meaning—find Emerson's "Supernal Oneness" as unsatisfying as Poe did. Yet both Poe's flirtation with the heart Divine and Emerson's glimpses of the Over-Soul place the source of final authority where Anne Hutchinson and all antinomians place it: within the self.

That is, Poe, in asserting in *Eureka* that the "heart Divine" is "our own," says (with a different emphasis, of course) what Emerson says in "Self-Reliance": when one trusts oneself, one trusts the God within. Anne Hutchinson's receiving "an immediate revelation . . . by the voice of his [God's] own spirit to my [her] soul" points to the same sort of spiritual/psychological experience.[13] If the divine speaks as unmistakably to one as *Eureka* and the sainted Anne suggest—as Emerson at his least careful seems to imply—then the separate self of an Ishmael or a Robin totally misunderstands its situation. Not struggle but passive relaxation into the womblike embrace of a universe that is at one with the self will suffice. But the laughter of America is not the laughter of a solipsist—who, of course, would have nothing to laugh at.

4. Thoreau's Recalcitrant Individual Fires His Pistols

The far more than Josiah Holland-like ideality of the solipsist elicits the laughter of an Ishmael, or of a Robin, and the ironic humor of a Thoreau. Indeed, it took the writer whom Melville, in *The Confidence Man,* ridiculed as nothing more than his master's disciple, whom James Russell Lowell dismissed as simply having picked up the windfalls in Emerson's orchard, to assert a kind of intellectual independence that goes beyond all slavish antinomianism and all dependent Arminianism, too. Paradoxically, as everyone now knows, Thoreau, who did surely travel a great deal in Concord, nevertheless spent a lot of time at the familial fireside. But however much the dinners and laundry may seem to have compromised his independence at the level of the mundane,

13. From "November 1637. The Examination of Mrs. Ann Hutchinson at The Court of Newtown:" in Thomas Hutchinson, *The History of the Province of Massachusetts-Bay, from the Charter of King William,* 508.

they lose significance in the context of his independent achievement in going beyond, and against, the views of his mentor. The natural fact, as Thoreau will suggest in *Walden*, does not always serve as symbol for the spiritual one. The mind of the Creator is not accessible to the created. The meaning of a symbol lies not in the divine order of the universe but in the mind of the solitary and self-disciplined observer.

Thoreau, in Emerson's final slight, stands accused of having been merely "the captain of a huckleberry-party" rather than "engineering for all America." Expressing his disappointment at what he considered Thoreau's lack of ambition, Emerson sighed, "Pounding beans is good to the end of pounding empires one of these days; but if, at the end of years, it is still only beans!" (393). But let us look at just two small pieces of Thoreau's greatest empire, *Walden*. In chapter 7, "The Bean-Field," not quite halfway through the chapter, Thoreau picks up one of those Emersonian windfalls and makes it into a delightful, as well as nourishing, apple soufflé. Emerson, in "The American Scholar"—young Henry Thoreau was part of the audience that heard it first—talks about the independent judgment of the scholar, who must pursue his own ends no matter how important the world may find some temporary distraction, "some fetish of government, some ephemeral trade, or war, or man." Instead of allowing himself to become distracted by popular uproar, "[i]n silence, in steadiness, in severe abstraction, let him hold to himself"; in this context, Emerson fashions one of those aphorisms for which he is justly renowned: "Let him not quit his belief that a popgun is a popgun, though the ancient and honorable of the earth affirm it to be the crack of doom" (73–74). For Thoreau, a decade later, hoeing his beans, the thought was as pertinent as the phrasing was memorable. Hearing the cannon fired in town as part of the militia exercises, Thoreau develops both idea and image freshly, and at length.

> On gala days the town fires its great guns, which echo like popguns to these woods, and some waifs of martial music occasionally penetrate thus far. To me, there in my bean-field at the other end of the town, the big guns sounded as if a puff ball had burst. . . .

If only for its delicious humor, the whole passage of three paragraphs deserves quotation, but perhaps a reminder of its drift will suffice. Thoreau likens the "trainers" to a swarm of bees and understands the cessation of sound at the end of the day as the sign "that they had got the last drone of them all into the Middlesex hive, and that now their minds were bent on the honey with which it was smeared." From this veiled image of the militia men at their drunken revels in the local tavern, Thoreau pretends to extract emotions of patriotic fervor. He feels "proud to know that the liberties of Massachusetts and of our Fatherland were in such safe keeping," and turns back to his "hoeing again . . . filled with an inexpressible confidence, and . . . a calm trust in the future." He goes so far in his response to "the trumpet that sings of fame" as to pretend to long after a proper target for his own martial spirit: "I felt as if I could spit a Mexican with a good relish,—for why should we always stand for trifles?—and looked round for a woodchuck or a skunk to exercise my chivalry upon." But then he concludes in the same "straight"—that is, non-ironic—tone with which he had begun to talk about those pathetic "waifs" of music drifting out from town: "This was one of the *great* days; though the sky had from my clearing only the same everlastingly great look that it wears daily, and I saw no difference in it."

Impeccable punctuator that he is, with a magnificent ear for the rhythms of prose as it sounds when read aloud—*Walden* remains one of the aural masterpieces of American literature—Thoreau's neglect of commas, here, can be no accident. "The sky had, from my clearing, only the same . . ." would have been far more conventional, far less aggressive, than "the sky had, from my clearing only, the same. . . ." Thoreau knows the difference between "the crack of doom" and the sound of "popguns," no matter what "the ancient and honorable of the earth affirm" the matter to be. But also he tells us that only from the perspective of his "bean-field" is it possible, or at least probable, for such a distinction to be made. He takes into account—he tries to force his reader to take into account—the effects upon perception of living a life so independent and self-disciplined as to enable one to escape the clichés of tradition. "Nature is hard to be overcome, but she must be overcome," he will say later on, in chapter 11 ("Higher Laws"). Because his "daily work" in "The Bean-Field" focuses his energies on "making the earth say beans instead of grass," as he asserts near the beginning of the chapter, his perception differs from that of the swarm of unthinking militia men. Only when individuals tend clearings as unattached to the conventions of the hive as Thoreau's bean-field can they absorb the true "greatness" by which they are surrounded.

This proper evaluation of the relative importance of things, Thoreau agrees with Emerson, comes down to a matter of consciousness properly developed. Emerson, however, would anchor the possibility of such development to the Over-Soul, and the legitimacy of the perception to the necessary correspondence of natural fact to spiritual fact, a correspondence existing "in the will of God" and not merely "fancied by some poet," a correspondence therefore "free to be known by all men," even though not all men know it: "It appears to men, or it does not appear" (35).

Thoreau and Emerson agree that not all individuals can arrive at truth. They also agree that any such arrival depends upon the individual's disciplined and courageous trust of self. They differ profoundly, not in trust of self, but in the basis for that trust. In "The Pond in Winter" (chapter 16 of *Walden*), Thoreau tells how he set about measuring the depth of Walden Pond, motivated, apparently, by a desire to scotch the superstition "that Walden reached quite through to the other side of the globe." He observes, with scorn for both the physical and intellectual laziness at issue: "It is remarkable how long men will believe in the bottomlessness of a pond without taking the trouble to sound it." Having taken the trouble, he "can assure [his] readers that Walden has a reasonably tight bottom at a not unreasonable, though at an unusual, depth." His information is all straightforward enough, but then Thoreau sums up his sense of the significance of the pond's hundred-foot-plus depth:

> . . . not an inch of it can be spared by the imagination. What if all ponds were shallow? Would it not react on the minds of men? I am thankful that this pond was made deep and pure for a symbol. While men believe in the infinite, some ponds will be thought to be bottomless.

Thoreau's use of the word "imagination" determines the meaning of the word "symbol." In direct contradiction of Emerson, symbols do not stand in the mind of God as indicators of an extrapersonal reality. Rather, "the minds of men" react to physical reality, to nature, outside of the self, and also project onto that reality physical symbols of their own preconceptions. No ponds are in truth bottomless, but "some ponds will be thought to be" so "while men believe in the infinite." Symbols depend for their significance not upon the nature of the universe but upon the poetic creativity of the human imagination.

The heavily ironic tone to Thoreau's prose and its argumentative bellicosity, both of which sound in such great contrast to Emerson's mild assertions of self-evident truth, underscore the crucial difference between the two. Emerson looks to Nature to find or to confirm promptings from the Divine. He would be at one with the Over-Soul. In contrast, Thoreau goes to nature in order to dive into depths within. "What would we really know the meaning of?" asks Emerson, and answers his rhetorical question in words that reveal his deep belief in the comprehensibility of the universe: "The meal in the firkin; the milk in the pan; the ballad in the street;" and so on, through the whole litany of subjects for a William Dean Howells (who will quote parts of this same passage) and for a Walt Whitman and Emily Dickinson, too. But Emerson's conclusion reveals that he wants to see "the ultimate reason of these matters; show me," he commands rather than asks,

> the sublime presence of the highest spiritual cause lurking, as always it does lurk, in these suburbs and extremities of nature; let me see every trifle

bristling with the polarity that ranges it instantly on an eternal law; . . . and
the world lies no longer a dull miscellany and lumber-room, but has form
and order; there is no trifle, there is no puzzle, but one design unites the
farthest pinnacle and the lowest trench. (78)

Emerson hunts through Nature to unlock the secrets of the universe
that are implicit for the divinely inspired thinker to perceive. Thoreau's
understanding of such hunting emphasizes its illusory, and therefore
superficial, nature:

> Our voyaging is only great-circle sailing, and the doctors prescribe for
> diseases of the skin merely. One hastens to Southern Africa to chase the
> giraffe; but surely that is not the game he would be after. How long, pray,
> would a man hunt giraffes if he could? Snipes and woodcocks also may
> afford rare sport; but I trust it would be nobler game to shoot one's self.

Thoreau goes to nature not to find the God within, but to find the
self. The above brief quotation from chapter 18, "Conclusion," brings
into the open what Thoreau has been up to all along, and what he has
said, in quite different words, near the beginning of *Walden*, in "Where
I lived, and What I Lived For" (chapter 2): "We must learn to reawaken
and keep ourselves awake. . . ." From evocations of Chanticleer to his
own proposal to brag, "if only to wake my neighbors up," to the pistol
shots of his explosive prose, Thoreau's effort is always to awaken the
self, both his own and his reader's. "Why level downward to our dullest
perception always, and praise that as common Sense?" he asks a few
pages from the end, with representative Thoreauvian arrogance: "The
commonest sense is the sense of men sleeping, which they express by
snoring." The humor shocks and surprises.

This shock of humor, this jolt into a self-conscious determination to
awake from the nap that too often grips us, Thoreau aims at himself as
much as at his readers. It is the self, not a transcendent Over-Soul, that
Thoreau is out to find, to liberate, to know. "Trust thyself," he well might
say along with Emerson, but not because he saw the world as the mind
of God made accessible to man or woman. Rather, hidden and at best
partly known though it might be, the self constituted the only value-
making machinery available. By going to the woods to live deliberately
so as to drive life into a corner and be able to publish its worth to the
world, Thoreau committed himself to a disciplined, focused effort to tell
the truth. "Say what you have to say, not what you ought. Any truth is
better than make-believe." As Thoreau's example makes clear, at issue
is truth-as-integrity, not truth-as-transcendental revelation: "Tom Hyde,
the tinker, standing on the gallows, was asked if he had anything to say:
'Tell the tailors,' said he, 'to remember to make a knot in their thread
before they take the first stitch.' His companion's prayer is forgotten."

5. AT THE HEART OF ALL, THE UNKNOWABLE REMAINS

Truth-telling turns out to be difficult. Even so unusual a maverick as
Thoreau sometimes tells it only by indirection, and one would have difficulty finding a book more seemingly personal yet more psychologically
reticent than *Walden*. Edgar Allan Poe recognized this truth about truth-
telling in one of his bits of magazine-filler, "The Impossibility of Writing
a Truthful Autobiography."[14] To achieve "immortal renown," all that
anyone "has to do is to write and publish a very little book. Its title
should be simple—a few plain words—*My Heart Laid Bare*. But—this
little book must be *true to its title*." And isn't it strange, Poe muses, that
not even those people "who care not a fig for what is thought of them
after death" can "write this little book?" For Poe, the writing itself is the
issue: "There are ten thousand men who, if the book were once written,
would laugh at the notion of being disturbed by its publication. . . . But
to write it—*there* is the rub. No man dare write it. No man ever will dare
write it. No man *could* write it, even if he dared." And then, in his last
sentence, Poe blows smoke in the reader's face: the reason why no one
could write the truth? "The paper would shrivel and blaze at every touch
of the fiery pen." But Poe has a different sort of resistance in mind.

Mark Twain, writing his *Autobiography* without much concern for any
"unconscious pulsations" (let us not forget Daniel Hoffman's phrase
concerning what makes Poe's tales tick),[15] sees the problem not as unconscious resistance but as lack of will, not all that different in substance
from Poe's sense of impossibility, but phrased differently. In his preface
(Volume 1, p. xv), Twain announces that he will be "literally speaking
from the grave," a decision about his book's publication that he has come
to in order to assure himself—and us—that he will be "speaking his
whole frank mind." Later on, this grand ambition withers in the heat of
a psychic reality not very different from the reality that Poe had evoked,
although Poe's wording suggests a more obvious, a very self-conscious,
euphemism. Twain's seems, on the surface, to be very simple. Twain
recounts his long-ago advice to his brother Orion, suggesting that anyone
who could "tell the straight truth" in an autobiography and "honorably
set down all the incidents of his life which he had found interesting to
him, including those which were burned into his memory because he was
ashamed of them," would produce "a most valuable piece of literature."

> I recognize now [Twain-the-autobiographer confesses] that I was trying to
> saddle him with an impossibility. I have been dictating this autobiography
> of mine daily for three months; I have thought of fifteen hundred or two

14. Poe, *The Viking Portable Edgar Allan Poe*, 650–51.
15. Hoffman, *Poe²*, 316.

thousand incidents in my life which I am ashamed of, but I have not gotten one of them to consent to go on paper yet.

Poe's metaphor of the burning page and Twain's evocation of burning shame can perhaps be taken as equivalents, although both strike me as curiously incomplete. I say "curiously" because my own belief is that both Poe and Twain, elsewhere in their writings, show awareness of the reality and unknowability of what Mark Twain at times labeled "the Dream-Self."[16] He shows in the story that this "dream self," as he spelled it in his notebook,[17] remains hidden from the "Waking-Self," and develops the idea in the *Notebook* in a context concerned with the "distinct duality" of the two and with the existence of the "wholly independent personage who resides in me—and whom I will call Watson." But this Watson and his implied Holmes—the conscious self—appear never to meet, for "the two persons in a man do not even *know* each other and are not aware of each other's existence."[18] For Poe, one has only to think of "William Wilson," especially in conjunction with Daniel Hoffman's implication that only through "images" (rather than direct statements) can "unconscious pulsations" be made accessible—but texts abound. Truth-telling—indeed, the very knowing of the truth—becomes possible only, as Emily Dickinson suggested, if one can tell it "slant" (Johnson #1129).

Among the constraints that inhibit and frustrate the most determined efforts to tell this "truth," the weight of tradition, of the past, of received wisdom, operates in ways often subtle and unrecognized. Poe, Thoreau, Twain: whoever gives much thought to the problem comes to an awareness that more than awareness is at issue. Twain, in, for example, *What Is Man?*, talks about the factor of self-interest as determining one's actions. Only insofar as one anticipates a boost to one's self-approval does one act. I am simplifying, but Twain's point, in context, is clear enough: one does at the time what, at that time, one judges to be most likely to produce comfort in the self about the self. A second later, and one's estimation of the effect of an action may have changed. Then one acts anew, perhaps in regret for the immediately previous deed.

Twain's formulation takes into account the immense force of public opinion. For Twain, the approval of others exerted power over most of an individual's choices and views. His famous "Corn-Pone Opinions" essay makes clear how vulnerable he saw human beings, including himself, to be to the "corn-pone" (the approval) of others. Although we may think

16. See especially the manuscript that he named "No. 44, The Mysterious Stranger," 342, et al., in *Mark Twain: The Mysterious Stranger*.

17. See *Mark Twain's Notebook*, ed. Paine, 348–52.

18. Ibid., 350.

we are independent, " 'You tell me whar a man gits his corn pone, en I'll tell you what his opinions is.' " This sort of conformity, he thought, sometimes has a quite conscious financial motive, "but not in most cases. . . . [I]n the majority of cases, it is unconscious and not calculated; . . . born of the human's natural yearning to stand well with his fellows. . . ."[19] So telling the truth in public puts at too great risk one's supply of nurturing "corn-pone." For Poe, among the unconscious forces that get in the way of truth, the principle of perversity ranks highest. This principle, laid out in "The Imp of the Perverse," accounts for the impulses toward self-destructive behavior that Poe almost systematically wrote into the protagonists of so many of his stories. When they confess to murder or cast themselves over precipices, they are enslaved by inner voices as surely as Twain's people are by internalized tradition or popular opinion. Poe cannot write "My Heart Laid Bare," nor can anyone, because no one can peel away all of the defensive layers that shroud those inner depths.

A kind of determinism operates, here, insofar as lack of awareness leaves individuals at the mercy of the past, whether individual or collective. Thoreau tackles this head-on in the first chapter of *Walden* in his distressed account of how what " 'They' " do and say affects the deeds and thoughts of individuals:

> I sometimes despair of getting anything quite simple and honest done in this world by the help of men. They would have to be passed through a powerful press first, to squeeze their old notions out of them, so that they would not soon get upon their legs again; and then there would be some one in the company with a maggot in his head, hatched from an egg deposited there nobody knows when, for not even fire kills these things, and you would have lost your labor.

But no matter how much aggression gets directed against individuals and their ideas, the vitality of old habits of thought continues to exert its force. And the last sentence of Thoreau's paragraph implies that this force need not, and cannot, always be seen as having a negative effect: "Nevertheless, we will not forget that some Egyptian wheat was handed down to us by a mummy."

Thoreau recognizes that his attack upon the forces of tradition, of convention, that his brave call for independence, cannot have an unqualified and universal success, but at best may make a glancing impact on the lives of peculiarly strenuous-minded individuals, like himself. Life at Walden Pond, his great metaphor for deliberate living and self-conscious confrontation with life and with that which interferes with one's encounters with it, is life in a corner of the world that "tolerates

---

19. *Mark Twain: Selected Writings of an American Skeptic*, 426, 428.

[but] one annual loon" (chapter 9), whose name is Henry David Thoreau. Such "lunatics" of nonconformity may threaten those who cling to the status quo, perhaps to the extent that someone will accuse them of promulgating "the latest form of infidelity," perhaps to the greater extent of being either ignored or misread as a simple conservationist of nature.

The notion that truth-telling becomes, finally, an impossibility lies at the heart of the opposition to the Genteel Tradition as American writers have found themselves, most often without quite knowing it, opposing the principal manifestations of that tradition. Willful lying, in all its disgusting immorality, does, to be sure, affront and insult, but poses no metaphysical threat: the liar knows the truth; those lied to will discover that truth, although perhaps too late to avoid immediate injury. Simon Suggs is a mendacious scalawag, but his victims, too, are lying about their piety or wealth or humility. The victims of Twain's king, however, imply no self-aggrandizing lies about themselves. Instead, they present themselves as easy victims because they fail to know themselves well enough; breaking none of the rules themselves, by their very nature they invite the con-game that robs them, thereby giving many of the genteel readers of Twain's day considerable discomfort. Superficially, they embodied the vulgarity that led librarians in Concord, Massachusetts, and Brooklyn, New York, to condemn the book.

More important, however, was their implicit subversion of genteel certainty. They believed lies, but the ones that contributed most to their victimization were not told by skillful confidence-persons but were instead a function of their failure to comprehend themselves. They believed untruths about themselves and about the nature of reality generally, but those untruths were less deliberate prevarications than comfortable assumptions based upon a structure of wish that encouraged the ignoring of the bedrock of uncomfortable experience. By presenting such easy victims upon the page, Twain no doubt made his readers squirm. With the hindsight of the years, one has an easy time understanding why Herman Melville's *The Confidence-Man,* appearing in 1857 and with a central figure operating in contexts and guises far less easily defended against than the blatant king and duke, persuaded its author that public demand for his long fiction had become non-existent. Curious, is it not, that both Melville and Twain should be in such agreement about the incapacity of dupes to know the truth not simply about the wicked other but about their own gullible selves?

Almost fifty years ago, in his preface to the Rinehart edition of *Huckleberry Finn,* Lionel Trilling pointed out that the really subversive force of the book lay in its calling into question the unthinking, perhaps not quite conscious, assumption that the social habits and prejudices of a particular time and place rightly had the force of moral absolutes, valid universally. The climax of such questioning occurs, as most readers now recognize, when Huck decides to do his best to free Jim, thereby condemning himself to hell for a decision that readers applaud. Certainty has disappeared long before then, however, as in chapter 23, when Huck makes the astounding discovery that Jim "cared just as much for his people as white folks does for their'n." What matters is not just the discovery, but Huck's rumination upon it: "It don't seem natural," he admits, "but I reckon it's so." By having Huck think in terms of what is "natural" and what isn't, Twain dramatized in his fiction the exposition of cultural conditioning, and of the assumptions people make about the privileged status of their own morality, that he was developing in his "certain sweet-smelling, sugar-coated lies" essay around the same time as he was finishing Huck's *Adventures*.[20]

But this was not something that most of his immediate readership was prepared to notice, much less understand. The genteel certainties of Josiah Holland's Timothy Titcomb remained in place. Only gradually, at least at first, and then with a rush, did the protective walls come crumbling down, even though the crumbling now seems to have been going on for a long time. And this brings me to my last reference to the Anglican heritage, a reference of which the value lies in its representative nature. Born in 1680, Nathan Marshall, D.D., in his position as "Canon of Windsor, and Chaplain . . . to His Majesty" George I (and then, until Marshall's death in the winter of 1729–1730, to George II), was neither exalted bishop nor ordinary vicar. Certainly he outranked most of his fellows of the cloth; and, equally certain, as George I's choice for royal chaplain, he could be expected to sympathize with his more Calvin-istically antinomian, less Arminianly Anglican, colleagues rather than otherwise. The representative nature of Marshall's utterances reflects how, by the early eighteenth century, the great Anglican compromise was working out in practice. Even though he stresses God's foreknowl-edge of human activities, Marshall preaches a "straight" Arminian-like Anglican line, for his era. More important for my purposes here is that he represents perfectly the smug and complacent certainty that on the other side of the Atlantic came to be perceived as part of the orthodoxy with which most of our enduring nineteenth-century writers struggled. Nathan Marshall—like a great number of his contemporaries—preached sermons of a sort that gives fresh resonance to the phrase, "the age of enlightenment." Enlightenment, to hear him tell it, is what Marshall values most. Preaching before the King at St. James's on November 5, 1714, he laments the effects of "Pride of Understanding . . . Prejudices

---

20. *Mark Twain's Autobiography*, ed. Paine, 2: 8–9.

of Education . . . an ignorant zeal . . . Indulgence to some one or more very vehement Affections," for "if the understanding be elated with Pride, be stopped up by Prejudice, be over-clouded with an ignorant zeal, or enslaved to vicious Affections; . . . how fatal must that darkness be?" To counteract such darkness, both "reason" and "the Authority of Revelation" come to our rescue: our reason tells us that God is always "true and gracious"; that God-given reason we are to trust:

> The Attributes of God are, in like manner, concurrent supports of all Revelation; and even the evidence of miracles consists upon them: For the truth and goodness of God are our great securities, that he would not lend out his power, in aid of a false Pretention, to cheat or to abuse us by it. A Revelation therefore which would represent God, otherwise than as true and gracious, would here again undermine one of its chief supports. . . . the eternal reason of things is contradicted, and Religion is made to turn against its own most avowed design and interest, whenever revealed and moral Truths are represented opposite to each other. It is as impossible that they be really so as it is that God should repent or lie.

What Marshall is really talking about does not emerge at all clearly from the above for reasons that will immediately come clear when one remembers that Queen Anne, daughter of the late and variously remembered James II, had died just three months earlier. November 5, a required occasion on which to preach thanksgivings for the national blessings of 1688 as well as of 1605, had raised problems for the clergy during her reign. As Marshall reminds his auditors, perhaps informing his king, Queen Anne

> was so well entitled to the Hearts of her People, that they could not be bold with a subject which carried an apparent Reproach along with it upon the conduct of her Royal Father. . . . Where-fore when the Praises due to the great Instrument of our Deliverance was unhappily mixed with the reproaches of her King and Father, what could with decency come from us, but the tenderest mention of the one and of the other?

The event of 1605 poses no problem, of course, but the "second Deliverance" of 1688 makes for hard going, especially in the context of insisting upon the obedience due to a monarch.

> Here indeed we confess a Difficulty, which obliges us always to speak of that whole Transaction with some reserve. . . . Yet within these reserves, we may be full of a grateful sense to God and to his instruments, for securing to us our happy Constitution; nor do we arraign the Means which were necessary to that great end; though we are cautious of forming rules upon anomalous emergencies; since whatever weakens the barrier of Majesty, will be found to impair the People's security; who never are in more imminent Danger of Ruin, than when they are entrusted with the Guardianship of their own Safety.

This last remark concerning what most puts the masses "in imminent danger" acquires special point when one remembers that democratically oriented John Wise had published his "reply in Satyre, to certain Proposals" (*The Churches Quarrel Espoused*) the previous year and would publish *A Vindication of the Government of New England Churches* less than three years later. Still, Marshall—who, like Wise, alludes to Pufendorf to support his own position[21]—takes a remarkable step in at least accepting the means by which the House of Hanover marched to the rescue and by which was secured "to us our happy Constitution." "The People" may be incapable either of understanding or of acting on behalf of their own best interest, but they could, and should, assist even in breaching "the barrier of Majesty" if the ends have importance sufficient to justify such "anomalous" means.

Seven years later, in the January 30 sermon for 1721/1722, Marshall once more raised the issue of the "means" employed in 1688 along with that of the intelligibility and reasonableness of the ways of God. His acceptance of the former depends precisely upon his assumption of the latter. He approaches both head-on, tackling first the vexing question of Charles's suffering in the context of God's justice. Like a magician about to pull a rabbit from an empty hat, Marshall begins by exhibiting the difficulties that he will have to overcome. First, he takes as his text Exodus 20:5, the passage asserting the nature and ways of "a jealous God, visiting the iniquity of the fathers upon the children unto the third and fourth generation of them that hate me." Then he sets himself the goal of "vindicat[ing] this (seemingly) harsh and unequitable dispensation," using "the three following particulars, as the Foundations. . . . 1. That God never punisheth any man, but for sin. 2. Never in strictness, (the Case of our Saviour alone excepted) but for his own sin. And 3. Never (then) any further, than his own sin deserveth." Marshall understands God's ways perfectly, and they just happen to coincide with a perfectly moral and "Arminianized" worldview. Even should the unlikely event occur that God sees fit to punish future generations a very little bit more than might seem proportionate to their sins,

> Whatever then the descendents from wicked ancestors may suffer, on account, or by occasion, of their forefathers and their guilt, cannot reflect the least disparagement upon the Justice or Goodness of God; because he can so easily, improve it to their profit, and render it thereby the object of a reasonable and prudent choice to them.

---

21. In *A Defense of Our Constitution in Church and State; or, An Answere to the late Charge of the Non-Jurors* (London, 1717, 97–98), Nathan Marshall finds in his source what he needs, although it is quite different from what Wise finds there: "Puffendorfe is a little more favourable [than Grotius] to the Rights of Monarchy. . . ."

That is, they can decide to mend their ways and thereby "add . . . to their future (eternal) Happiness. . . ." This kind of moral and metaphysical smugness, usually associated with Job's comforters, lies at the heart of the genteel tradition. God's universe conforms to ideas in human minds; "the poet's ideal is the embodiment of God's will."[22]

At the same time, Marshall acknowledges the truth that a "righteous man hath, more than once, been given up into wicked hands; as a righteous Prince was, this Day, made a sacrifice to the meanest and vilest of his People." Although he avoids the suggestion that Charles achieved Christ-like perfection, he does assert that "every thing was redressed by the King which could be called a grievance, before the sword of war was drawn."

> Yet at last some errors in the government of this gracious Prince, tho' magnified beyond all proportion, the Laws of truth will not permit us utterly to deny; as I am sure, the rules of decency will not allow us to publish, nor to blazon them upon this sorrowful occasion. [So much for Charles.] Much rather would I choose to intreat your farther patience, whilst two sorts of People are here reminded of their common error. For surely the Wet Martyrdom [the bloody decollation of Charles I] and the Dry One [James II, although driven into exile, lost no blood] (as some of late have affected to distinguish) differ more essentially than they are willing to allow on either side, who would mitigate on one hand, the horrors of this Day's Tragedy; or would blacken, on the other, the Means and Methods of our present Establishment. Both should remember, that the one preserved our Monarchy, whilst the other subverted it; that the one secured to us our holy Religion, and the Profession of our Faith in its ancient purity; whilst the other tore up its fences, threw open its enclosures, and let in upon us a sweeping deluge of Enthusiasm, Bigottry, and Superstition.[23]

He never actually says, "Wherefore by their fruits ye shall know them," but he probably expected his auditors to remember Matthew 7:20 on their own. The result of 1648 reveals how bankrupt were the means used then:

> We feel, to this Day, the genuine consequences of that detested year. . . . For this is plainly the destructive Root, which hath scattered amongst us such pestilent seeds of Discord and animosity, as threatens all public spirit, all common honesty, all virtue, learning, and religion, with their malignant and fatal influence. For, when men saw Religion abused; when (as a Nobel Historian—Lord Clarendon—very smartly observes) Praying and Preaching were the talents and employments of all, but scholars; it could be no great wonder, if the rising generation were scandalized at these

22. Josiah G. Holland, "The Poetic Test," from *Lessons in Life*.
23. This is from a later January 30 sermon, the year of which I have not been able to determine.

nauseous pretensions, and fell quite out with a Religion, whose loudest Professors were, in the main, directed either by very naughty hearts, or else by very sickly brains.

Given God's "truth and goodness" (spelled out in Marshall's sermon for November 5, 1714, as quoted above), the results of the "Wet Martyrdom" —so objectively set forth by Lord Clarendon—should lead all sensible readers to a proper condemnation of the means then employed. The results of the "Dry Martyrdom" being so conspicuously salutary, Jacobite sympathies reveal a wicked as well as an unpatriotic heart.

The characteristic most prominently shared by this very representative Anglican of the early eighteenth century and by prominent Puritans of the early seventeenth manifests itself as a committed, an involved, even an involuted, seriousness about the world, the Lord, and their relations with each other. Their certainty that they knew the truth, that their party or religion had exclusive possession of the truth, seems often to have overridden all other considerations. Behind H. L. Mencken's famously barbed definition ("Puritanism—The haunting fear that someone, somewhere, may be happy.")[24] lies something more than wrongheadedness alone. We know from his journal that John Winthrop, serious civic leader though he was, took time now and then to appreciate a jest of his own making; we have seen that Nathaniel Ward could exaggerate his cobbler's rage to a laughable extent and that he enjoyed playing on words. But that Puritans and their descendants in the main distrusted humor seems true beyond any cavil. The 1872 biographer of Johnson Jones Hooper spoke for a number of generations when he observed that "[w]hile Mr. Hooper gained celebrity as a humorist, he lost something of a higher value in public estimation. . . . Here let him stand as a beaconlight, to give warning of the rock on which the manly ambition of his youth perished."[25]

Lord Chesterfield's famous concern for decorum, his condemnation of laughter as a kind of behavior "characteristic of folly and ill manners, . . . so illiberal, and so ill-bred" that Chesterfield could "heartily wish that you [his natural son] may often be seen to smile, but never to laugh while you live,"[26] helped to establish the standard of respectability by which Hooper and his fellow humorists were measured. Bonamy Dobrée, from whose edition of Lord Chesterfield's letters I have just quoted, adds a footnote attributing the same sentiments to Swift, Pope, Congreve, and Fontenelle, the latter of whom "was proud that during his reasoning life he had never 'fait ha! ha!'" The perspective shared by these gentlemen

---

24. H. L. Mencken, *A Mencken Chrestomathy,* 624.
25. Blair, *Native American Humor,* 108–9.
26. Chesterfield, *The Letters of Philip Dormer Stanhope, 4th Earl of Chesterfield,* 3: 1115.

assumes their antidemocratic repugnance not only to laughter but also to vernacular characteristics in general. To laugh at the vulgar becomes in due course to laugh with them. Finding entertainment in the antics of the low is not an immense step from finding a belief, a trust, not so much in a rule of the common people (a political *demo cracy*) but in the intelligence, perceptions, and perhaps finally the tastes of such boors, too.

But, clearly, Lord Chesterfield and others similarly educated and sophisticated make up the pool from which should come those competent, proper, genteel adults, those Major Molineauxes, whom God has equipped, and called, to govern the rabble. No? No: the rabble, let us not forget, finds its apotheosis in Huckleberry Finn—whose "real-life" model, Tom Blankenship, became a respected Justice of the Peace in the Wyoming Territory—as well as in Sut Lovingood, in the "edge-tools" who are John Wise's church members as well as in the victims of Hooper's and Twain's camp meetings. Americans today, accustomed to finding the "experts" routinely divided as to what course to pursue—whether in foreign affairs, domestic economy, or social morality—should have little trouble recognizing the long-hidden virtues of democratic decision-making. The aristocratic pretensions of a Lord Chesterfield no longer compel attention, with regard either to government or to laughter.

6. PURITAN REJECTION OF PURITAN REALITY — AND WHAT ABOUT US?

But there is another basis for the rejection that humor and laughter have to overcome. Let us remember that, just as assumptions about being God's New Israel turned out to have strong British Anglican as well as colonial Puritan backing, so, too, British Puritans themselves shared later Anglican aversion to laughter, albeit for different reasons. Is it possible to remain unreservedly committed to doing God's will on this earth if one also finds amusement in the doings of one's fellow human beings? Is it possible to take worthy matters seriously if one acquires the habit of laughing at what is unworthy? This query evokes a perspective quite different from that of the worldly Lord Chesterfield. Like his, it, too, helped directly to shape the nineteenth-century attitude toward humor. It finds its weightiest embodiment in the principal Puritan document in the war on laughter, a "pamphlet" (as it is usually called by those who quote it) of more than 1,150 pages, *Histrio-Mastix. The players scourge, or, actors tragedie, . . . wherein it is largely evidenced, by divers arguments, . . . that popular stage-playes . . . are sinfull, heathenish, lewde, ungodly spectacles, and most pernicious corruptions . . . to the manners, mindes, and soules of men* [and on and on]. Published in London, in 1633, its author was the same William Prynne whose ears the Court of Star Chamber so brutally ordered removed as partial punishment for his having dared publish this same volume.

It cannot be said that Prynne's attack on laughter stimulated the total seriousness with which his production was viewed, but the immediate results of Prynne's words were very serious indeed. Because *Histrio-Mastix* appeared "almost simultaneous with the appearance of Queen Henrietta Maria and her ladies in a court performance . . . (January, 1633)," the apparent insult to Charles II's wife in "Prynne's unfortunate invective against actresses" led to "a trial for sedition and libel" that totally discounted the eight years in which the book had been in the works and, instead, saw it as an immediate and deliberate effort at subversion of the royal authority.[27] The Court of Star Chamber had no capacity for perceiving itself and its concerns as anything but of central importance. The same absence of humor tends to characterize all groups and individuals whose endeavors seem to them to matter cosmically. For Puritans and Anglicans of the seventeenth century, assured as they were that their own polity and belief bore the burden and privilege of God's special concern, to fail to take themselves seriously would have been to affront their God. But Prynne insists, and shows, that others besides Puritans were in principled opposition to the theater and to the laughter it occasioned. Those who find him and others who shared his views, including numerous church fathers (whom he cites),

> more than puritanically rigid in this point of laughter, let them hearken what some Pagan Authors have resolved of it, whom none dare tax of Puritanisme. "No man" (writes Plato) "ought to be affected with the desire of laughter." . . . Catullus, as wanton a poet as any, records; "That there is nothing more unseemly than wanton foolish laughter." (296)

And, as if to underscore his objectivity, here, Prynne later numbers Catullus among those writers whose works "Christians are expressly condemned and prohibited" from reading (916).

Prynne, to be sure, objects to "Stage-playes" for the standard Puritan reasons that they waste time and money (302, 311, et al.), and also that they have among their many deleterious effects "the irritation, the inflamation, the fomentation of divers sinful lusts, of many lewde, unchaste adulterous affections" (327), not only adultery itself, but, because of the appearance of boys and men in women's apparel, "that unnaturall Sodomiticall sinne of uncleanesse" (208). More than one hundred pages of *Histrio-Mastix*, however, urge in order to condemn (well beyond the

27. See Arthur Freeman's preface to the 1974 facsimile edition of William Prynne, *Histrio-Mastix*.

point of redundancy) the necessary connection between theatrical pre-
sentations and laughter, Prynne's end being to discredit the laughter and
therefore the plays:

> [T]he laughter Playes occasion, (which is their chiefest end,) is a sufficient
> evidence of their excessive folly; and so is ground enough for Christians,
> for all men to condemne them as vanities, as fooleries, as Clements Alexan-
> drinus, and other Fathers doe at large declare [175]. Stage-laughter . . .
> is altogether unseemely, unseasonable unto Christians . . . [because] alto-
> gether inconsistent with the gravity, modesty, and sobriety of a Christian,
> whose affections should be more sublime, more serious and composed,
> then to be immoderately tickled with meere lascivious vanities, or to lash
> out in excessive cachinnations in the publike view of dissolute gracelesse
> persons, who will be hardened and encouraged in their lascivious courses,
> by their ill example. (293)

Histrio-Mastix stands mainly as a monument to Puritan rejection of
the theater; but in Prynne's objection to laughter we find at work an
expression, if not quite a consciousness, of a concern that finds full voice
in nineteenth-century American calls for "reverence" and that accounts
for a fair part of Prynne's own rejection of dramatic performance.

This part of his dim view of the theater, with laughter as its "chiefest
end," focuses on the laughers, the audience. On the one hand, and
with several references to John 11:35 ("Jesus wept"), Prynne insists
that "Christ Jesus our patterne, our example, whose steps we all must
follow, if ever we expect salvation from him; was always mourning,
never laughing . . ." (294). "Paul likewise wept night and day for yeeres
together," Prynne claims, "but that he ever laughed, neither doth he
himselfe shew any where nor any other for him" (403). Beyond Paul
and Jesus and their brief moment, Prynne, struggling toward a worldly,
practical objection to laughter, also surveys the subject historically, and
concludes that those "who were very studious of jesting Comedies, were
so accustomed to laugh at Playes, that they could not forbeare laughter
in their solemne sacrifices, nor their most serious affairs" (300). That is,
having acquired the habit of laughing, they can be seen to have turned
matters of high importance, both religious and civil, into mere spectacles
to which they could respond as distanced spectators.

Not only does laughter at vice encourage the vicious; of more importance is the effect of the laughter upon the laughers. To laugh in the
midst of one's "solemne sacrifices" or "most serious affairs" suggests a
distancing, a sudden change of perspective. What should be of supreme
importance shrinks for a moment—perhaps for more than a moment—
to comparative unimportance. When young Goodman Brown's howls
of laughter fill the forest, Brown, no longer vacillating between curiosity
and repugnance, has become "the chief horror of the scene," roaring

back at the sounds that afflict his ears, " 'Come witch, come wizard, come Indian powwow, come devil himself, and here comes Goodman Brown. You may as well fear him as he fear you.' " Brown laughs in self-disgust as he gives up his spiritual independence. Similarly, Hawthorne's Robin, as I began by trying to suggest, laughs in equal self-disgust at the dependence to which he has clung. In each case, a young man concerned with very serious affairs indeed suddenly sees them in a new light.

If we wrench our minds from Hawthorne's bitter laughers to the 1877 *Atlantic* dinner and the response to Mark Twain's address, we can see that the writers of both editorial and letter in the Springfield *Republican* shared William Prynne's concern about the effect of laughter on laughers. Twain, in using serious, revered poetry to encourage Prynne's loathed "cachinnations," brings out not the best but the beast in his hearers, leading them—according to the damning, damaging old assumption—to treat lightly matters of weight and majesty. The Truth in the lines of poetry that Twain ripped out of context corresponds to the ideal world in the poet's head, the world that works according to God's plan.

To step back from the vision of the ideal so as to see the measles and squabbles and animosities that beset real people means either to weep at the discrepancy or to laugh at the incongruity. Humor, therefore, suggests detachment. Psychologist William McDougall in 1923 saw laughter as " 'Nature's' antidote for the sympathetic tendencies";[28] Henri Bergson insisted that "laughter has no greater foe than emotion," and saw that "the comic" insists on "something like a momentary anesthesia of the heart."[29] Dr. Holland, presumably content with his formulation of ideality, and concerned to explain away, rather than disinterestedly enjoy, the discrepancy between things "as they are" and things "as they ought to be," seems to have intended no humor in his mention of measles, just as the "much good will it do" in the concluding words of his "The Poetic Test" seems only unintentionally ironic, from our not very reverent perspective: "When the world shall reach the poet's ideal, it will arrive at perfection; and much good will it do the world to measure itself by this ideal, and struggle to lift the real to its lofty level." Holland's emotional investment in his sense of the ideal precluded his amusement.

As Mark Twain's Satan observed,[30] laughter alone can free us from the bondage to the past that we so often perceive—both rightly and

---

28. William McDougall, in *Outline of Psychology*, 165–68, as brilliantly summed up by Ralph Piddington, *The Psychology of Laughter: A Study in Social Adaptation*, 206.

29. See John Morreall, "Humor and Emotion" (1983), and Henri Bergson, from *Laughter: An Essay on the Meaning of the Comic* (1900), both in *The Philosophy of Laughter and Humor*, ed. Morreall.

30. "The Chronicle of Young Satan," in *The Mysterious Stranger*, ed. Gibson, 166, as read in Covici, *Mark Twain's Humor*, 240–41, 246–47.

wrongly—to be the source of our strength. But such freedom, by the very nature of our all-too-human psyches, can be at best fleeting and incomplete. Our ties to our various pasts we seem perpetually to ignore and deny and distort, and always to our peril. George Santayana's sense that "modern American[s]" are compulsive in their predilection for "joking"[31] no doubt has to do with an outsider's sense that we laugh in order not to think about what lies behind us, about what may be gaining on us. "Borne back ceaselessly into the past," as F. Scott Fitzgerald said, we can perhaps empathize with the struggles of our predecessors to acknowledge and to resist, to discover and to hide from view. Never to laugh, or always to laugh? At different times we have tried both ways: Prynne and Josiah Holland, Jim Doggett and the inhabitants of the world of situation comedy. Holland and Prynne wanted people to understand the truth. The "truths" that they wanted understood seem, now, to have been truncated, selective, skewed. At the other extreme, Jim Doggett preferred to laugh so as not to have to understand; we last see him as he prepares to return to the incomprehensible wilderness from which he has so recently emerged to visit the at least equally opaque city.

Never to laugh, or always to laugh? When our writers succeed in putting before us (and in pushing us to experience) violent shifts of perspective like those that we have been examining, they may perhaps make us smile; they certainly make us think. Robin's sense of his kinsman, Melville's narrator's sense of a world that contains both Paradise and Tartarus, Mark Twain's sudden forcing of the language of genteel poetry out of the ideal and into the literal realm (as when "Longfellow" steals real shoes in order to leave real footprints): whether or not we laugh, we have to think and we have to look. What we often see is that Americans, finally, may be human beings writ large, individuals who keep on denying part of what they have been, becoming, in part, what they have denied. Our writers make this clear. Who runs may read. More to the point, when we stop running and pause for a while, we find ourselves able to read.

31. Santayana, "The Genteel Tradition," 43.

Bibliography

Bergson, Henri. *Laughter: An Essay on the Meaning of the Comic*. New York, 1900.

Binckes, William. *A Prefatory Discourse to an Examination of a late Book, Entitled An Exposition of the Thirty-Nine Articles of the Church of England, by Gilbert, Bishop of Sarum*. London, 1702.

Blair, Walter. *Native American Humor, 1800–1900*. New York: American Book Company, 1937.

Bohi, Janette. "Nathaniel Ward, A Sage of Old Ipswich," *Essex Institute Historical Collection* 99: 3–32.

Bozeman, Theodore Dwight. *To Live Ancient Lives: The Primitivist Dimension in Puritanism*. Chapel Hill: University of North Carolina Press, 1988.

Burnet, Gilbert. *An Exposition of the Thirty-Nine Articles of the Church of England*. London, 1699, and at least 11 later editions.

Chase, Richard. *The American Novel and Its Tradition*. Garden City: Doubleday Anchor, 1957.

Chesterfield, Earl of. *The Letters of Philip Dormer Stanhope, 4th Earl of Chesterfield*. Ed. Bonamy Dobrée. Six volumes. New York: Viking, 1932.

Cohen, Hennig, and William B. Dillingham, eds. *The Humor of the Old Southwest*. Boston: Houghton Mifflin, Riverside, 1964; reprinted Athens: University of Georgia Press, 1975.

Comber, Thomas, D.D. (Dean of Durham). *A Discourse on The Offices for the Vth of November, the XXXth of January, and the XXIX of May.* London, 1696.

Cotton, John. "Christian Calling," from *The Way of Life*. London, 1641.

Covici, Pascal, Jr. "God's Chosen People: Anglican Views, 1607–1807." *Studies in Puritan American Spirituality* 1 (December 1990): 97–128.

———. *Mark Twain's Humor: The Image of a World*. Dallas: Southern Methodist University Press, 1962.

Cross, Amanda [Carolyn Heilbrun]. *No Word from Winifred*. New York: Ballantine, 1988.

Dickinson, Emily. *Final Harvest*. Ed. Thomas H. Johnson. Boston: Little, Brown, 1962.

Donovan, Frank, ed. *The Benjamin Franklin Papers*. New York: Dodd, Mead, 1962.

Emerson, Ralph Waldo. *Selections from Ralph Waldo Emerson: An Organic Anthology*. Ed. Stephen E. Whicher. Boston: Houghton Mifflin, 1960.

Franklin, Benjamin. *Autobiography and Selected Writings*. Ed. Larzer Ziff. New York: Holt, Rinehart and Winston, 1963.

———. *Benjamin Franklin's Autobiographical Writings*. Ed. Carl Van Doren. New York: Viking, 1945.

———. Number 4 of "The Dogood Papers," *New-England Courant* for "Monday March 26 to Monday April 2. 1722." Widely reprinted.

Hall, Max. *Benjamin Franklin and Polly Baker: The History of a Literary Deception*. Chapel Hill: University of North Carolina Press, 1960.

Harris, George Washington. *Sut Lovingood. Yarns Spun by a "Nat'ral Born Durn'd Fool.["] Warped and Wove for Public Wear*. New York, 1867.

Heimert, Alan, and Andrew Delbanco, eds. *The Puritans in America: A Narrative Anthology*. Cambridge: Harvard University Press, 1985.

Hirose, Norio. "Humor in *The Big Bear of Arkansas*." *Studies in American Literature* (17: 1–20). Kyoto: American Literature Society of Japan, 1980.

Hoffman, Daniel. *Poe Poe Poe Poe Poe Poe Poe*. Garden City: Doubleday, 1972; Anchor Press edition, 1973.

Holland, Josiah Gilbert. *Lessons in Life: A Series of Familiar Essays*. New York: Charles Scribner's Sons, 1861. Reprinted in 1881 and 1893.

Holland, Norman N. *Laughing: A Psychology of Humor*. Ithaca: Cornell University Press, 1982.

Holmes, Geoffrey. *The Trial of Dr. Sacheverell*. London: Eyre Methuen, 1973.

Hoole, W. Stanley. *Alias Simon Suggs: The Life and Times of Johnson Jones Hooper*. Tuscaloosa: University of Alabama Press, 1952.

Hooper, Johnson Jones. *Some Adventures of Captain Simon Suggs*. Philadelphia, 1846.

Houston, Neal B., and Fred A. Rodewald. " 'My Kinsman, Major Molineux': A Re-Evaluation." *Proceedings of the CCTE [College Conference of Teachers of English] of Texas* 34 (1969): 18–22.

Howells, William Dean. *Criticism and Fiction*. New York: Harper and Brothers, 1891.

Hutchinson, Thomas. *The History of the Province of Massachusetts-Bay, from the Charter of King William*. Boston, 1767.

Inge, M. Thomas, ed. *High Times and Hard Times*. Knoxville: Vanderbilt University Press, 1967.

———. *The Frontier Humorists: Critical Views*. Hamden: Archon, 1975.

Kaplan, Justin. *Mr. Clemens and Mark Twain*. New York: Simon and Schuster, 1966.

Kenyon, J. P. *Revolution Principles: The Politics of Party, 1689–1720*. Cambridge: Cambridge University Press, 1977.

Lawrence, D. H. *Studies in Classic American Literature*. New York: Thomas Seltzer, 1923.

Lemay, J. A. Leo. "Rhetorical Strategies in *Sinners in the Hands of an Angry God* and *Narration of the Late Massacres in Lancaster County*." In *Benjamin Franklin, Jonathan Edwards, and the Representation of American Culture*, ed. Barbara Oberg and Harry S. Stout, 186–203. New York: Oxford University Press, 1993.

Longstreet, Augustus Baldwin. *Georgia Scenes*. Augusta: 1835.

Lynn, Kenneth S. *Mark Twain and Southwestern Humor*. Boston: Little, Brown, 1959.

Madan, F. F. *A Critical Bibliography of Dr. Henry Sacheverell*. Ed. W. A. Speck. Lawrence: University of Kansas Libraries, 1978.

Mather, Cotton. *Bonifacius. An Essay upon the Good that is to be Devised.* . . . London, 1710.

———. *Magnalia Christi Americana*. London, 1702.

Matthiessen, F. O. *Theodore Dreiser*. New York: William Sloane, 1951.

McDougall, William. *Outline of Psychology*. New York: Charles Scribner's Sons, 1923.

Mencken, H. L. *A Mencken Chrestomathy*. New York: Alfred J. Knopf, 1949.

Miller, Perry G. E. "The Marrow of Puritan Divinity," in *Errand into the Wilderness*. Cambridge: Harvard University Press, 1956.

———. *The New England Mind: From Colony to Province*. Cambridge: Harvard University Press, 1953.

Miller, Perry G. E., ed. *The American Puritans*. Garden City: Doubleday Anchor, 1956.

————. *The American Transcendentalists: Their Prose and Poetry.* Garden City: Doubleday Anchor, 1957.

Miller, Perry G. E., and Thomas H. Johnson, eds. *The Puritans.* New York: American Book Company, 1938.

Morreall, John, ed. *The Philosophy of Laughter and Humor.* Albany: State University of New York Press, 1987.

Mulford, Carla. "Caritas and Capital: Franklin's Narrative of the Late Massacres," in *Reappraising Benjamin Franklin: A Bicentennial Perspective.* Ed. J. A. Leo LeMay, 347–58. Newark: University of Delaware Press, 1993.

Peckham, Harry Houston. *Josiah Gilbert Holland in Relation to His Times.* Philadelphia: University of Pennsylvania Press, 1940.

Pettit, Norman. Review of *The New England Soul . . .* in *The New England Quarterly* 60 (1987): 604–8.

Piddington, Ralph. *The Psychology of Laughter: A Study in Social Adaptation.* New York: Gamut Press, 1963.

Plunkett, Harriette M. *Josiah Gilbert Holland.* New York, 1894.

Poe, Edgar Allen. *The Viking Portable Edgar Allan Poe.* Ed. Philip Van Doren Stern. New York: Viking, 1945.

Prynne, William. *Histrio-Mastix.* London, 1633. Facsimile edition. Ed. Arthur Freeman. New York: Garland, 1974.

Rickels, Milton. *George Washington Harris.* New York: Twayne Publishers, 1965.

Rusk, Ralph R. *The Life of Ralph Waldo Emerson.* New York: Charles Scribner's Sons, 1949.

Santayana, George. "The Genteel Tradition in American Philosophy," in *The Genteel Tradition: Nine Essays by George Santayana.* Ed. Douglas L. Wilson. Cambridge: Harvard University Press, 1967.

Sloane, David E. E., ed. *Mark Twain's Humor: Critical Essays.* New York: Garland, 1993.

Smith, Henry Nash. *Mark Twain: The Development of A Writer.* Cambridge: Harvard University Press, 1962.

Smolinski, Reiner. "*Israel Redivivus*: The Eschatological Limits of Puritan Typology in New England." *NEQ* 63 (September 1990): 357–95.

Stout, Harry S. *The New England Soul: Preaching and Religious Culture in Colonial New England.* New York: Oxford University Press, 1986.

Thoreau, Henry David. "Letter to Harrison Blake, December 7, 1956," in *The American Transcendentalists: Their Prose and Poetry.* Ed. Perry Miller. Garden City: Doubleday Anchor, 1957.

Thorpe, Thomas Bangs. "The Big Bear of Arkansas," 1841; reprinted in *The Big Bear of Arkansas and Other Sketches of Character and Incident in the South and South-West.* Ed. William T. Porter. Philadelphia, 1843.

Trevor-Roper, Hugh. "Laudianism and Political Power," in *Catholics, Anglicans and Puritans: Seventeenth Century Essays.* Chicago: University of Chicago Press, 1988.

Twain, Mark. "Early Rising as Regards Excursions to the Cliff House." San Francisco *Golden Era,* July 3, 1864; reprinted in *Mark Twain's San Francisco,* ed. Bernard Taper. New York: McGraw-Hill, 1963.

———. *Mark Twain: The Mysterious Stranger.* Ed. William M. Gibson. Berkeley and Los Angeles: University of California Press, 1977.

———. *Mark Twain: Selected Writings of an American Skeptic.* Ed. Victor Doyno. Buffalo: Prometheus Books, 1983.

———. *Mark Twain's Autobiography,* in two volumes. Ed. Albert Bigelow Paine. New York: Harper and Brothers, 1924.

———. *Mark Twain's Notebook.* Ed. Albert Bigelow Paine. New York: Harper and Brothers, 1935.

———. *Mark Twain's San Francisco.* Ed. Bernard Taper. New York: McGraw-Hill, 1963.

———. *Selected Shorter Writings of Mark Twain.* Ed. Walter Blair. Boston: Houghton Mifflin, 1962.

Twain, Mark, and William Dean Howells. *Mark Twain–Howells Letters.* Ed. Henry Nash Smith and William M. Gibson, with the assistance of Frederick Anderson. 2 Vols. Cambridge: Harvard University Press, 1960.

Van Doren, Carl. *Benjamin Franklin.* New York: Viking, 1938; reprinted 1945.

Walker, John Huber. "A Descriptive Bibliography of the Early Printed Works of Peter Heylyn." Ph.D. diss., Shakespeare Institute, University of Birmingham, 1978.

Ward, Nathaniel. *The Simple Cobler of Aggawam in America.* London, 1647. Ed. P. M. Zall. Lincoln: University of Nebraska Press, 1969.

Whicher, George F., ed. *Poetry of the New England Renaissance, 1790–1890.* New York: Rinehart, 1950.

Williams, Roger. *The Bloody Tenent.* Printed in *The Puritans,* ed. Miller and Johnson, *q.v.*

Wilson, Edmund. *Patriotic Gore: Studies in the Literature of the American Civil War.* New York: Oxford University Press, 1962.

Winthrop, John. "A Model of Christian Charity" (1630), in *The Puritans in America: A Narrative Anthology.* Ed. Alan Heimert and Andrew Delbanco. Cambridge: Harvard University Press, 1985.

———. "Speech to the General Court, July 3, 1645," from *The Journal.*

In *The American Puritans*, ed. Perry Miller. Garden City: Doubleday
Anchor, 1956.

Wise, John. *The Churches Quarrel Espoused: or, A Reply in Satyre, to certain
Proposals*. New York, 1713; Boston, 1715. Facsimile edition, ed.
George A. Cook. Gainesville, Fla.: Scholars Facsimiles and Reprints,
1966.

————. *A Vindication of the Government of New England Churches*. Boston,
1717. Facsimile edition, ed. Perry Miller. Gainesville, Fla.: Scholars
Facsimiles and Reprints, 1958.

Index

Affectation, 1, 7, 137, 144, 146, 148, 151, 154, 163, 165, 184

Anglicans: Chosen People, 3, 6, 47–72 *passim*, 73, 74–75; mystery, absence of, 1, 45, 69

Antinomianism, 197; colonial, 61, 71; Emerson's, 194, 195, 197; frontier, 92

Arminianism, 197; Anglican, 6, 61, 68–70, 91, 101, 193, 206; Emerson's, 193, 194; frontier, 70, 71

Atlantic Monthly. See Howells, William Dean; Twain, Mark ("Whittier Birthday Speech")

Bercovitch, Sacvan, 48, 49, 51, 68

Burnet, Bishop Gilbert, 6–7, 89–97 *passim*, 99–100, 122, 130, 132

Byrd, William II, 11, 47

Calvinism, 7, 44, 52, 68–69, 71, 90–92, 100, 101, 103, 131, 195

Cambridge Platform of 1648, 111, 112–13, 114, 115

Chase, Richard: American vs. British novel, 6; *The American Novel and Its Tradition*, 39–40, 41–42, 43, 43–44

Chesterfield, Lord, 210–11

Child, Francis James, 23

Cooper, James Fenimore, 159–60; *The Prairie* as romance, 40; *The Spy* and sensibility, 180

Cotton, John: "Christian Calling," 129; to Roger Williams, 121, 196

Crane, Stephen: *Maggie: A Girl of the Street,* vs. Josiah Holland's "poetic justice," 172; "The Open Boat," 178

Cross, Amanda, 172

DeFoe, Daniel, 83, 97

De Toqueville, Alexis, 70–71

Dickinson, Emily: "One Need not be a Chamber to be Haunted," 181; "Tell All the Truth But Tell it Slant," 203; mentioned, 200

Edwards, Jonathan, 89

Emerson, Ralph Waldo, 26, 29, 155, 190–97; "The American Scholar Address," 4, 193–94, 195, 196, 198; antidemocratic bias, 196; as devil, 190–91; "The Divinity School Address," 155, 191 (*see also* Norton, Andrews); "Experience," 195, 196; inconsistency of, 191; *Nature*, 191–93, 195, 199, 200; revelation without humor, 190, 196; "Self-Reliance," 197; on Thoreau, 198

Faulkner, William: *The Bear,* 159
Fielding, Henry, 1, 133, 137, 144, 145, 147, 148, 151, 172
Fitzgerald, F. Scott: *The Great Gatsby,* 156–58, 160, 173, 215; mentioned, 138
Fleetwood, Bishop William, 78–79, 82; his "Curate of Salop," 6, 84–87, 135
Fortescue, "our Learned," 97
Franklin, Benjamin, 124–33; "Dialogue Between Franklin and the Gout," 127, 132; on the Indians at Carlisle, 126, 130–32; "Narrative of the Late Massacres in Lancaster County," 125; "The Speech of Polly Baker," 119, 127–30, 137, 138–39, 143; Twain's view of, 125–26; vernacular, avoidance of, 132–33; mentioned, 9

Genteel tradition: certainty, 2, 8; humor, 7, 13–14, 210–11; the Ideal, 5, 8, 13, 16, 137–38; opposition to, 17, 205; reverence, 6, 12, 20–21, 22–25, 45, 154; and transcendentalism, 13; and vernacular, 12, 13, 22–25, 139, 149–51, 154, 205; vulgarity, disgust with, 7, 147, 148, 149–51, 154, 167, 205
God's Chosen People: British Anglicans, 3, 6, 47–72 *passim,* 73, 74–75; New England Puritans, 47–50
Griswold, Rufus. *See* Poe, Edgar Allan

Harris, George Washington: Sut Lovingood, 27–28, 147, 148, 149–54, 167; mentioned, 7, 157
Hawthorne, Nathaniel: "The Maypole of Merrymount," 36; "My Kinsman, Major Molineux," 5, 28–36, 37, 175, 176, 215; *The Scarlet Letter,* 31, 36; "Young Goodman Brown," 176
Heilbrun, Carolyn, 172
Hemingway, Ernest, 138
Hobbes, Thomas: laughter as "sudden glory," 135, 143
Holland, Josiah G., Dr.: and "the embodiment of God's will," 16, 172, 193; and the genteel tradition, 5; *Lessons in Life,* 16–17; and "the poet's ideal," 16, 25, 138, 168–72, 214, 215; and reverence, 20–21, 151; mentioned, 206, 215
Holland, Norman N., 143–44
Holmes, Oliver Wendell, "AT THE 'ATLANTIC' DINNER, December 15, 1874," 19

Hooper, Johnson Jones: antidemocratic thrust, 149, 185–86; humorist, 14, 149–50, 210; Simon Suggs, 15, 145–46, 148–49, 165, 205
Howells, William Dean, 12; and *Criticism and Fiction,* 177; "Editha," 13; editor of the *Atlantic,* 17; the Real, 12, 13; *The Rise of Silas Lapham,* 133–34; mentioned, 200
Humor: British roots of American, 4; and democracy, 5, 104–5, 108–9, 113, 115, 123, 211; Ishamel's, 179; as "low," 13–14, 211; Poe's, 179, 180–81, 183–86; Puritan roots of American, 4, 7; as revelation, 3, 8, 123, 126–28, 131–32, 173, 174, 179, 201, 214–15; no sense of, 173, 179, 212; theories of, 143, 163, 214; Thoreau's, 198–99, 201; and Twain's view of *Atlantic* readers, 18, 162; and the vernacular, 5, 15, 22, 123
Humor of the Old Southwest, 15, 144–45, 157, 158; antidemocratic bias, 15, 161–62, 185–86, 186–87
Hutchinson, Anne, 45, 197

Independence: ambivalence toward, 5, 8, 11, 26–27, 34–36, 45–46, 73, 117, 119, 179, 189, 214–15
Irreverence, 122, 130–32

Laud, Archbishop, 44, 45, 56, 74, 87, 91–92, 101
Laughter: as detachment, 214; Genteel American view of, 22–25, 214; Goodman Brown's, 176–77, 213; Hobbes's "sudden glory," 135; Ishmael's, 175, 176; Jim Doggett's, 177, 215; Lord Chesterfield's view of, 210–11; Nietzsche on, 33; Pip's, 176; Prynne's view of, 211–13; Puritans' view of, 123–24; Robin's, 29–31, 33–35, 176, 177, 214; as self-awareness, 35, 175–76
Lawrence, D. H., 125, 126, 130, 131, 138
Lowell, James Russell: "The Courtin'," 153; mentioned, 12, 18, 197

Marvell, Andrew: "To His Coy Mistress," 50
Mather, Cotton: *Bonifacius, or Essays to do Good,* 128, 132; *Golden Street,* 111; "Life of John Winthrop," 58; *Proposals* of November 5, 1705, 102–14 *passim*

Mather, Increase: "The Day of Trouble is Near," 60–61
Melville, Herman: *The Confidence-Man,* 205; England vs. America, 38, 41–44, 45; *Mardi,* 36; *Moby-Dick,* 36, 40, 41, 43, 159, 160, 169, 174–75, 176, 177, 179; "The Paradise of Bachelors and the Tartarus of Maids," 6, 36–43, 215; and Thomas Bangs Thorpe, 160; *Typee,* 36
Mencken, H. L.: "*Boobus Americanus,*" 140; Puritans, 210
Milbourne, Luke, 6, 61–62, 76, 78, 79
Miller, Perry G. E., 51, 52–53, 68, 102, 190–91
Milton, John, 50, 99
Morreall, John, 143

Nathan, Marshall, 193, 206–10
Norton, Andrews: "The Latest Form of Infidelity in Cambridge," 155, 171, 191. *See also* Emerson, Ralph Waldo

Occasional sermons, 52, 53, 61; January 30 (31), 6, 54–55, 61, 63, 66–67, 75–81, 83, 87–88, 97, 99, 208; May 29, 6, 54, 56–57, 60, 63, 67, 76, 97–99; November 5, 6, 54, 55, 57–58, 59, 60, 64, 67, 68, 76, 82–84, 87–88, 96–98, 109, 110, 115–17, 119, 206–10; other occasions, 59, 63, 71; special to England and to Israel, 67

Pettit, Norman, 48
Poe, Edgar Allan: antidemocratic bias, 185–87; *Eureka: A Prose Poem,* 182, 189, 197; Griswold's (Rufus) view of, 189; humor, 179, 180–82, 183–87; humor in "How to Write A Blackwood Article," 179, 180, 196; humor in "A Predicament," 180–81, 184; humor in "The Premature Burial," 184; humor and the Old Southwest, 184; humor in "The Sphinx," 184–85; "The Imp of the Perverse," 204; "The Impossibility of Writing a Truthful Autobiography," 202, 203; "Ligeia," 182–83; "The Oblong Box," 184; "The Purloined Letter," 183, 187–89; terror, 72, 181; the uncanny, 189; "unconscious pulsations," 181–82, 189, 202, 203; "William Wilson," 203
Poetic justice: Josiah Holland vs. Stephen Crane, 170–72
Porter, William Trotter: *The Spirit of the Times,* 144, 158

Prynne, William: *Histrio-Mastix,* 123, 211–13, 215
Pufendorf, Baron von: and Marshall, 208; and Wise, 118–19
Puritans: God's New Chosen People, 3, 47–72 *passim,* 73; sense of certainty, 2, 45; sense of mystery, 1

Ridiculous, the, 1, 148

Sacheverell, Dr. Henry, 55, 83–84, 85
Santayana, George: on Emerson, 193, 194; "The Genteel Tradition in American Philosophy," 2, 5, 12, 137–38, 153–54, 155, 167, 174, 177–78, 215
Sartre, Jean Paul: *La Nausée* and horror, 177
Sensibility, 180–81
Sewell, Samuel: *Phaenomena . . .* (Plum Island), 159, 178–79
Stevens, Wallace: "Anecdote of the Jar," 160
Stout, Harry S., *The New England Soul,* 48, 52, 53
Swift, Jonathan: the Houyhnhnms, 138; "A Modest Proposal," 129; and John Partridge, 124

Thoreau, Henry David, 197–202; "The Bean-Field," 198–99; "Conclusion," 201; vs. Emerson, 200–201; nonconformity, 205; "The Pond in Winter," 200; shock, 77–78, 145; *Walden,* 198, 202; weight of tradition, 204
Thorpe, Thomas Bangs, 138; "The Big Bear of Arkansas," 158–63, 177; and Melville, 160
Titcomb, Timothy. *See* Holland, Josiah G., Dr.
Toleration, 44–45, 74–75, 76, 77, 85–85, 87, 89, 92, 94–95, 95, 99, 121–22, 124, 156, 196
Trilling, Lionel, 205–6
Twain, Mark: *Adventures of Huckleberry Finn,* 12, 40, 140, 162, 165–66, 205, 211, and Lionel Trilling, 205–6; *The Adventures of Tom Sawyer,* 22; *Autobiography,* 147–48, 202–3; "The Celebrated Jumping Frog," 15, 26, 126, 136, 139, and "The Notorious Jumping Frog," 134–35, 140; *A*

Connecticut Yankee in King Arthur's Court, 12; "Corn-Pone Opinions," 203–4; "The Dandy Frightening the Squatter," 14–15; dream-state, 25–26; Franklin, view of Ben, 125–26; "His Grandfather's Old Ram," 126, 134; vs. humor of Old Southwest, 2, 143; humorist, attitude as, 18; and "lie" of "moral medicine chest," 147, 162, 172, 206; "The Mysterious Stranger," 167, 214–15; *Pudd'nhead Wilson,* 162; *Roughing It,* 26–27, 134, 139; "Sabbath Reflections," 17; "The $30,000 Bequest," 25, 167; *Tom Sawyer Abroad,* 139–43, 162–65; "Tom Sawyer, Detective," 140; and the unconscious, 203, 204; *What Is Man?,* 203; "Whittier Birthday Speech," 5, 12, 14, 18–26, 149, 215

Vernacular, 12, 13, 14, 15, 22–23, 24, 25, 26, 27–28, 133
—avoidance of: by Bishop Fleetwood,

135; by Franklin, 132–33, 135; by Ward, 119–20, 135, 154; by Wise, 135
—and democracy, 211
—use by: Hooper, 149; by Howells, 133; by Twain, 14–15, 21–22, 22–27, 28, 134–35, 136, 139; by Wise, 102, 113, 115, 116, 154
Vernacular characters. *See* Fleetwood, Bishop William; Franklin, Benjamin; Harris, George Washington; Hooper, Johnson Jones; Howells, William Dean; Thorpe, Thomas Bangs; Twain, Mark; Wise, John

Ward, Nathaniel: *The Simple Cobler of Aggawam,* 6, 44, 45, 75, 119–22, 123, 124, 147, 154, 210
Weaned affections, 129
Williams, Roger, 45, 62, 74, 89, 99, 121, 131, 196
Wilson, Edmund, 150–51, 167
Winthrop, John, 58, 70, 81, 95, 103
Wise, John, 6, 7, 49, 102–19, 120, 122–23, 124, 130, 147, 154, 158, 171, 208, 211